TOM HORN

Blood on the Moon

Dark History of the
Murderous Cattle Detective

Other books by Chip Carlson:

Tom Horn: "Killing men is my specialty…"
Joe LeFors: "I slickered Tom Horn…"

TOM HORN

Blood on the Moon

Dark History of the
Murderous Cattle Detective

CHIP CARLSON

with a foreword by
Larry D. Ball

HIGH PLAINS PRESS

Cover art © L.D Edgar
"Trouble at Big Horn Crossing"
For prints or information contact: Western Heritage Studio
P. O. Box 68, Meeteetse, WY 82433-0068
www.WesternHeritageStudio.com

Library of Congress Cataloging-in-Publication Data
Carlson, Chip.
Tom Horn : blood on the moon : dark history of the murderous cattle
detective / Chip Carlson ; with a foreword by Larry D. Ball.
p. cm
Includes bibliographical references and index.
ISBN 0-931271-58-4 (hard : alk. paper)
ISBN 0-931271-59-2 (pbk. : alk. paper
ISBN 0-931271-60-6 (collectors : alk. paper)
1. Horn, Tom 1860-1903.
2. Frontier and pioneer life--Wyoming.
3. Scouts and scouting--Wyoming--Biography.
4. Apache Indians--Wars, 1883-1886.
I. Title.

E83.88.H67 C37 2001
979'.03'092--dc21
[B]   2001024830

His Wyoming advent was during a troublous era....

there was "blood on the moon"

and Horn was to add to it.

— *John Charles Thompson*

For Susan,

and my parents, Roy and Lois Carlson.

And for our children,

John, Lisa, Alan, Ken, Jenna and Tina

and theirs.

Contents

A CONSPICUOUS PLACE IN HISTORY

AMONG THE NOTABLE personalities of the nineteenth century frontier, Tom Horn occupies a conspicuous place. Born Thomas H. Horn, Jr., in Missouri, in 1860, he traveled west in his early teens. Horn knocked about as a day laborer, prospector, and cowhand, until he settled in southeastern Arizona in the early 1880s. While herding cattle contracted to the San Carlos Indian Reservation, he served occasional hitches as a civilian packer for the army and, finally, as a chief of scouts in the final campaign against Geronimo in 1885–86.

At the conclusion of this conflict, Horn returned to his previous pursuits. He excelled as a cowhand and became a notable performer in the pioneer rodeo movement in Arizona. Occasional stints as a deputy sheriff led to employment by the Pinkerton National Detective Agency in 1890. While assigned to the company's Denver office, he became associated with the large cattle companies in southern Wyoming in their feud with small ranchers and homesteaders, whom the barons accused of being in league with rustlers. Aside from short absences—once, as a packer in Cuba, in 1898—Horn now made Wyoming his home. He may have occasionally hired out his gun in the past, but Horn's services as a range detective for the powerful cattlemen soon led him into the grim business of hired assassin. While controversy still surrounds his role in the Wyoming range war, he was eventually tried and convicted of murder. Tom Horn was hanged in Cheyenne, Wyoming, in 1903.

Upon his death, Tom Horn entered the realm of frontier legend, and he has been the subject of numerous books, articles, and Hollywood scripts. In a strange twist, Horn contributed to this popularity through his own—highly exaggerated—*Life of Tom Horn: Government Scout and Interpreter, Written by Himself: a Vindication* (1904). Written while awaiting the hangman's noose, Horn sought to convince readers that his services in the Apache campaigns "vindicated" him of the present murder conviction. (He carefully avoided writing about his years as a range detective in Wyoming.)

In the century since his death, much of the writing about Tom Horn has been inaccurate and unreliable. Authors such as Arthur Chapman, Dane Coolidge and Owen P. White, who first popularized his life in the 1920s and '30s, relied uncritically upon *The Life of Tom Horn*. Since Horn was very selective when writing about his past, and left much out, these "wild west" writers added little of value to the story.

At the same time, Horn became the subject of a heated debate in the 1930s when aging veterans of the Apache campaigns made strenuous efforts to diminish the services of Horn (and other civilian scouts) in the pursuit of Geronimo. The old bluecoats claimed all the credit. Charles B. Gatewood, Jr., son of Lieutenant Charles B. Gatewood, who negotiated the warrior's surrender in 1886, led this crusade. While the lieutenant was clearly in command, Tom Horn was present and ran the same risks when they entered the Apache camp. Unfortunately, Horn played into the hands of these military detractors with his ridiculous claims that he was in charge and ordered Lieutenant Gatewood around as though the soldier his subordinate.

Fortunately, a few writers have assumed a more restrained attitude and have begun to arrive at a more balanced picture of the former scout. Painstaking research has been necessary, since Tom Horn's background and movements were often very obscure. Jay Monaghan's pioneer biography, *The Legend of Tom Horn: Last of the Badmen* (1946), represented the first serious effort at a complete story. Dean Krakel's *The Saga of Tom Horn: The Story of a Cattlemen's War* (1954), which concentrated upon Horn's trial and execution, is also useful for its documentary approach.

Chip Carlson took up the subject of Tom Horn late in life, but he quickly became a leading authority. Carlson, who became interested in this frontiersman while promoting the Tom Horn Kick & Growl tourist event in Cheyenne, Wyoming, in the late 1980s, is well-known from two previous books on this subject: *Tom Horn: "Killing men is my specialty..." The Definitive History of the Notorious Wyoming Stock Detective* (1991); and *Joe LeFors: "I slickered Tom Horn..." The History of the Texas Cowboy Turned Montana-Wyoming Lawman: A Sequel* (1995). This latter work is a study of the range detective and deputy United States marshal who was responsible for the arrest of Tom Horn.

In *Tom Horn: Blood on the Moon, Dark History of the Murderous Cattle Detective*, Chip Carlson has produced an updated version of his earlier biography. While he devotes the majority of the book to Horn's years in Wyoming, Carlson does not ignore his subject's early years. The author's exploration of the range detective's early life helps us go beyond the brief statements in *The Life of Tom Horn* and to better understand Horn's origins, as well as his family relationships. In addition, Carlson brings into clearer perspective the various violent episodes associated with Horn's career as an alleged assassin in Wyoming and assesses the surviving sources fully.

This does not mean that the controversial nature of Tom Horn's life is removed—far from it. He will continue to provoke discussion and debate among persons interested in the violent aspects of the American Frontier. However, Chip Carlson's well-researched volume represents a significant advance in our knowledge. Not only does Carlson bring Tom Horn's life into much sharper relief, but the author presents mature and persuasive arguments on various points in Horn's career. Readers of *Tom Horn: Blood on the Moon* will find this volume entertainingly written and the fullest account of this controversial frontiersman's life.

LARRY D. BALL
ARKANSAS STATE UNIVERSITY

Preface

Following publication of my first book on Tom Horn, I became aware that more research on the range detective and the events surrounding him remained to be done. Some of the resulting information appeared in my second book, *Joe LeFors: "I slickered Tom Horn...."* but even more material has come to the surface. Much of that is presented here.

A great deal of what follows is new—not previously published nor widely disseminated. My focus again is roughly on the period from 1892 until Tom's hanging in Cheyenne on the day before his forty-third birthday in 1903. Material that precedes those years is presented here as background. Significant work is being done on Horn's earlier years by Larry D. Ball.

Some of the background information here relates facts that I and others have previously written about, but Stephen Ambrose and Dale Walker are right: The most important part of history is the last five letters.

The Controversy is Two-Fold

Tom Horn, the preeminent name in Wyoming history, remains a figure wrapped in controversy. The controversy is twofold: first, did Horn kill Willie Nickell and, second, was justice served in his trial? Horn was hanged for the Nickell murder, but the controversy continues. Horn is an even more compelling figure because of his dark, enigmatic, mysterious nature.

Leaving home in 1873 at only thirteen, he headed to the American Southwest where he served with distinction as a civilian employee for the Army in the Apache struggles of the 1880s. He was a champion rodeo contestant and mined silver before heading north to continue mining, but more significantly to embark on a career as a lawman, primarily a manhunter. He worked for Pinkerton's National Detective Agency in Colorado and Wyoming and was a deputy U.S. marshal.

He arrived in Wyoming late in 1891 or early 1892, where he became effective—exceedingly effective—as a stock detective. John Charles "Charley" Thompson, the Cheyenne newspaperman who was part of the background to the unfolding drama, accurately described the scenario:

> His Wyoming advent was during a troublous era there. The famous and infamous "Johnson County invasion" was little more than three years past; the lynching of Jim Averill and "Cattle Kate" had been perpetrated only five or six years previously; there had been numerous other dark crimes to avenge alleged cattle stealing. There was "blood on the moon" and Horn was to add to it.

But conditions were not favorable. Tom Horn's path began to spiral downward starting in the mid-1890s, until the political and social changes of the late nineteenth and early twentieth centuries literally and figuratively "put him under."

To paraphrase Will Henry who said it well in *I, Tom Horn*: "history wrote it dark for him and called it by another name. It was Wyoming."

The Poem Unfinished

He strangled to death in a hangman's noose

On a cold, November morn.

Brave at the gallows, the coolest man present

The detective, the legend, Tom Horn.

Chapter One

INNOCENT!

THE WORD RANG OUT like a gunshot in the crowded Cheyenne courtroom in September 1993, almost a hundred years after Tom Horn's hanging for first-degree murder. "Innocent!"

Light is fading on the early twentieth century, but even as that light dims it has become more apparent that Tom Horn quite likely was not the killer of Willie Nickell on July 18, 1901. It took a hundred years for him to be exonerated, if only in a mock trial at the same locale where he was convicted.

No one witnessed Willie Nickell's murder. At the first trial—the only trial that really matters—the prosecution used an alcohol-induced "confession," weak circumstantial evidence, and perjured testimony. But it was enough.

Tom Horn, a man often found in close proximity to violence, had been working as a range detective in the general area at the time of the murder. The morning before the shooting he had been visiting the James Miller ranch, the homestead of a family who had maintained a long-running mutual feud with the neighboring Nickell family. The prosecution built their case from this circumstance and added other questionable scraps of circumstantial evidence to the mixture.

The linchpin for the prosecution was a "confession" given by a drunken Tom Horn to a federal officer operating out of his jurisdiction, Joe LeFors. A deputy sheriff and a legal reporter, hidden from view, witnessed the conversation and the reporter recorded parts of it. LeFors had arranged for them to be there for a single purpose—as witnesses if Tom talked. LeFors himself acknowledged that he was operating under the instructions of the district attorney, Walter Stoll, who had his own ambitions—perhaps exceeding Joe LeFors's. The conviction assured his reelection to office.

The prosecution empanelled a jury tainted with prejudice against the cattlemen who hired Tom Horn as a range detective and the power they represented. The presiding judge, an elected official with a clouded history, gave rulings during the trial and instructions to the jury that were anything but impartial. His loyalty to the electorate led to his election to a seat on the Wyoming Supreme Court.

The lawyer who represented Tom Horn in the 1993 retrial described the work of Horn's real-life 1902 legal defense team as the "worst he had ever studied." And Tom Horn's own foolish statements in cross examination, driven by his ego and played like a musical instrument by prosecutor Walter Stoll, helped seal his own dark fate.

Willie Nickell was the second fourteen-year-old boy from Iron Mountain, a ranching community northwest of Cheyenne, to die of gunshot wounds within months. The previous summer Frank Miller, the son of Jim Miller, had died when a shotgun in a spring wagon in which he and a younger sister were playing accidentally discharged. His sister Maude carried the buckshot and scars from her wounds the rest of her life. Believing the feud had led to the accident, Jim Miller placed the blame for Frank's death solely on his neighbor Kels Nickell and swore that if the law did not avenge the death, he would.

Willie Nickell saddled his father's horse at six-thirty the morning of July 18, 1901. Kels, Willie's father, had sent Willie on an errand to find a man who had ridden through the area looking for work. Nickell's sheepherder had unexpectedly quit and he needed a replacement. The errand led to Willie's death.

Willie mounted his father's bay and headed from the family house toward a wire gate three-quarters of a mile to the west. Reaching the gate, he dismounted, led the horse through, and turned to loop the gate closed.

Three shots rang out—two in quick succession, then a pause, and then another. Two reached their mark. They smashed into the boy's left back and exited. Blood sprayed on the gate, the ground, and the tree used as a gatepost. Willie stumbled sixty-five feet toward home before he dropped face-down on the rough granite gravel. Blood seeped from the exit wounds.

Someone, probably the killer, rolled Willie's body over and pulled open his shirt.

The reverberations of that gunfire through the Wyoming hills signaled the beginning of a long search for Willie Nickell's killer. And they marked perhaps the largest setback for the so-called cattle barons, one of several that began with the lynching of Ellen "Cattle Kate" Watson in 1888 and continued through the Johnson County War of 1892. These ranchers who controlled large portions of public land, along with the industrial, railroad and mining barons, were players in the drama of economic and social change marking the evolution in America from an agrarian to an industrial society. The three shots that rang out in an early summer morning in 1901 near remote Iron Mountain, Wyoming, were more than mere gunfire. They were, figuratively, the sound of a hammer driving nails into the coffin of the Wyoming cattle business as it had existed for nearly thirty years.

Two years, three months, and two days after Willie Nickell's assassination Tom Horn strangled to death in a hangman's noose in the Laramie County jail on November 20, 1903. He would have been forty-three years old the next day.

Tom Horn's execution may symbolically mark the passing of the Old West in Wyoming, poignantly described in the foreword of Owen Wister's *The Virginian*, written while Tom was in jail in 1902:

> It is a vanished world.... A transition has followed the horseman of the plains; a shapeless state, a condition of men and manners unlovely as that bald moment in the year when winter is gone and spring not come, and the face of nature is ugly....

The controversy over whether Tom Horn shot Willie Nickell, his so-called confession ("...the best shot that I ever made and the dirtiest trick I ever done"), the trial, the failed appeals, and his hanging still rages on in Wyoming a century later.

Chapter Two

TROUBLESOME

"TROUBLESOME." It was a word Tom Horn himself used, first to describe the times at his birth and his early years, and later to describe Willie Nickell's father. It was appropriate.

The trouble for Tom Horn's father and grandfather started in the 1840s in Ohio, where both Tom's father and mother were born. Father Thomas Horn was born in Knox County in 1825, and mother Mary Ann Miller was born in Coshocton County in 1831. Thomas's father, Hartman Horn,[1] was born in Washington County, Pennsylvania, in 1794 and was a descendant of German immigrants who had settled in that part of Pennsylvania.

Years after Thomas and Mary had secretly left Ohio for Scotland County, Missouri, in 1852, a former partner of Thomas's continued legal action against him. On November 21, 1867, John Thompson filed suit against Thomas Horn at the Scotland County Circuit Court for $1,650.[2] Thompson had entered a bill in chancery[3] sixteen years previously in 1851 in the Knox County Court of Common Pleas in Mount Vernon against Horn and others, requesting settlement of a dispute that dated to a transaction in October 1849, when Horn was still living there.

Thompson's suit alleged that he and Horn had been partners in a deal to buy cattle in Knox County, drive them to Baltimore, sell them, and split the proceeds. Hartman Horn, Elijah Patterson, and Harris Thompson, John's brother, were part of the arrangement.

Thomas Horn was to buy the cattle but had to borrow a thousand dollars from the Knox County Bank in Mount Vernon to finance the deal. He proposed that Thompson borrow a similar amount and that each provide a guarantor. The arrangement proceeded; John Thompson's guarantor was his brother Harris, while Horn's was his father

Hartman.[4] Thompson's experience in the cattle business was of major importance, "to some extent skill offsetting capital,"[5] but both men agreed to give equal attention to the project. The loan was finally procured at the Bank of Baltimore, Maryland. The cost of the cattle plus expenses of the drive to Baltimore was $1,927.93 plus a few small expenses paid in Baltimore by Horn.

Horn left the cattle with a man "by the name of Gregory," according to the Knox County court records. Gregory was to sell the cattle and deposit the money into an account Horn had set up in his own name at the Bank of Baltimore. The cattle were sold for $2,110.72, and Gregory deposited the amount to Horn's account.

Horn, together with his father and Elijah Patterson, then withdrew the money, without paying off the loan at the bank. Thompson claimed that Horn next purchased a drove of hogs that Hartman and Patterson were already feeding; Horn drove them to the East, sold them, and loaned the proceeds to his father and Patterson. Apparently Thomas Horn's plan was to make the money inaccessible to John Thompson by loaning it to Hartman and Patterson—a plot that implies that the three had set it up in advance.

Thompson confronted Thomas Horn at Dresden, Ohio, where the latter was in charge of the hogs. Horn replied that he would speak with his father, who would clear up the matter with the bank. Horn assured Thompson that this "would be the last...he would ever hear of it," and Thompson "rested for a time satisfied that he would not be further troubled about the matter."[6]

Then Hartman and Thomas Horn filed a suit against Thompson requiring Thompson to pay the debt in Baltimore himself. In the meantime, Thompson said, Thomas Horn was "giving out in speeches that he [Horn] is insolvent...." He added that both Thomas and Hartman Horn were combining together to compel him to pay the whole amount.

The final outcome of the whole matter, with its charges and countercharges, as mandated by the court in Ohio late in 1851, was that Thomas Horn was to pay Thompson $838.95 plus interest and court costs within ten days, which would settle the matter once and for all.

*Tom Horn's father, Thomas Horn (*From *Life of Tom Horn, Government Scout and Interpreter*, original 1904 edition)

Horn apparently never paid a penny of the amount due and soon left the state. But Thompson did not forget, and the matter was not settled "once and for all."

Additional affidavits show that Thomas was under a shadow of debt both before he left Ohio in the fall of 1852 and for most of the rest of his life. Young Tom, born in 1860 after the family fled Ohio, was apparently raised in a milieu of financial trouble stirred continually by his father's financial shenanigans.

Court testimony from the 1867 case further attests to the Horn family's ill repute. Washington Houck, a grocer, stated that he had known Horn for eight or nine years before he left in 1852, and that he owed him about three hundred dollars in addition to two thousand dollars he had in other debts. Houck said that Horn "ran away or left without his neighbors knowing when or how he went."[7] He continued that Horn "had passed counterfeit money and a warrant was issued against him." He left no belongings of any kind when he suddenly departed.

Tom Horn's mother, Mary Ann Miller Horn (*From Life of Tom Horn, Government Scout and Interpreter,* original 1904 edition)

William Houck stated that he had known Horn for fourteen or fifteen years in 1852 in both Knox and Coshocton counties, that Horn had left "clandestinely," and that he was insolvent when he left.

Physician A. C. Scott, who had known Horn for six or eight years, said Horn owed him several hundred dollars and that he knew of other debts. He added that Horn had left suddenly and was wanted for passing "counterfeit bank paper."

Sheriff Thomas Wade stated that he had a warrant for Horn and had a "large number of executions against him on which I was unable to collect a cent." The sheriff said Horn had returned to Ohio briefly in 1864 while Wade had an attachment against him. He said that Horn settled the attachment and then asked him repeatedly if there were any other attachments; Wade had none but Horn "started off through the woods" stating that no one would ever see him in Ohio again.

By accident Thompson finally learned that Horn was back in Scotland County in 1867, thus leading to his pursuing his claims against Horn.

Summons issued in 1889 against Tom Horn's parents by his brother, Martin, as part of the action to foreclose on the property they had sold him. (Scotland County Circuit Court, Anita Watkins, Clerk)

The case ended with the court in Scotland County ordering the sheriff to attach any and all of Thomas Horn's property to satisfy the sum of $1,650. Sheriff H. H. Byrne then attached a large amount of land owned by Horn.

This case was only one of twenty-two in which Thomas Horn, often along with others, were defendants in Scotland County. Frequently his wife, uncle Martin Horn, and Charles Horn (not his oldest son Charles, but a more distant relative, a second cousin) were also named.

When Thomas and Mary Horn left Ohio for Missouri in 1852, they were accompanied by Thomas's brother, Martin C. Horn, and his father, Hartman. Mary purchased their first parcel of land, approximately 240 acres of rural farmland east of Memphis, in Harrison Township northeast of a small hamlet, Etna. They invested a two-hundred-dollar down payment and signed a mortgage for six hundred dollars. They probably purchased the property in Mary's name to shield it from their creditors in Ohio.

As their troubles mounted, Mary arranged for Thomas's name to be on the title of the original land, with a note due in one year. They "sold" it to son Martin on March 1, 1888, for eight hundred dollars, the amount of the note that had been signed the previous month.

Martin filed a Petition in Ejectment and followed on January 16, 1889, by obtaining a court order against Mary and Thomas. The sheriff served it on each of them two days later. Foreclosure proceeded in March. While the exact motivation of the parties is not clear, it seems as if it was "set up" so that the property, against which there were no legal actions, could be passed to Martin without Thomas and Mary paying the note.

One final court case incident involved what has been described as "a shady deal on a pair of white horses."[8] Thomas left hurriedly for Arkansas, where he had a second cousin, Aaron, apparently hoping to avoid further troubles.

Clearly, young Tom's growing-up years were spent with his parents embroiled in financial and legal turmoil, though how much Tom knew or participated is unknown.

But as Tom later said, their times were troublesome.

Chapter Three

BOUND TO SEE TROUBLE

T HERE MIGHT NOT HAVE been a worse time to be born or a better family at creating trouble for itself. And baby Tom's instincts, ostensibly already flowing through his veins, seem to have destined him for trials enough for the "fifteen ordinary lives" he felt he lived.

Tom Horn was born in northeast Missouri east of the Scotland County seat, Memphis, on November 21, 1860.[1] And as old west journalist Bill Nye once said, "anyone born in Missouri is bound to see trouble." [2]

Northeast Missouri was neutral during the Civil War. As the war ebbed and flowed, locals tended to favor "the side of the uniform that was knocking at the front door," one local historian said.[3] The Horn family sided with the confederacy, since the section of Pennsylvania where its German ancestors came from was originally part of Virginia.[4] At one point during the war, a Confederate captain and enlisted man stayed at the Horn home. After leaving, they were ambushed and the enlisted man was killed.

In 1869 Hartman was taken ill, and moved into the family home with Thomas, Mary, and their family. They cared for him until his death in 1874, when Thomas was named administrator of his estate, valued at $275.75.[5]

In 1874 they started selling some of their land to sons Charles and Martin. By 1876 their holdings had grown to 1,250 acres in the Etna area that were estimated to be worth over twenty thousand dollars. On January 16, 1884, they purchased four lots in the southeast part of Memphis for $1,700.

Young Tom was the child of a large family. At least one of Thomas and Mary's children died at a young age—a son, whose name is not known, died on October 20, 1854, and is buried in the Dennis Church cemetery in Knox County, Ohio.[6]

HORN'S BIRTHPLACE

The birthplace of Tom Horn. It still stands and is used as a home on a farm in Missouri. (From *Life of Tom Horn, Government Scout and Interpreter*, original 1904 edition)

The 1860 census was taken during the summer, before Tom's birth. The family household, including hired help living with them, consisted of [7] the parents and:

> Charles,[8] who was born in 1854;
> William, born in 1856, (Died on January 14, 1864. Buried in Etna Cemetery)[9]
> Nancy, born in 1858;
> Also living in the household were:
> John Wilson, twenty-four, from Indiana, engaged in farming;
> John Wage, twenty-two, from Pennsylvania, engaged in farming;
> Miller Barnes, twenty-one, from Pennsylvania, engaged in farming;
> John Dean, nineteen, from Canada, engaged in farming;
> Sarah Scott, seventeen, from Ireland, a domestic;
> A second woman, whose name, age, and origin are not legible, a domestic.

For 1870 available census records do not show occupations. In addition to the parents and the two older children, the members of the household in 1870 were:

Thomas (Tom), born in 1860;
Martin, born in 1862;
Harriet, born in 1863, (who may be "Hannah" or "Fanny"
    born in 1864);[10]
Austin, born in 1866;
Mary, born in 1869;
Rey Markley, age twelve, a cousin from Arkansas.[11]

⚬—⚬—⚬—⚬—⚬—⚬

Religion was an important element in the household. Both parents were Campbellites, a fundamentalist sect of the Disciples of Christ. Apparently Mary was the stricter of the two. The family was said to be very reclusive.

Young Tom, elaborating on his childhood, said in his autobiography:

Up to the time I left home I suppose I had more trouble than any man or boy in Missouri. We had Sunday schools and church, and as my mother was a good old-fashioned Campbellite, I was supposed to go to church and Sunday school...I had nothing particular against going, if it had not been for the 'coon, turkey, quail...and other game...I would steal out the gun and take the dog and hunt all day Sunday and many a night through the week, knowing full well that whenever I did show up at home I would get a whipping or a scolding from my mother or a regular thumping from father.[12]

Evidently religious convictions became part of his evolving personality, but his father's stern, if excessive, discipline played a greater role. Another trait that stayed with him from childhood was his attraction to excitement.

An early hint of this attraction is evident in his autobiography. His best boyhood friend, he wrote, was his dog Shedrick. They were "the designated hunters of the country:"

The Etna church attended by Tom Horn's family. (Sandy Remley)

…When our neighbors would complain of losing a chicken (and that was a serious loss to them), mother would tell them that whenever any varmint bothered their hen-roost, she just sent out Tom and Shed, and when they came back they always brought the pelt of the varmint with them…. There was never a better dog….[13]

…I would always be finding fresh rabbit or coon or cat tracks crossing the trail to school. I never could cross a fresh track, for I would see one, and the rest of the children would pay no attention to it, so, I would follow it a little ways just to see which way it went, and then I would go on a little farther, and then I would say to myself, "I will be late for school and get licked." Then an overpowering desire…would overcome me, and I would go back, call the dog, and as he would come running to me, the stuff for school was all off, and Shed and I would go hunting…. I could see far more advantage in having a good string of pelts than in learning to read, write, and cipher….[14]

After the Civil War ended in 1865, emigrants heading west traveled through the Horn farm. One day Tom and Shedrick came across two boys on a horse who were traveling west with their family. One of them carried a single-shot scattergun. Tom, never one to watch his mouth, remarked caustically that a man who shot game with a shotgun was no good. A fight ensued, with Tom barely holding his own against the two until Shed jumped into the fray. When Tom pulled the dog off, the two emigrant boys climbed back on their mare. They then shot Tom's dog:

> Shed whined and I could scarcely believe such a thing had been done. I carried Shed home, which was about a quarter of a mile away, and he died that night. I believe that was the first and only real sorrow of my life.[15]

In his early teens, Tom challenged his father, who had set out to give him a thrashing. The older man prevailed.

At that point, Tom decided to leave. So, at the age of thirteen, he headed west, searching for adventure.

After he left home, Tom worked on the railroad in Newton, Kansas. He and brother Charles may have been involved in a livery stable in Burrton, Kansas, for a short period, and Tom scuffled with cowboys in Dodge City.[16]

By late 1874, according to his account, he was in the New Mexico territorial capital of Santa Fe. In January 1875, he landed a job as a stage driver for the Overland Mail Route from Santa Fe to Prescott, Arizona Territory.

A few months later he was sent with a herd of mules, replacements for stock stolen by Apaches, to Beaver Head Station near the Verde River, in the heart of Indian Country. He moved on to Camp Verde, an Army post. He found work there as a night livestock drover:

> My feelings were so different and my life was so different from what it was at home that it seemed to me then as though I had been all my life on a stage line.... It had taken me just about a year to get from Santa Fe to Prescott, but I had learned more in that year than in all my previous life.[17]

Interacting frequently with Mexicans, Tom soon became fluent in Spanish. In July 1876, when Tom was fifteen, Al Sieber, chief of army scouts of the Fifth Cavalry, hired him as a Spanish-English interpreter at the San Carlos Indian Agency in southern Arizona. His duties additionally included night herding, cooking, and running the camp. Sieber may have become something of a surrogate father to him.

At age sixteen he was boss of the Army Quartermaster's herd, managing droves of animals at Fort Whipple, the headquarters of the Department of the Army Department at Prescott.

A growing interest in mining prompted him to visit the Colorado mountains, for he appears in Gunnison, Colorado, in the 1880 census.[18] His name is also listed in the Cripple Creek City Directory in 1880.[19]

The same year he was also back home in Missouri, working there for a period that year.[20] That year the Horn household included, in addition to the parents:

> Martin, age seventeen, born in 1863, engaged in farming;
> Tom, age nineteen, born in 1860, engaged in farming;
> Hannah, fifteen, born in 1865, at school;
> "Oss" [Austin], a son age fourteen, at school;
> Maude [Mary], eleven, born in 1869, at school;
> "Alliss" [Alice], five, born in 1875, at school;
> William Woods, age twenty-two, a boarder.

Verification of Horn's tenure in the Southwest came in a letter written to Mrs. John Coble, the widow of Horn's close friend during his last few years in Wyoming. Henry W. Daly met Tom Horn at the San Carlos Agency in Arizona Territory, he said, in 1880 or 1881 while Tom was a packer under James Cook, better known as "Long Jim" Cook.[21]

Horn and Billy Harrison were the only two Anglos working under Cook, Daly said, and Horn stayed with Cook until November 1885.[22]

Continuing skirmishes with Apaches and Mexicans flared up during this period. The approaching campaign against the Apaches was organized at Fort Bowie, Arizona Territory, in November 1885. Tom Horn was named chief of scouts for Lieutenant Marion Maus, under the overall command of Captain Emmet Crawford.[23] One reason for his appointment was his fluency in Spanish.

Tom Horn (seated) with two unidentified men. This photograph was probably taken in the southwest about 1883. (Author's photo, courtesy Ray John de Aragon)

The expedition crossed into Mexico and proceeded two hundred miles south. Near Nácori it encountered a group of Mexican irregular troops. Tom Horn called to the Mexicans, attempting to convince them that his group was a part of the U.S. Army and that the Apache scouts accompanying them were working for the army. Suddenly the Mexicans shot Crawford through the head, killing him. Tom Horn was shot through the arm.

In other encounters during the previous two years Horn had been wounded two other times. He wrote from Sonora, Mexico, to his parents on February 20, 1886:[24]

> Dear Father and Mother:
>
> It has been a long time since I wrote you a letter, and you have no doubt been very uneasy about me. I am, as you are doubtless aware, employed by the government as Chief of Scouts for Arizona and New Mexico, and interpreter of the Mexican and Apache languages. Am well and hearty and get good pay for my services. I was wounded in the fight in which Capt. Crawford was killed, but it is not a serious wound. Was shot through the arm above the elbow, but it is nearly well now. I used to run great many risks in this country and the United States, but it is getting so there is no danger any more. The last of the Apaches will surrender in six weeks, I am sure.... After these Indians come in I promise you I will write oftener, and will get a good job and be stationed on the post.
>
> Don't think I am a hard case because I am a scout. I try to be [illegible] and am always sober. I speak the Spanish language as fluently as a Mexican.
>
> I will send you the report of Gen. Crook and Lieut. Maus, when the Indian troubles are over, so you can see what they say about me. It is useless for me to say I will come home and live on the farm for I could not do it now.
>
> I would like to see you very much and as soon as war is over, Lieut. says he will give me leave for a month or two to visit home....
>
> I had about 100 head of cattle and 26 good horses ten months ago, but the Indians and Mexicans cleaned me out—killed my

partner and left me dead broke, so there was nothing left except
to follow their trail and get satisfaction…. At the time my partner was killed, I was slightly wounded, and also again about two
years ago.

I close by sending kind regards to all the children and friends.
Write to me oftener. Everybody in the command gets letters
from home but me. When the Courier comes in with the mail
they always say there is nothing for you, Tom!

Rep'y Your Son,

Tom Horn

While some army contemporaries and historians have made
attempts to discredit Horn's role in the Crawford episode, Lieutenant
Marion Maus's letter (as printed in the *Arizona Daily Star*) to Captain
C. S. Roberts at Camp Bowie on January 21, 1886, from Sonora,
Mexico, clearly points to the value of Horn's contributions.[25] Further,
Maus recommended Horn for honorable mention, but the request was
denied simply because only soldiers could receive honorable mention.
Horn, of course, was a civilian employee.[26]

Shortly after the episode when Crawford was killed, Horn became
Chief of Scouts. General Nelson Miles succeeded Crook and sum-
marily dismissed Sieber and Horn.

Shortly after that hasty decision, Miles was forced to recall Horn
to help catch Geronimo when the army's independent efforts to
apprehend the Apache proved futile. Horn's efforts, in part, in the
campaign led to the capture of Geronimo for the last time.

In 1887, Horn mined silver for a short time in Arizona, and then
became involved in the Pleasant Valley War. This feud—the biggest
of Arizona's range wars—involved alleged cattle rustlers and sheepmen warring against cattle outfits over private and government lands.

Tom Horn's first killing may have been Mart "Old Man" Blevins in
July 1887. Blevins mysteriously disappeared, and nothing was found
of him except a skull in the hollow of a dead tree two years later. An
old rifle was leaning against the tree, and locals identified it as one the
man habitually carried. The rifle itself disappeared soon thereafter.

Horn's drunken bragging years later referred to a "coarse son of a
bitch" he'd murdered at age twenty-six, but referred to him as a Mexican

lieutenant. This may have been part of a dispute over a prostitute. Another version of the account is that Horn grew fond of an attractive young Mexican woman who lived near the ranch where he worked. An officer in the Mexican army was similarly attracted to her, and one evening as both men approached her home, they quarreled. The quarrel ended in the shooting death of the Mexican.

Late in 1888 Horn entered a rodeo in Globe and won the steer-roping event. It became common knowledge that he was a proficient rodeo contestant.

At this point Horn began to wind down his activities in Arizona.

About that time, Tom Horn's parents and siblings were living in the Delta-Ladner section of British Columbia. Archives show that living in the province on May 23, 1891[27] were:

> Thomas, age sixty-six, born in the U.S.;
> Mary A., age sixty, born in the U.S.;
> A. (probably Austin) H. Horn, age twenty-three, born in the
>   U.S.; and
> Alice Horn, age sixteen, born in the U.S.

The archives further reveal that Thomas died on November 20, 1891, in "Ladners Landing," at age sixty-six of inflammation of the lungs complicated with pleurisy. In the space on the death record for religion, a firm line was scrawled through it as if to say "none." Information on the deceased was given by Alice Horn.

B.C. Archives also indicate Mary Ann Maricha Horn[28] died in Surrey (which is in the same region as Ladners Landing) on November 26, 1908, at age seventy-seven of a chronic intestinal obstruction. Her religion, as provided by son-in-law J. B. Loney, Alice's husband, was "Christian Camble ite [sic] Church."

Alice, too, died in British Columbia. Austin was lost at sea on a sealing expedition in the Bering Strait before Tom's execution. Speculation within the family was that Japanese pirates played a role in the loss of all the men and the ship.

The Etna Cemetery in Scotland County, Missouri, holds, in addition to the remains of Thomas and Mary's infant son William, the remains of:

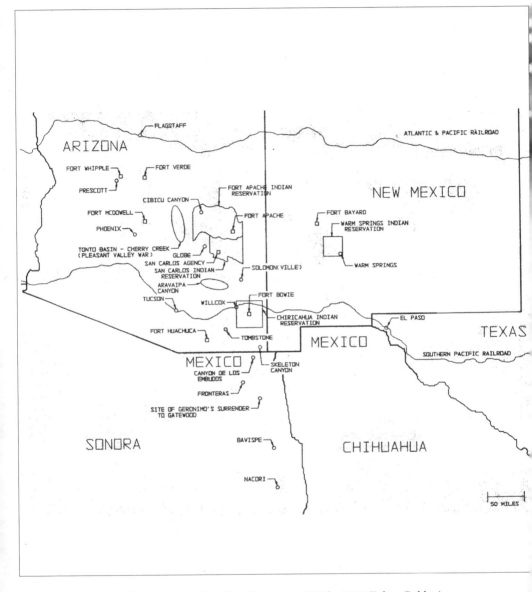

Region in the southwest where Tom Horn spent 1874–1890 (Johan Bakker)

Hartman Horn, the father of the elder Thomas;

Alice L. Horn, the first wife of Martin Horn, who died at age twenty-nine (no date of death shown);

Martin Horn, Thomas's brother, died January 1, 1896, at age eighty-four;

Druzilla Horn, the second wife of Martin, died January 20, 1872, at age fifty-four;.

Charley Horn, a son of Thomas and Mary's son Charles and his wife, Elizabeth Blattner Horn. Charley was born April 6, 1890, and died August 5, 1891;

Ima and Ina Horn, twin daughters of Thomas and Mary, who were born November 20, 1871. Both died on September 3, 1872;

Charles Horn, born February 1851 and died August 8, 1915. His relationship to the family is not known, and he is known as the "mystery man" among local historians;

Christena C. Horn, wife of this Charles, born April 9, 1857; died October 27, 1924.

Yes, it seems the Horns were bound to see trouble. And most of them fulfilled the prophecy, including the infamous Tom Horn.

Chapter Four

Black, Shifty Eyes

I T WASN'T LONG BEFORE more adventure sought Tom Horn out. Late in 1890 C. W. "Doc" Shores, a deputy U.S. marshal, sheriff of Gunnison County, Colorado, and part-time Pinkerton's agent, was on the trail of thieves who had driven stolen Colorado horses into Arizona. In December he received a letter from the postmaster of Solomonville, in southeastern Arizona. The postmaster and his brother owned the Dunlap Brothers' Ranch where Tom Horn was foreman. Both he and Horn had seen the thieves who had been described on a "Wanted" poster that had been distributed in the region. Shores said, "Being in the cattle business himself [the postmaster] appreciated what I was doing and would have his foreman appointed as deputy sheriff to assist…in making the arrests. He praised Tom Horn highly as a capable cattleman, rodeo star, and a former Indian Scout." [1]

Shores answered Dunlap's letter and arranged to meet Tom at Willcox, forty miles south of Solomonville. They met in the lobby of the hotel where the Colorado sheriff stayed after arriving. Shores described his new acquaintance as "a tall, dark-complected man with a black mustache…. He was around thirty years of age and presented an imposing figure of a man—deep-chested, lean-loined, and arrow-straight. He was wearing a plaid shirt, woolen trousers and high-heeled boots. A wide-brimmed sombrero covered his head." Shores also said Horn had "black, shifty eyes." [2]

As they traveled by buckboard to the location where the horse thieves had been seen, the two men became engaged in discussions on various matters. Shores described his partner as an "interesting conversationalist…[but] not the type of man one liked to argue with." [3]

After capturing the horse rustlers without trouble, the two men went their separate ways. Shores wrote a letter to James McParland, superintendent of Pinkerton's National Detective Agency in Denver. He praised Horn's work in helping him run down the horse thieves and recommended that the agency hire Tom.

Within months Tom Horn left his job at the Dunlap ranch and sold his interest in an Arizona silver mine. He went to Denver and, as he said, was "initiated into the mysteries of the Pinkerton institution." His superintendent, McParland, asked him what he would do if he were assigned a train robbery case. Tom told him simply that if he had the help of another good man, he would catch the robbers.

Around midnight on August 31, 1891, unidentified men robbed a train on the Denver and Rio Grande Railway between Cotopaxi and Texas Creek, roughly midway between Salida and Cañón City on the Arkansas River. The agency sent Horn out on the job, where his partner would be none other than "Doc" Shores. When Shores caught up with him, Horn:

> ...asked me how I was getting on. I told him I had struck the trail, but there were so many men scouring the country that I myself was being held up all the time; that I had been arrested twice in two days and taken in to Salida to be identified.
>
> Eventually all the sheriff's posses quit, and then Mr. W. A. Pinkerton and Mr. McParland told Shores and me to go at 'em. We took up the trail where I had left it several days before and we never left it till we got the robbers.[4]

The robbers went west across the Sangre de Cristo range in southern Colorado. They proceeded into an iron mining area and crossed back to the east side of the Sangre de Cristos at Mosca Pass, just southeast of the present-day Great Sand Dunes National Monument. Horn and Shores then chased them through Huérfano Cañón, out by Cucharas and east of Trinidad near the New Mexico line. The robbers dropped down into Clayton, New Mexico, and "got into a shooting scrape there in a gin mill. They then turned east again toward the 'Neutral Strip' and close to Beaver City, then across into...a place in Texas called Ochiltree" in the northeast part of the Texas Panhandle.

The robbers proceeded toward Oklahoma Indian Territory and entered it below Canadian City, going to the head of the Washita River and following it downstream to their final destination.

The two Pinkerton's men chased the robbers on horseback to Paul's Valley, south of Oklahoma City, more than three hundred miles from where they had first picked up the trail. At Washita station they located and captured one of them, Burt Curtis, in a house owned by a man named Wolfe. Shores hauled Curtis back to Denver, leaving Tom Horn to wait and see if the other robber would come back to Wolfe's:

> After several days of waiting on my part, he did come back, and as he came riding up to the house I stepped out and told him someone had come! He was 'Peg Leg' Watson, and considered by everyone in Colorado as a very desperate character. I had no trouble with him.[5]

Early in the investigation, Horn and Shores had suspected that Joe McCoy, who was wanted in Cañón City by the Fremont County, Colorado, sheriff for murder, had participated in the Denver and Rio Grande robbery. That was not the case; while the McCoys may have masterminded the event, they did not participate. McCoy and his father, Dick, had been tried and convicted of murdering a stock detective. Joe escaped from jail before he was sentenced, and Dick was out on bail at the time of the Denver and Rio Grande incident. Dick's ranch was across the river from the place where the train had been robbed, and it was natural that the lawmen would suspect him and his boys.

The train had been robbed in order to get money for attorneys' fees to carry the McCoys' case up to the Supreme Court, an early indication that men will go to unusual lengths to pay for a legal defense. In the McCoys' case it was for naught, as the father ended up with an eighteen-year sentence in the Cañón City penitentiary.

After apprehending Curtis and Watson, Tom Horn and "Doc" Shores ended their partnership. Horn, however, notified James McParland that he had an idea where Joe McCoy might be. McParland contacted the Fremont County sheriff, who went to Denver to accompany Tom in pursuit of the robber.

Horn wrote:

> We left Denver on Christmas Eve and went direct to Rifle, from there to Meeker, and on down White River. When we got to where McCoy had been, we learned that he had gone to Ashley, in Utah, for the Christmas festivities. We pushed on over there, reaching the town late at night, and could not locate our man. Next morning I learned where he got his meals, and as he went in to get his breakfast, I followed him in and arrested him. He had a big Colt's pistol, but did not shoot me.[6]

The next year, Tom Horn was arrested in Reno for robbing a Faro dealer on April 9.

The Pinkerton's Agency had sent him by train to Salem, Oregon, in December 1890, to apprehend one Jim McCabe. McCabe was wanted for attempting to wreck a train in order to rob it. Horn worked his way in with ditch diggers, who were all ex-convicts, even sleeping with them, in an attempt to locate McCabe. Early in April Pinkerton's dispatched Horn to Truckee, California, in the belief that McCabe was there. From that point Horn went to Reno.

Since McCabe was known as a tinhorn gambler, Reno seemed a natural place for him to hang out. Horn searched all through saloons and gambling halls, but came up with nothing.

After gambling for a while Horn returned to his boarding room and wrote his daily report to "J. S. Mack" (the code name for McParland, his chief). He proceeded to the post office, mailed it, and when he heard the train whistle he quickly packed his bag, went to the depot, and boarded.

Just before this, around 11:30 P.M., James Conroy, the faro dealer for the Palace Hotel Club Room, was robbed as he counted his cash while closing for the night. A masked man came up the stairs, waved guard Tom Pollard aside, and leveled a pistol at Conroy. He swept several hundred dollars into a bag and left.

Conroy reported the crime to lawmen; he, Pollard, and the officers rushed to the depot:

In about fifteen minutes the westbound train arrived and
Conroy and the officers with Tim Pollard were on hand to
watch for any suspected person boarding the train. Just as the
conductor said, "all aboard," the thief coolly walked past…with
a grip in his hand, stepped on to the car and took a seat. Conroy
knew him and stepped on at once with the officers, walked past
him, and turning quickly, said "Yes, that's the man." The officers ordered him to throw up his hands, which he did without
any hesitation…. He was hustled off the car and handcuffed
just as the train pulled out, and marched off to jail…. He said
his name was Thomas Hale and claimed to be an agent of the
Pinkerton's detectives.[7]

The trial commenced on July 14, with the defendant now being
called "Thomas C. Horn," [8] who, the paper said, was a Pinkerton's
detective. Horn had been released on bail, probably paid by Pinkerton's. Lieutenant J. M. Neal testified that he had known Horn since
1885 and described how he had served with merit in Arizona and
earned a "sterling reputation." [9]
Horn testified that Pinkerton's had hired him in 1890:

My duties have been various, running down robbers and
roping in gangs of toughs. Went to Salem, Or., to rope in some
train wreckers. I was doing the 'hobo act,' that is, eating, sleeping, drinking and gambling with 'tinhorn gamblers' for the purpose of catching crooked men. I came to Truckee and then to
Reno, hoping to catch one Jim McCabe….[10]

He described how he had filed his report, boarded the train, and
been arrested. He continued that he was worth in real estate and
horses about twenty-five hundred to three thousand dollars. He indicated he wanted to square things, but the officers told him Conroy
was an honest individual and they believed him to be telling the
truth. The proceedings ended with a hung jury.
Horn was again freed on bail, pending a new trial. The second
trial commenced two months later on September 29.

The prosecution attempted to establish firmly that Horn was the robber, but his defense team on cross-examination obtained acknowledgments of confusion as to the robber's identity.

The defense first introduced depositions:

> ...among them from General Nelson A. Miles, which was a high testimonial of his [Horn's] honesty, efficiency and bravery.... The other depositions were from prominent men in Arizona, ex-Sheriffs, U.S. Marshalls and Judges. All tended to the same point, and were to the effect that Horn was always well and favorably known as an honest and upright citizen, upon whom there had never been attached the slightest suspicion in any way.[11]

William A. Pinkerton testified that he had known the defendant and "he had been in my employ *for several years*...[emphasis added]. He has been a trusted employee of ours and while in our employ has been an honest and efficient employee."[12]

Horn testified that he was born in Missouri and was thirty-one years old. He described his experiences in the Southwest in considerable detail, and then went into his investigation in the McCabe affair. A Mr. Fraser, assistant superintendent of the Pinkerton's Agency, testified on the details of Horn's assignment to search for McCabe, and introduced a letter and telegram as further evidence.[13]

The defense rested without a closing argument. The jury returned a verdict of not guilty within a few minutes.

The Willcox, Arizona, *Southwestern Stockman* published an article on Saturday, October 17, 1891:

> W. A. Pinkerton, the head of the famous detective agency, arrived at the Palace hotel yesterday from Reno, Nev., where he attended the trial of one of his men, Thomas H. Horn, who was charged with robbing a faro bank. Horn was discharged, as Pinkerton secured a number of witnesses who proved it was a clear case of mistaken identity. In speaking of the case last night, Pinkerton said that he would travel 20,000 miles to get one of his men out of trouble, if he knew he was innocent.—*San Francisco Chronicle*.

Mr. Thomas H. Horn, mentioned in the above, is well known in Graham county, especially in the western portion, where he was for a long time foreman for Hon. Bart Dunlap.... His many friends here will be glad to hear of his acquittal of the charge of robbery. A number of depositions were taken here as to Mr. Horn's excellent character and forwarded to Reno.[14]

The Reno experience seemingly soured Tom Horn on the judicial system and its delays. He never mentioned it in his autobiography, nor did it come out in his murder trial in Wyoming. Horn was apparently able to work on the Cotopaxi train robbery while he was free, pending the second trial in Reno. He did a masterful job of juggling time and places.

In his autobiography Horn said that he left Pinkerton's and came to Wyoming in 1894.[15] This is almost certainly not correct. In all probability he arrived late in 1891 or early in 1892 when he was still associated with the Pinkerton's Agency. In the appendix to Horn's autobiography, Glendolene Kimmell, the Iron Mountain schoolteacher, stated that he arrived in 1892.[16]

Horn was in Wyoming for at least the aftermath of the Johnson County Cattle War.

The Johnson County War, launched in April 1892, was an effort by large cattlemen to solve what they perceived as their major problem: rustling in central Wyoming. The failed effort involved gunmen hired from Texas and a special train from Denver that surreptitiously picked up the cattlemen in Cheyenne. The cattlemen's intent was to murder or drive out all the suspected rustlers and install their own politicians to power.

From Cheyenne they proceeded to Casper, where they disembarked and continued north via horseback and wagon toward Buffalo. They sidetracked to Kaycee, where they murdered Nick Ray and Nate Champion. The delay allowed their adversaries to learn of the foray, organize, and advance toward the south from Buffalo. The cattlemen's expedition ended with a gunfight when locals surrounded the invaders at the TA Ranch.

Horn worked as a deputy U.S. marshal starting in May 1892, after the murder of George Wellman in Johnson County. He again used the alias Hale.

Wellman had been named a foreman for Henry Blair, a major rancher who was involved in the Johnson County Invasion, after the army took custody of the invaders following their defeat at the TA Ranch. On May 4, 1892, U.S. Marshal Joseph P. Rankin deputized Thomas H. Hale. Rankin also deputized Frank Grouard, Robert Lee Gibson, and others to investigate Wellman's murder.

Rankin came under pressure later in the year from the U.S. Attorney General to pursue the situation in Johnson County more aggressively. Senators Joseph M. Carey and Francis E. Warren, at the behest of the cattlemen, had urged the Attorney General to fire Rankin. Rankin defended himself in voluminous correspondence to the Attorney General. He said that Hale would not obey orders. In a letter to the Attorney General in Washington dated October 31, 1892, Rankin wrote:

> About the time of the killing of Wellman, at the request of the cattlemen, I appointed a man by the name of Hale a deputy for Johnson County. He had been obtained by the cattlemen from the Pinkerton Agency at Denver, and was selected by them because of his peculiar fitness for the work. He was to remain in Johnson County and watch for the parties against whom warrants were to be sworn out, and also to secure evidence as to who killed Wellman. He remained in Johnson County during all this trouble, having gone up there with me at the time Mr. Carr [Thomas Jefferson Carr, another deputy] and I took the injunction papers.[17] When I was in Johnson County in September I questioned Mr. Hale as to why he had been unable to accomplish anything in the arrest of the six or seven men for whom we then had warrants, and rather complained to him because he had not done something in the matter. He said, "I will be frank with you and state that I am instructed, through my [Pinkerton's] office in Denver, to take no instructions from you whatever; that the cattlemen are our clients, and we are working for their best interests. My instructions from the Denver office were to try to

drive these men out of the country and not arrest them. If they were arrested, and taken to Cheyenne and the evidence was not sufficient against them, they would be turned loose and the cattlemen would be in a worse fix than ever. I have carried out my instructions from the Denver office, and have rather tried to drive these men out of the country than arrest them." [18]

The marshal continued by repeating that Hale was a Pinkerton's agent. He further alluded to the perilous, shifting sands of the political scenario in Wyoming and the risks of antagonizing the then-powerful cattle interests:

Hale was, and is, a Pinkerton man, brought from Denver by the cattlemen, and appointed a deputy at their solicitation. I had appointed him about May 5th, 1892, and went up to Johnson County with him at the time he commenced work.... He has been in Johnson County ever since the date of his appointment, ostensibly trying to arrest the seven men for whom we have warrants. I say "ostensibly trying to arrest" the parties, for I have some ground for believing that he is instanced by the parties—except possibly the three charged with the killing of Wellman—but to hold the warrants against them and thus drive them out of the country. I would discontinue his services at once, if it were not for the fact that I do not want to do anything that will give the cattlemen the least ground for further complaint against me." [19]

The U.S. Attorney for Wyoming, Benjamin F. Fowler, had written to the Attorney General in Washington on June 27, 1892, regarding warrants to be served for setting fire to a barracks at Fort McKinney. The warrants were to be served on Charles Taylor, Henry Smith, and Johnson Long in May. He wrote:

In the cases named above, for obstructing process, Deputy Marshals Thomas B. Smith, Howard Roles and Thomas H. Hale were stopped by the defendants, who compelled the marshals to dismount and disarm and approach the defendants with hands up. When the marshals made known the object of their visit they were told by the defendants that they would not be permitted to serve the papers, and were driven away. [20]

U.S. Marshal Joseph P. Rankin. (Wyoming Division of Cultural Resources)

Significantly, Fowler cited a different name when he filed a document with the Clerk of the U.S. District Court on November 22, 1893, with respect to the trial for the killing of Wellman: "You are hereby notified that I have this day excused from further service as a witness, the following persons: Thomas Horn, Chugwater, Wyo."[21]

Horn's personality seems to have undergone considerable change during this period. Previously, no one had said anything derogatory about him—until "Doc" Shores made his observations, that he had no conscience.

An argument can be made that Tom Horn was exhibiting psychopathic tendencies. Certain traits that were first noted in 1890 became more apparent as the decade progressed.

According to Don Patterson, former chief of police in Cheyenne and an authority on criminal behavior, psychopaths exhibit characteristics seen in Horn:

> A superficial display of charm and average to above-average intellect.
>
> Psychopaths seem immune to neurotic, psychotic, or emotional problems such as anxiety and worry. There are usually viewed as very cool customers. They could very well view their own execution with cold disdain or clinical interest, but no fear.
>
> The psychopath exhibits a "flat" emotional reaction...he may be able to mimic emotion.... He lacks a true understanding of humor and is not able to laugh at himself.
>
> Psychopaths are totally unable to feel remorse or guilt. They would be ideal stock detectives.... A body count would be nothing more than an example of a job well done....
>
> Alcohol, even small amounts, prompts most psychopaths to become loud, boisterous and domineering....
>
> Perhaps most importantly, psychopaths all seem to require something "extra" in the way of sensory stimulation. The world of school, home, family, and regular work is not enough. Skydiving, car racing, or "man-hunting," now that's the ticket.

Patterson adds that a psychopath may well profess a dedication to truth and honesty. However, moral and ethical concepts are ignored if they do not serve the purpose.[22]

U.S. Attorney Benjamin Fowler. (Wyoming Division of Cultural Resources)

Regardless, by November 1893 Tom Horn had moved to Chugwater and begun a long career as an off-and-on employee of the Swan Land and Cattle Company and other major cattle outfits, while at the same time serving in various capacities as a lawman.

Chapter Five

CONSIDERABLE CATTLE STEALING

F ROM DEPUTY U.S. marshal to stock detective and sometime-sheriff was not a big jump. Tom Horn may have been first hired as a stock detective and graduated easily to deputy marshal, without leaving the first job.

When first hired by the Swan Land and Cattle Company, Tom Horn was based at the Two Bar Ranch. The Swan's headquarters were in Chugwater, thirty-five miles north of Cheyenne. The Two Bar home ranch is another twenty miles or so northwest of Chugwater, off and to the north of present-day Wyoming Highway 34.

The Swan's other ranches, the Mule Shoe, TY, M Bar, and Forty Bar, were major operating centers of one of the largest livestock operations in the history of the West, controlling over five hundred thousand acres of land and tens of thousands of cattle by 1885. The empire stretched from Sidney, Nebraska, ninety miles east of Cheyenne, to Rock River, Wyoming, ninety miles to the northwest.

The first documentation of Tom Horn's work as a stock detective involved the Langhoffs, a small cattle outfit. He had been specifically directed to gather evidence that could be used to obtain legal convictions against rustlers like the Langhoffs. At the time, John Clay was manager of the Swan operations.

Ferdinand Albert Langhoff (a derivative spelling of the original German "Langholf"[1]) was born in Wisconsin in 1856. In 1869 he moved to the Dakota Territory and by 1878 was working as a cowhand in North Park, Colorado. His employer at the time was Charley Hutton, a pioneer Laramie Valley ranchman.[2]

By 1880 Langhoff was in Wyoming, living at Dale Creek, fifteen miles south of Ames Monument to the west of Cheyenne.[3] In 1882, he settled on the main Sybille Creek forty miles southwest of Wheatland

Fred Langhoff. (Wyoming Division of Cultural Resources)

and northwest of Iron Mountain. He had married Evalina "Eva" Farrell in 1881 at her family's ranch in the Little Laramie Valley.

Eva's father, a Civil War veteran, had moved to Wyoming shortly after the war. By 1870 he was one of the largest cattlemen in Albany County.

Within a short period of time Fred and Eva had developed a substantial operation on 360 acres they owned outright. They were proving up on another 160 acres. They had three children.

Fred's brother, Henry (Hank), had moved from Wisconsin with their mother and lived for a short period with Fred and Eva. Hank worked at times with young Gus Rosentreter for people moving into the Sybille valley. Hank and Fred seemed not to get along, and Hank and their mother moved to another cabin nearby. Hank ended his own life in 1892 when he hanged himself in a shed on his brother's place. Their mother died shortly thereafter.

The Langhoff place, along with other homesteads that were springing up in the area, was located between large ranch operations in the Laramie Valley to the west and the vast Swan holdings to the east, primarily the Two Bar. Other substantial cattlemen also were situated near Langhoff's outfit, including William L. "Billy" Clay, whose place lay to the southeast on Mule Creek.

Other early settlers on the Sybille included many whose names later turned up in the Tom Horn/Willie Nickell episode. They included Mike Fitzmorris and many of German descent: Rudolf and Raymond Henke; the Plaga brothers, Otto and Albion; and the Berner and Waechter clans, who all homesteaded there in the 1880s. To the southeast were the families of Jim Miller and Kels Nickell, the former on Spring Creek and the latter on North Chugwater south of Clay's ranch.

Fred Langhoff was perhaps a focal point and an example of the larger struggle between the so-called cattle barons and more recently-arriving homesteaders. The homesteaders who had legally filed on their land felt they had a right to use the land and water resources. The big outfits that had used the open range for years believed otherwise; they did whatever they could to squeeze the "nesters" out. Their actions, including the lynching of Cattle Kate and Jim Averill in 1889, the lynching of Tom Waggoner shortly afterward, and the Johnson County Invasion in April 1892, resulted in a spreading animosity toward them on the part of an increasing middle class.

Fred developed a reputation as a horse trader, but was arrested for horse theft in 1892.[4] He had shipped twenty-six horses to Owensboro, Kentucky in June 1892. His problem was that he did not own them. The owners included John C. Coble, a prominent cowman, and two other major outfits.

The law pursued him to Kentucky, only to learn he had fled after selling the horses. A deputy sheriff remained in Kentucky to reacquire the horses, while a sheriff pursued Fred to Wisconsin. Fred was returned to Cheyenne to await prosecution. Also charged were Eva and two hired hands, Thomas Boucher and Louis Bath. Bath was the son of a prominent Laramie Valley family whose place was located near the Farrell ranch.

While Fred was engaging in casual or more serious thievery, and his neighbors, including Leslie Sommer, knew what was going on. Sommer wrote, "There were whispers that the Langhoffs' prosperity far exceeded their visible livelihood."[5]

Fred's log house and ranch became a gathering place for various purposes. People from as far as Chicago and farther east arrived to take advantage of the horse-trading opportunities at the LF Bar, as his place was known. At first Fred's business seemed to be legitimate, but as time went on there was talk that Fred seemed to do far better than one might expect, considering his modest start.

Other aspects of the Langhoff operation also attracted attention. Eva's charm sometimes diverted customers from obtaining a clear title to the horses they acquired. Leslie Sommer continued:

> There were rumors of the lure Mrs. Langhoff had for the strangers that came within their gates with horses or cattle to sell. Some of these strangers, falling under her spell, fell so deeply in love with her they figured they had received value personally, regardless of the profitless deal they may have made on their business arrangements....[6]

The 1892 incident with the stolen horse was the nadir of Fred's questionable actions as things turned completely sour. Things had not been going well beforehand, either.

Sommer wrote that hearsay indicated an earlier visitor, a Frenchman named Zu (or Susette), had a number of fancy horses for sale. He evidently had made some kind of a deal with the Langhoffs, since they had possession of his horses.

Susette disappeared from familiar haunts after he had complained to the law about the rawness of the deal. It was later reported that he'd hanged himself in the area.

By this time, however, the authorities in Cheyenne had begun an investigation of the Langhoff operation's more extensive activities. After a series of legal proceedings that ended in Eva's being acquitted of butchering neat cattle, Fred suddenly disappeared. He left Eva in charge of the ranch.

It was said that she graciously entertained the investigating committee that was trying to learn of Fred's whereabouts, but coyly denied knowing where he might have gone.

Sommer continued:

> Evelyn managed quite well on her own, and operated the ranch alone for some time after that, having as a foreman a boy of nineteen by the name of Lou Bath. He made no secret of his infatuation for his beautiful employer, but it was noticeable that no steadily employed men were hired to work on the ranch after Lou was made foreman....
>
> As things developed, it seemed that the outfit did unusually well in the cattle business.
>
> At that time Alexander "Al" Bowie was foreman of the Two Bar. Tom Horn was acting as a stock detective and a deputy sheriff in Laramie County [which had been arranged by Bowie and Clay]. There had been considerable cattle stealing around the country, and the big outfits were again hiring men as detectives, as they had been for years when rustling got out of hand.[7]

Horn had been lying in the hills around the Langhoff place for several weeks, watching for evidence that Eva and her hands were taking liberties with other outfits' cattle. When the time arrived, he moved into action:

Eva Langhoff. (Wyoming Division of Cultural Resources)

Al Bowie and Tom Horn decided to visit the ranch unexpectedly, with witnesses, and have a look at the cattle being dressed for market, which, strangely enough, seemed to be only done at night. They had brought as witnesses and deputized Raymond and Rudolph Henke, and young Gus Rosentreter—then only in his teens but already considered a good cowpuncher. They all hid out in the brush to watch the proceedings.

There were only three people working by lantern light, Lou, Mrs. Langhoff, and a man by the name of Bill Taylor, a drifter. [As a point of fact, Bill and Nellie Cleve also participated in the Langhoff shenanigans.[8]] The lawmen waited until the beef dressing was well under way before they approached the group. There was no chance of a getaway or to hide any evidence, as they were caught indisputably in the act of butchering stolen cattle.

Bill and Mrs. Langhoff stood quietly when the men with Tom Horn and Bowie in the lead came forward. Young Lou lost his head and started chattering, using the knife he was holding as a defense weapon. Horn ordered him to drop the knife, and on Lou's refusal, Horn gave him the ultimatum of dropping the knife by the count of three, or of being shot without parlaying.[9]

Tom Horn arrested the group and hauled them into town for prosecution.

This effectively marked the end of the line for Eva Langhoff. The family's previous and subsequent legal proceedings left her penniless, and she ultimately lost all her holdings there.

At the trial, Taylor swore that he only held the lantern and had no knowledge that the cattle were stolen, so he was not charged. Bath swore that he alone was guilty of the cattle stealing—that Eva could not be held even as an accessory to the crime, as she did not know the cattle were stolen. Taylor and the "Cow-Belle," as Evelyn was called, went free.

Louis Bath was sentenced on January 30, 1894, for killing cattle.[10] He was given an eighteen-month term in the state penitentiary, then located in Laramie, and was granted a pardon on January 8, 1895 by Governor John E. Osborne, a Democrat—just before the newly-elected Republican

Gus Rosentreter on his horse Raven. (Wyoming Division of Cultural Resources)

Governor, William A. Richards, was sworn into office. Richards was a strong supporter of the cattlemen.

In a broader context, the Langhoff incident reflected the ongoing struggle between the big outfits and homesteaders to control the best land and water, and the frequency with which the big ones prevailed.

As it later turned out, Tom Horn's recollection of the affair contributed to his own demise. His testimony during the Langhoff case stating that he had more faith in calves than in courts was used against him during his murder trial, as an illustration of his disdain for the legal system.

Gus Rosentreter's own life story adds color to the Langhoff incident. At sixteen, he arrived in Laramie from Germany in July 1890, after rebelling against a doctor's prognosis that he would never fully recover from a bout of typhoid fever. He went to the Sybille area where he earned room and board as he learned the basics of ranching. The clean dry air, nutritious food and physical ranch work restored his health, and he subsequently became a muleskinner, crew member of a surveying outfit, and cowboy.

Gus Rosentreter wrote of the Langhoffs in his memoirs:

> One day when I rode into the Plaga Ranch, I found the Two Bar manager, Al Bowie, and Tom Horn there. They were watching a neighbor who had been butchering Two Bar cattle, and they wanted me to go with them.
>
> I told them I did not care about going, but Raymond [Henke] spoke up and said, "You had about as well make up your mind to go as Tom Horn will deputize you anyway."
>
> I went, and when we got to the place, they had several beef hanging up in a shed. One man had a big butcher knife in his hand and talked big. Tom Horn told him, "Drop that knife or I'll put a bullet through your head." The knife dropped and the show was over, except for watching the prisoners.
>
> I was then told to go to several of the Swan Ranches—the Jones Ranch, Two Bar, and Mule Shoe—and tell the ranchers to be there early the next morning with their teams. They took the beef and the prisoners to Laramie....
>
> That was all I had to do with it. I heard later that one of the prisoners was sent to the penitentiary for a year, and the rest of the guilty ones left the country.[11]

Laurence Rosentreter, Gus's son, furnished an interesting addendum to the account.[12]

> In the territorial days of Wyoming, the Axford family squatted on upper Deadhead Creek on my present-day ranch. They had a dugout house, small rock barn, and started a ditch and meadow. They also had a small band of sheep. Tom Horn supposedly tacked a note on their door, to leave. The next day they pulled out to the Wheatland flats and settled on a farm.[13]

Chapter Six

No Better Man

F RANK M. CANTON, who had himself been a deputy U.S. marshal and sheriff of Johnson County and who subsequently lost an election to rustler-sympathizer William "Red" Angus, is believed to have murdered John Tisdale in Johnson County. Tisdale was gunned down in a wagon as he drove toward home in December 1891. He was an honest homesteader who had gone to Buffalo to handle some business matters and purchase Christmas gifts for his wife and children.

Canton participated in the Johnson County Invasion in April 1892, siding with the cattlemen. That alliance added to the enmity the homesteading community had already developed toward him. He then moved to Oklahoma which, in terms of geography, provided him with a measure of safety from the homesteader/rustler element in central Wyoming.

Canton worked as an undersheriff in Pawnee County, Indian Territory. In 1895 he pursued John "Jack Smith" Tregoning, who had escaped from the penitentiary in Laramie on November 15, 1894.[1]

Canton wrote to William A. Pinkerton in Chicago on April 7, 1895, asking for help from a Pinkerton's agent who was a good tracker and sleuth.

On April 12, William Pinkerton replied:

I am in receipt of your very full and complete letter of April 7th and note contents. As we have not got the right kind of man for this rough work out there, I have referred the matter to Supt. McParland at Denver, sending him a copy of your letter. I was greatly pleased to hear from you and did not know of your change of place. I imagine that whoever goes out on this work will find it rather difficult to do and we have not got at this

Frank Canton with his wife and daughter, while living in Buffalo. (Jim Gatchell Museum, Buffalo, Wyoming)

office available such a man as I feel satisfied would fill the bill in every particular.

Tom Horn who used to be with our Denver office would be a good man for the place, and I will ask McParland to communicate with him and see if he cannot be got for the service and for the length of time you want him. He is not in our service now. You probably know of him. He is well acquainted all through the western country among cattle rustlers and all that class of men, and is a thorough horseman and plainsman in every sense of the word. I note particularly that you want to get Jack Treganing [*sic*] who escaped from the Laramie penitentiary where you sent him for life and that he is down in that country. I should be very glad to hear of his capture....

William "Red" Angus, Johnson County sheriff who allegedly sympathized with rustlers. (Wyoming Division of Cultural Resources)

James A. McParland wrote to Canton in Pawnee from Denver on April 13, discretely avoiding the mention of any names:

> Yours of the 7th to Mr. W. A. Pinkerton has been forwarded to me with instructions that if any of the Operatives at this office who were capable of doing work of this kind were available that I should at once send him forward to you.
>
> You are well aware that it will take a peculiar man to do this work, in fact a man as it were, to the Manor born. I have such men at this office but at the present time they are engaged on other operations. In fact I have three that could do this work or that I could detail upon it but at present they are unavailable and it is impossible for me to say when they would be at liberty. I know of a man although not working for me but I could recommend

Frank Canton. (Wyoming Division of Cultural
Resources)

him as he formerly did work for me. I have not got his address at
the present time but he is liable to write me at any time and as
soon as he does I will suggest to him the fact that this matter is
ready to be taken up and will have him communicate with you. I
can guarantee the man. If he undertakes this matter no better man
could be found for the work that you wish to have done. I, like
you, would very much like to get hold of Tregoning as poor Henderson was an intimate friend of mine.[2]

The "no better man" was, little doubt, Tom Horn.

Chapter Seven

A System That Never Fails

NO BETTER MAN than Tom Horn could have been available to investigate the cattle thievery that was occurring northwest of Cheyenne along Horse Creek.

The years before and after the Langhoff episode reflected continuing problems with rustling for the cattleman. The Langhoff case of cattle theft, which resulted in only Louis Bath being jailed, was simply another in which the homesteaders and associated middle class again prevailed.

For years the courts had been lenient with cattle thieves. The Wyoming Stock Growers Association (WSGA) and large independent cattle ranchers had hired as brand inspectors and stock detectives reputable men like N. K. Boswell and W. C. Lykins—and still others who had earned dubious reputations—in an effort to gather evidence and arrest the thieves. However, their efforts were frustrated by juries that were often made up of working men—including rustlers—and by lenient judges. The judges, who were elected, understood their own electorate.

Thomas Sturgis, secretary of the stock growers association (WSGA), had said in 1886:

> Whenever a special case [of cattle stealing] comes to our notice, we always push it if the evidence is sufficient to get even a hearing before the proper authorities…[but] it is very difficult to get an indictment from a grand jury [even] with pretty definite evidence as to the guilt of the party charged with stealing cattle. Unfortunately, it is almost completely useless to bring matters to the court even after an indictment has been obtained and the evidence pretty well gathered. There seems to be a morbid sympathy with cattle thieves both on the bench and in the jury room....[1]

William C. Irvine, president of the Wyoming Stock Growers Association. (Pioneer Museum, Douglas, Wyoming)

Even hiring independent detectives to procure courtroom evidence proved to be wasted effort. WSGA Secretary Thomas Adams, describing the frustrations and sorry financial situation in which the large outfits found themselves, said:

> It would be impossible for the Association…to undertake to bring the parties referred to, to justice. In the first place, we have no money at our disposal. In the second place, if we had the means to enter into any investigation of the matter, we would be obliged to act through private detectives. We already have tried this system, and have been thrown out of court and laughed at for our pains. *Circumstances have forced cattlemen to look to themselves for protection outside of any association*….[Emphasis added] [2]

"Looking to themselves" meant taking whatever measures became necessary. William Lewis was one of those who invited those measures upon himself.

Many of the big ranch owners recognized that most homesteaders were honest, law-abiding citizens, simply trying to start a new life. However, they could not allow the rustling to continue unabated. And while in some areas the big outfits were determined to run the "nesters" out using any means, most of them did not have the time or the manpower to harass the settlers. Their main focus was keeping their outfits in business. But their patience and frustration had limits.

By 1895, the frustration reached the highest levels. Tom Horn had a meeting with the governor himself, William A. Richards, which Charles B. Penrose described. Penrose, a young physician who had accompanied the Johnson County Invaders, wrote[3] that W. C. Irvine, head of the Wyoming Stock Growers Association, told him:

> Ex-Governor W. A. Richards [in office from 1895 until 1899]…was the Governor when our office was in the Capitol Building. He was a part owner of a ranch and quite a number of cattle in Big Horn County. It finally dawned on him that cattle thieves were not respecters of persons, and that he was losing an animal occasionally. One day I met him as I was walking up to the Capitol. When we reached the building he said, "Come into my office; I want to see you." He immediately laid his troubles at the ranch before me, and we discussed the situation quite fully.

It was at this point that the Governor spoke of what was really on his mind:

> He finally said he would like to meet Tom Horn, but hesitated to have him come to the Governor's office. I said, "Stroll in my office at the other end of the hall at three o'clock this afternoon, and I will have him there…." [When the three of us met] I opened the conversation by stating the trouble they were having in Big Horn County, and that the Governor wanted to talk to him [Horn] as to the best way of stopping the stealing

Governor William A. Richards. (Wyoming Division of Cultural Resources)

there. The Governor was quite nervous, so was I, Horn perfectly cool. He talked generally, was careful of his ground; he told the Governor he would either drive every rustler out of Big Horn County, or take no pay other than $350 advanced to buy two horses and a pack outfit.

Then Tom Horn alluded to how he would solve the problem. He did not need to go into specifics:

> When he had finished the job to the Governor's satisfaction, he should receive $5,000, because, he said in conclusion, "whenever everything else fails, I have a system which never does." He placed no limit on the number of men to be gotten rid of. This almost stunned the Governor. He immediately showed an inclination to shorten the interview.... [After Horn left] the Governor said to me, "So that is Tom Horn! A very different man from what I expected to meet. Why, he is not bad-looking, and is quite intelligent; but a cool devil, ain't he?"

It has been written that another meeting occurred though no documentation seems to exist.[4] This meeting allegedly took place at the original Cheyenne Club, on Seventeenth Street, with leaders of the cattle industry attending. Horn made a simple proposition. His plan was that he would do whatever was necessary to rid the country of thieves. His actions would require no legal defense and no appeals. His words were said to be, "Gentlemen, I have a system that never fails. Yours has."

The proposal created more than soul-searching. The meeting broke up with the chairman stating that arrests were one thing, but outright assassination was another. Nevertheless, the conventional wisdom is that more than one outfit took Tom Horn up on his proposal to clear out the thieves, as long as they were not implicated.

Within the space of six weeks in 1895, two suspected rustlers, William E. Lewis and Fred U. Powell, were dead. Lewis was the first to die.

William Lewis was an English immigrant who had settled near Horse Creek northwest of Cheyenne. His age has never been determined, but he apparently came to the United States in the early 1880s and applied for citizenship in 1882.[5] He received citizenship in 1888.

Lewis was an unsavory character. In 1883 he was indicted in Albany County for stealing a minor's money after persuading the youth to try his hand at faro. Three years later he was charged with stealing clothing from two different men in Cheyenne and ended up spending two months in jail for the misdeeds.

Over a period of time he became involved in rustling cattle from neighbors in the Iron Mountain area where he owned a small ranch. In mid-May 1893 seven cattlemen charged him with stealing a calf. He was arrested, charged, and found guilty. The court, however, granted his lawyers a motion for a new trial.

The case dragged on, with him now being charged separately for stealing cattle by the Swan Land and Cattle Company, one of the plaintiffs in the first case. The prosecution, for reasons unknown, dropped the first case. In the second case the jury found him not guilty.

This was another serious blow to the cattlemen. Lewis then became a much bigger problem. He struck back by suing the Swan, Al Bowie (a Swan foreman), John Coble, Van Gilford, Samuel Moses, and a party by the name of Pierce for fifteen thousand dollars. His allegations were that the parties who had charged him had damaged him financially.

Fifteen thousand dollars in 1895 was a lot of money—equivalent to perhaps three hundred thousand in today's dollars. If the defendants lost they would be in deeper financial water, and a precedent would be established.

And there was a good chance he would win the case, since Lewis had prevailed in the two earlier cases, and the winds of change were blowing against the barons. Speculation even today exists that his enemies, who numbered more than the six parties he had sued, decided it was time to solve the problem of William E. Lewis once and for all.

Lewis received death threats; twice someone fired shots at him, and then someone burned down his ranch house. He moved southeast to Horse Creek where he worked for the Montgomery Ranch. He was also deeply in debt for his legal bills and to the creditors who had posted bail for him. Most, if not all, of his property was mortgaged. He had received notes telling him to cease his activities, leave the area, or face the consequences.

On the morning of July 31 he was loading a skinned beef into a wagon. As he prepared to go to town, three shots hit him. Any would have been fatal.

Ranchers J. Whittaker, George Shanton, and John Harding discovered his decomposed body on August 3.

News of his death reached Cheyenne when a young man rode up to the courthouse at 2:00 P.M. that day with a note Whittaker had written to the sheriff. Together with the county prosecuting attorney, coroner, and physician, the sheriff took two teams of horses and a vehicle and left the same afternoon for the site of the killing. Lewis's body, it was said, had decomposed so badly it had turned coal black by the time the inquest was completed the next day. He was buried where he was gunned down.

The *Laramie Boomerang* reported the Lewis killing in its August 5, 1895, issue.[6] It indicated that Lewis had been tried and acquitted four weeks earlier in Cheyenne, but the article did not specifically describe the charges he had faced.

The investigation of Lewis's murder revealed he had no business butchering or in any way disposing of cattle. Frank Boehm of Cheyenne held a chattel mortgage to all of his cattle as collateral on a loan. Any sales should have gone to help settle the note. However, investigators found a number of old hides bearing his HDK brand in a shed nearby. Officials also found that Lewis had considerable debts in Cheyenne and that he kept spare clothes hidden in a trunk at Nimmo's meat market. Shanton and Whittaker commented to the newspapers that Lewis was a disagreeable type. People said he had not a friend in the area.

A grand jury investigation called over a dozen witnesses, including Tom Horn and William L. (Billy) Clay. Clay had been subpoenaed and arrived in the company of a deputy sheriff who had gone to Bates Hole to find him. Bates Hole, where the Swan Land and Cattle Company had holdings, is southeast of Casper in Natrona County and over eighty miles from the site of the murder. Rumors circulated that

Tom Horn would not appear, but he arrived on the scene after he sent a telegram from Glenrock on October 2 indicating that he would be on the Northern Railroad and in Cheyenne shortly.[7]

Horn and Clay testified at the inquest that they had been in Bates Hole. No further action was taken. Local speculation was that Clay had been in Bates Hole simply to provide an alibi for Horn.

Lewis's meager assets were sold at auction to local interests, but they were not sufficient to cover his debts.

So, who killed William Lewis? A descendant of a prominent Laramie County rancher who had employed Tom Horn provided information to the author in confidence. He said, "I have reason to believe my grandfather killed William Lewis, because he was stealing our cattle."

Perhaps a greater significance lies in the way that the public attempted to tie Tom Horn to the killing. His brash proposals, his heavy-handed methods, and his braggadocio concerning the Langhoff incident contributed to his reputation as an intimidating, fearsome detective. And rightly so.

At the Lewis auction Fred U. Powell, who ranched southwest of the Montgomery place in Albany County, was warned to leave the country by parties who were looking out for his best interests. He was the next to take a bullet.

Chapter Eight

THE DESIRED EFFECT

THE MURDER OF William Lewis was not the last tied to Tom Horn that summer.

The second homesteader to be killed was Fred U. Powell. Old-timers have argued about who deserved killing more, Lewis or Powell, and Powell usually comes out on top. There is reason for it; he got into more trouble with more people. During his entire tenure in Wyoming he went out of his way to find trouble, and perhaps trouble found a way to find him.

Powell was born in Virginia[1] and became well known in southeast Wyoming virtually from the time of his arrival in the mid-to-late 1870s, by becoming a sort of pariah. He married Mary Keane in December 1882, the daughter of John and Mary Keane, well-known pioneers who had come to Laramie from Colorado in 1868.

Fred and Mary had a son, William E. "Billy," who, according to one legend, as a small child witnessed his father's murder on September 10, 1895. Fred was only thirty-seven at the time of his death.

⟶⟶⟶⟶

As a young man, Fred had lost an arm in an accident working for the Union Pacific. The railroad then gave him a job as a night watchman until he was fired for robbing a traveler (probably a drifter), who was working his way across the country, of twenty dollars.

He then took up ranching on the west side of the Laramie Range in Albany County, upstream on Horse Creek about seven miles southwest of the spot where William Lewis had been shot. He became proficient with a rope and horse in spite of his handicap, and was generally considered a rustler. He was the only person in the area who was friendly with Lewis. Fred, however, was in most ways an anathema to the ranching community and even the populace in general because of his continuing propensity to steal, trespass, and destroy property. He thought it was fun to taunt his neighbors—in a manner he felt was more humorous than did they—with invitations to have their own beef for dinner at his place.

From pre-statehood days before 1890, the charges against him read like a self-defeating chant:[2]

> *Territory of Wyoming v. Fredrick U. Powell,* Stealing and Killing Neat Cattle, Albany County;
> *State of Wyoming*...Grand Larceny, Cheyenne Justice of the Peace;
> *State of Wyoming*...Stealing Live Stock, Albany County;
> *State of Wyoming*...Malicious Trespass and Destruction of Property, Albany County;
> *State of Wyoming*...Incendiarism and Malicious Trespass, Albany County;
> *State of Wyoming*...Criminal Trespass, Albany County.

First he stole four horses in Albany County in July 1889. He was arrested and jailed in September. After the grand jury held its proceedings, the charges were dropped.

In August 1890 he was charged with grand larceny in Cheyenne. The justice of the peace accepted a motion by Powell's lawyer that there was not enough evidence to show any crime had been committed, and Fred was released.

In January 1892 Mary Powell filed for divorce on grounds that for seven years he had not supported her or their son, who was then seven. The divorce was granted the next month. Mary however continued to live with Fred for years after that, although perhaps only intermittently.

The summer after the divorce he was charged with stealing a horse in Albany County. Fred pleaded not guilty, and after four days of legal arguments he was bound over for trial. At the trial in September, the jury returned with a verdict of not guilty.

In July the next year Fred was charged with malicious trespass and destroying fences belonging to Etherton P. Baker.[3] First he was convicted but filed an appeal, and in September the jury found him not guilty.

That was not the last Etherton P. Baker heard from Fred U. Powell, however.

The next spring, in April 1894, Powell set fire to personal property belonging to Baker and another neighbor, Joseph Trugillo, who was apparently living with Baker. Powell was hauled into court, but this was not to be his best day in his encounters with the law. He appealed the light sentence that was meted out and was released on a hundred-dollar bond.

In July Powell stole a horse, was arrested, and tried. The judge found him guilty and fined him forty-five dollars. Again he appealed and was released on bond. When the next trial for incendiarism came up in September, he was convicted and sentenced to four months in jail. The charges were dropped in the horse-stealing charge.

When Powell was released in early 1895 he started to receive letters. The letters carried the then-familiar theme to stop stealing, leave the country, or be killed. For a while he seemed to disregard the threats.

After the Lewis murder, he started selling his stock.

Powell met the same fate as Lewis the morning of September 10, 1895. Laramie's *Boomerang* reported the afternoon of his murder that:

> During the past three months Powell has received three threatening letters without signature. The last one was received on Tuesday of last week, and according to the remembrance of a gentleman who read it it ran as follows:
>
> *Laramie, Wyo., Sept. 2, 1895*
>
> *Mr. Powell: This is your third and last warning. There are three things for you to do—quit killing other people's cattle or be killed yourself, or leave the country yourself at once.*
>
> There was no signature to the above letter, which was written in ink and with a disguised hand.

The *Boomerang* continued that the writing was in a "backhand style" and appeared to be an attempt to disguise the author's true handwriting—and "the work of a fairly good pensman."

The paper indicated that the first of the three letters had arrived about three months previously, and the second shortly after the Lewis

Mary Powell. (Wyoming Division of Cultural Resources)

killing. Upon receiving the third letter, Powell "tried to induce one of his friends to accompany him home, stating that he was afraid for his life."

The only witness to Powell's murder was a hired hand, Andrew Ross. Ross testified at the inquest that he had gone to cut a stick near a creek, on orders from Powell, to repair an enclosure around a haystack. He heard one shot, found his employer's body, and fled to the nearby Fay Ranch. He informed a Miss Richardson, who carried the mail, of the killing. She in turn took the news to Laramie.

※※※※

Mary was in Laramie, probably accompanied by Billy, at the time of the incident.

The rumor that Billy pointed out the man who had killed his father, arguably Tom Horn, does not stand up under scrutiny. However, the prosecution effectively used it in closing arguments in Tom Horn's murder trial in the Nickell murder in 1902.

T. Blake Kennedy, who became a key player on Tom Horn's legal defense team and later a U.S. District Judge, mentioned in his memoirs, "It had been reported that at a coroner's [Powell's] inquest the small son of the murdered man, who was perhaps five years old, made the remark in identifying Horn, 'That's the man that killed Daddy.'"

However, Fred's hired hand Andrew Ross, stated at Fred's inquest that the two were alone on the ranch the morning of his killing.

※※※※

Powell's brother-in-law, Charles Keane, later returned to the ranch to run it. He left shortly after he arrived after receiving a threatening note himself. Mary and her son continued to run the ranch.

The question lingers: who killed Fred Powell?

Under conditions of anonymity, a Laramie county researcher and historian told the author, "E. P. Baker. Fred Powell had set fire to Baker's haystacks."

However, the "system that never fails" and the man who first proposed it to Governor Richards were suspected of being behind both murders. The system worked—whether Horn committed the murders or not, people believed he did. Fergie Mitchell, a rancher of the North Laramie River, said:

We had been having a lot of trouble with rustling on the North Laramie. One of our neighbors up the creek arrived in the spring with eleven cows, and that fall marketed forty yearlings. He made serious inroads upon our herds, but no matter how hard we tried, we could not catch him in the act of stealing cattle. He would take them before our eyes, secret them some place, we never could find where, and that would the last of them. He was so brazen he asked one of the neighbors if he wouldn't like to come over and eat some of his own branded steak.

So one day Tom Horn visited the North Laramie. I saw him ride by. He didn't stop, but went straight on up the creek in plain sight of everyone. All he wanted was to be seen, as his reputation was so great that his presence in a community had the desired effect. Within a week three settlers in the neighborhood sold their holdings and moved out. That was the end of cattle rustling on the North Laramie.[4]

Horn's dissatisfaction with the judicial system seemed to grow as a result of his arrest in Reno and the Langhoff case. He had to know of the continuing leniency toward lawlessness in the courts. His own overconfidence in his prowess with "the system that never fails," coupled with his boasting (part of his intimidation tactics), eventually led to his own undoing.

A local rancher who is a descendant of Iron Mountain/Horse Creek pioneers told the author, "Tom Horn was hired to clean up the rustling situation, not to murder people." And clean it up he did.

"Fritz" Mueller, who was raised by stepparents on Horse Creek, knew Mary Powell for many years when he was growing up. Mary worked for his family and told Fritz on many occasions that it was not Tom Horn who killed her husband, but another local with whom Fred had been feuding.

After Fred's death, Mary Powell went to work as a cook at the Two Bar. Mary became notoriously ill-tempered, in keeping with a tradition of ranch cooks. One noon during dinner, an indiscreet cowboy at the long table began griping about the food. Mary walked up behind him, pulled a six-shooter out from under her apron, and stuck the muzzle in his ear. She said, "Now, you are going to eat that meal, and then, you son of a bitch, you are going to tell me how good it was."

Following Fred's murder, Mary's life continued to be as tempestuous as it had beforehand. She had continuing brushes with the law. Between 1895 and 1914 she was charged at least ten times for burglary, stealing livestock (with Billy), arson, assault and battery, malicious mischief, trespass, twice for disturbance and breach of peace, and assault and battery. She died in 1941.

Fred and Mary Powell's son, Billy, had at least three scrapes with the law himself, including two charges of owning a still, manufacturing and possessing liquor, and violation of the white slave act. He served thirty days for that offense in 1925. Locals spoke of the high quality of his bootleg. "You'd never feel bad after an overdose of Billy's stuff," one Iron Mountain rancher said.

Billy met death in gunplay in 1935 at the hands of his fifteen-year-old stepson, Lon Phelps. The two argued over Lon's need of a bath at their ranch home on a Saturday night in January, and the boy ran into a bedroom, drawing a twenty-two caliber automatic from a holster lying on the floor.

The Cheyenne *Daily Sun* reported on January 7, 1935:[5]

> He [Lon] warned Powell to stay away but his stepfather leaped at him and struck him, knocking him across the bed, the officers said.
>
> Lying across the bed he fired twice, one of the bullets striking Powell's mother [Mary]...when she ran into the room and inflicting a superficial wound in the left arm....

Powell died in Laramie hospital after his stepson and wife transported him there in a pickup.

At the time of Billy Powell's death—and over forty years after Tom Horn put the "system that never fails" into effect—big cattlemen still justified Tom Horn's work. An executive of the largest bank in Denver, who was raised on a Wyoming ranch, said in 1936 that Tom Horn had been a big part of his family's heritage. He said that his father had told him that if it had not been for Tom Horn every cowman in the state would have gone bankrupt. He emphasized his point by stating that Tom Horn helped more boys get a college education than Phillips Brooks or Horace Mann ever did.

Although, apparently, Horn had no role in the actual murders of either Lewis or Powell, his shadow—that of the devil incarnate to the smaller ranchers in southeast Wyoming—hung heavy over Wyoming.

Chapter Nine

No Cure, No Pay

B Y 1896 Tom Horn had left the Wyoming range and returned to working in the Southwest. His earlier role in the capture of Geronimo had earned him a positive reputation. As the Indian depredations in Arizona continued, he was once again called upon. Or, perhaps, he injected himself into an opportunity and excitement.

Although Geronimo had surrendered in 1886, while he was being transported to Fort Bowie, Arizona Territory, six of his Apache companions, three men and three women, escaped in the night before arriving at the fort. At least one or two of the escapees took part in a fight in 1896 with the Seventh Cavalry in the vicinity of Guadalupe Canyon at the junction of the borders of Arizona, New Mexico, and Mexico.

The fight with the Apaches in 1896 was the largest since the year of Geronimo's imprisonment. Tom Horn took part in the episode.

The Adjutant General's office prepared a brief on the situation on May 15, 1896.[1] It indicated that since 1890 bands of renegades had been making incursions from Mexico that resulted in killings, stealing, and pillaging. An Apache called "Kid" headed the band, which returned to the Sierra Madre mountains in Mexico after the raids, according to the brief.

Mexicans were similarly troubled by the Apaches' deeds. In December of 1892 the governments of Mexico and the United States entered into an agreement whereby forces of either country could enter the other to pursue renegades.

On February 23, 1893, the commanding general of the Department of Arizona was notified that "Renegade Kid" had kidnapped a woman the previous day. The First Cavalry pursued the Kid, causing him to leave the woman behind, but lost the trail between Rock Canyon and Ash Creek Canyon.

On December 8, 1893, the governor of Arizona wrote to the Secretary of War, requesting assistance to run down the Kid. He stated that:

> …this renegade with a small band of followers had continually for the past 3 years kept the frontier settlers of Southeastern Arizona, Southwestern New Mexico and Northern Sonora and Chihuahua, Mexico, in a constant state of unrest, had killed many people and destroyed and stolen a large amount of property….

The brief continued that on December 5, 1893, "Mr. Merrill and daughter of Pima were killed by Indians at Ash Springs, 20 miles east of Solomonville. Six Indians from Mexico were reported to have committed the crime, and gone north." It said that an Indian known as "Old George" was suspected in the murders.

On March 31, 1896, correspondence from the commanding officer at Fort Grant stated that Apaches had murdered Alfred Hands and that the commander had given orders to destroy the killers. It said, "The man Hands was killed by Indians and cut to pieces on the 28th of March at mouth of Cave Creek, 25 miles south of San Simón." It continued that Lieutenant Rice had driven the Indians back across the border near the Cloverdale ranch.

On April 27, the brief continued, the commanding general of the Department of the Colorado received a report from the commanding officer at Fort Grant, who had returned from the southern part of his district. By this point Tom Horn had entered the picture. The report indicated that the Chiricahuas were camped in Mexico near the border:

> …From necessity for food, or from a malicious desire to plunder and murder citizens of the United States the different members of this band cross the border periodically when they think it safe to do so, waylay any defenseless citizen on their route, steal horses and plunder ranches. It is supposed that they cross the border on foot and at night [,] hide in the mountains on our side of the line for days and when an opportunity presents itself they gather a sufficient number of animals to carry their plunder and return to Mexico.

The settlers were partly at fault. With the Indians apparently crossing the border on foot and hiding until opportunities arose, the settlers over a period of time became lax and negligent in taking sufficient measures to ensure their own safety:

> That portion of our border lying between San Barnardino [sic] and the Animas Valley to the East is like a door left wide open, and the carelessness of the citizens, in their defenseless condition, is simply an invitation to these renegades to plunder and murder them.

This brief from Colonel Sumner of the Seventh Cavalry at Fort Grant ended with a request for "employing Mr. Thomas Horn and 2 Chiricahua Indians at Fort Sill," and stating that five hundred dollars would be necessary to accomplish their mission. It reported that "Mr. Horn desires only one Indian from Fort Sill (Nochi by name) to assist in capturing the renegades...." The brief was heartily commended by the commanding general of the Department of Colorado.

A second brief dated May 20, 1896, was called "A plan for the capture of renegade Indians, 'Kid,' 'Massai' and followers." The brief stated that on April 29 Senator William M. Stewart wrote to the Adjutant General requesting that the situation be investigated. He said that "a colored person called 'Jim'" had driven H. G. Howe of Tombstone through mining properties in Arizona and Mexico and that Jim knew where the Kid stashed supplies and went for water.

The commanding officer at Fort Grant, E. Johnson, had written to the Adjutant General of the Department of Colorado in Denver on May 4 that he wanted to employ:

> ...Mr. Thomas Horn, the man that went into Geronimo's camp alone and persuaded him to see and talk to Lt. Gatewood, all of which was preliminary to the surrender to Colonel Lawton. The government could save money and probably many lives by expending five thousand dollars to catch these renegades and I may be able to accomplish it for much less. Still, I want money enough to pay well for success or at least enough to pay Mr. Horn for the attempt be it successful or not....

Mr. Horn is supposed to be the only white man with whom the renegade Masse [Massai] will hold any communication. This may or may not be true at any rate he is willing to ask it and may meet with success.... I respectfully request prompt action in the matter as Mr. Horn intends leaving the country but will wait a reasonable time.... I will want instructions as to what promises I can authorize Mr. Horn to make the renegades in case of surrender.[2]

The major general commanding the army submitted the recommendation to the Secretary of War, who approved it on May 21, 1896. Only the "negro Jim" was to be employed with Horn, at no more than seventy-five dollars per month for four months. Horn's pay was to be one hundred dollars monthly on a similar temporary basis.

On July 1 a detachment left for San Bernardino, including five enlisted men of Troop K of the Seventh Cavalry, two Indian scouts, three civilian packers, twenty-one pack animals, and Tom Horn as guide.

Heavy seasonal rains slowed the effort to track the Indians. The commanding officer left the outfit at a camp near Batipeta while he and Horn attempted to find their quarry on foot; the country was so rough it was impossible to use the pack animals through much of it. When they didn't find the Indians, the entire troop continued in pursuit.

Lieutenant Michalson of the Seventh Cavalry reported that the expedition had gone through no fewer than seventy horse and mule shoes. He recommended that any future expedition be well outfitted with a farrier, plenty of shoes for the animals, that all men be mounted on mules, and that no attempts be made to do any trailing during the rainy season, July through September.

Tom Horn's presence on the Mexican border in June 1896 in the service of the army was well covered by local newspapers. The *Sulphur Valley News*[3] in Willcox stated on June 2, 1896, that Horn had been there for a week, having come in from Aravaipa Canyon where he was foreman for Burt Dunlap, one of his employers from his previous stint in the Southwest. On June 16 the paper reported, under the headline "Real Campaigning," Horn's presence at the San Bernardino ranch with the Seventh. It added that "Horn had charge of the scouts in the ill-fated expedition against Geronimo, which cost the life of the gallant Captain Crawford at the hands of Mexico soldiers."

The *Graham County Bulletin* reported on June 19, 1896, that the headquarters of the Seventh Cavalry was at the San Bernardino ranch, "right on the line between the United States and Mexico, preparing to chase into Mexico." It stated:

> Tom Horn, one of the best known Indian fighters in Arizona, was with the outfit, having been engaged by the United States at a very fancy salary to give the officers of the 7th the benefit of his experience gathered during many years of Apache warfare, in fights with the wily redskins and following them over the rocky mountains and burning deserts of Arizona and Mexico from the San Carlos clear down to the Sierra Madre mountains.[4]

No skirmishes resulted from the army's pursuit of the renegades; the Indians evidently reached the relative safety of Mexico. Over a period of time, relentless pressure from the military brought a semblance of peace. However, Tom Horn's expertise was perhaps a factor in subduing the Apaches.

Later that year Tom Horn was running a ranch for E. A. Jones at Aravaipa, northeast of Tucson. He wrote a letter to U.S. Marshal William K. Meade from Jones's ranch on November 7, 1896, offering his services to run down the Black Jack Christian gang. William T. (Black Jack) Christian and Robert (Bob) Christian had broken out of jail and, along with the members of their band, were robbing virtually every establishment in sight.

Horn wrote:

> ...If there is anything in it for me...I can stand a better show to get them by going alone and will go and get some of them at least and drive the rest out of the country.... No cure no pay is my motto. So if I don't get them it costs no one a cent.[5]

The same issue of the *Graham County Bulletin* reported that Marshal Meade had been complimented during the session of the

Quartermaster General documents reflecting Tom Horn's employment during the Spanish-American War. (Courtesy Larry D. Ball, from the National Archives)

U.S. court "on the promptness with which every duty of his office was performed.... Marshal Meade conducts his office on strictly business principles."

The army solicited Tom Horn's services late in 1897 or early in 1898, as a mule packer for an expedition to Cuba. His ability with stock and knowledge of Spanish served the military well.

Glendolene Kimmell, the schoolteacher who boarded at the Miller homestead in 1901 and who was a peripheral figure in the Willie Nickell episode, wrote of Horn's experiences in Cuba in an extensive appendix to Horn's autobiography. Her comments are believable, since she and Horn spoke at length during the two days he was at Millers, and she spoke with him further before the second session of the coroner's inquest of the Nickell murder. Although Horn exaggerated his role in the war, telling Kimmell of his alleged achievements for Theodore Roosevelt, her account is largely corroborated by other sources. She wrote, "Too great emphasis can not be given to the fact but for...Tom Horn, there would have been no supplies nor ammunition at...San Juan Hill."[6]

She said General Marion P. Maus solicited Horn's services to organize the pack train that would transport supplies for the army after it landed in Cuba. The pack train, made up of 520 mules, was delayed on the sea trip from Tampa after traveling by land from Saint Louis. The result was that Roosevelt and his Rough Riders landed ahead of the supplies and pack train that the men needed.

Kimmell continued that only because of Tom Horn's efforts were the mules ever landed at all. The transport ships were not able to get close enough to the landing to disembark the animals by gangplanks, so Tom obtained orders to use his own methods. At the gangway of each ship, four men with ropes secured each animal, and then pushed it into the bay. Following its instincts, virtually every animal swam to shore. Thus it was, she believed, that the pack train reached the beach and helped Roosevelt achieve his victory.

Kimmell also said that Roosevelt, with Leonard Wood (with whom Tom Horn served in Arizona) met Horn as they approached San Juan Hill and that Horn supplied the two with fresh mounts. She said, too, that Horn's eyewitness description of the San Juan fight was "the best in detail ever given."

A number of independent accounts verify that Horn served capably in Cuba. He enlisted as a packmaster in Tampa on April 23, 1898.[7] He landed with the Fifth Army Corps at Santiago, and on August 1 was promoted to chief packer. He was discharged on September 6.

Horn contracted the "Cuban" (yellow) fever while in Cuba. Traveling by way of New York, Horn returned to Wyoming where he recuperated at John C. Coble's Iron Mountain Ranch northwest of Cheyenne during the winter of 1898–1899.

On October 5, 1898, Horn wrote from the Iron Mountain ranch to the Quartermaster General in Washington about going to the Philippines, a territory ceded to the United States by Spain as part of the war reparations:

> Sir: I understand that there are to be some Pack Trains organized to be stationed in Wyoming.
>
> I think for the services that I rendered in Cuba as Chief Packer of the 5th Army Corps that I should be entitled to Pack Mastership of one of the trains organized here as this is my home. Colonel Jacobs, Chief Quartermaster at Santiago has known me many years and will, I believe, recommend my work in Cuba and elsewhere. I am well and personally known by nearly all the Generals of the Army. I was Chief of Scouts for Genls Miles, Lawton and General Wood in the Apache Indian wars.
>
> Now if you can give me one of these Pack Trains I will fully appreciate it and I think you will never have cause to regret it.

Yours truly,

Tom Horn

I have been sick every day since my return from Cuba but am improving now.   —H.[8]

⚓

Aide-de-Camp Marion Maus, with whom Horn served in Arizona and Cuba, wrote to the Quartermaster General from Army Headquarters in Washington on February 28, 1899:

General:

I beg to commend to your kind consideration the name of Tom Horn, who was employed as Chief Packer in Cuba, and has high testimonials from Colonel Jacobs.

I can say this of Horn: that he is one of the bravest men I ever saw. He was with me in Arizona; distinguished himself for gallantry in action with Mexican troops and Apache Indians with my command of scouts in the Sierra Madre Mountains. He is energetic, speaks Spanish fluently, and would be invaluable as a scout, or packer, or whatever you could give him. He is an experienced cow herder, packer, and an all-around good man. He was my chief of scouts, and I have a high regard for him.

He wants to go to Manila as a packer, or a scout, or in some position that you might give him.... I would be especially appreciative if you could give this man employment, and permit him to go with the next of your transports to Manila.[9]

Nothing came of Tom Horn's attempt at more service for the military. However, later that year the War Department wrote of him, referring to "Horn, Tom, Ex Chief Packer 5th Army." It referred to a letter from Tom at Iron Mountain dated September 30, 1898:

Tom Horn desires to know whether he can obtain pay and commutation of rations from the time he left Santiago September 6 till September 23 when he reported to Colonel Atwood at Denver, Colo. The claim was denied by the War Department on November 16, saying "that in the absence of official evidence

Manager, J. C. Coble.   Range and P. O.
Foreman, Duncan Clark.   Iron Mountain, Wyo.

CATTLE BRANDS.

Iron Mountain
INCORPORATED **Ranch Company**

Iron Mountain, Wyo., Oct 5" 1898—

Quarter Master General
Washington D.C.
U.S.A.

Sir

I understand that there are going to be some Pack Trains organized to be stationd in Wyoming I think for the service that I rendered in Cuba as Chief Packer of the 5th Army corps that I should be entitled to Pack Mastership of one of the Trains organized here as this is my home. Col Jacobs Chief Quartermaster at Santiago has known me many years and will I believe recommend my work in Cuba and elsewhere. I am well and personaly known by nearly all the Generals of the Army. I was Chief of Scouts for Genls Miles Lawton & Genl Wood in the Apache Indian war.

Now if you can give me one of these Pack Trains I will fully appreciate it and I think you will never have cause to regret it.
Yours Truly
Tom Horn
Iron Mountain
Wyoming
I have been sick every day since my return from Cuba but am improving now.

Letter written by Tom Horn to the Quartermaster General October 5, 1898, requesting a position as packmaster for horses from Wyoming that were to go to the Philippines. (Courtesy Larry D. Ball, from the National Archives)

that there is pay due him his claim cannot be considered by this office. Attention is invited to the complimentary endorsement hereon by Colonel Jacobs." [10]

＊＊＊＊＊＊＊＊

Larry Jordan's grandfather, John L. Jordan, was an employer and friend of Tom Horn in the Iron Mountain country. Larry relates a story about Horn's recovery from the fever and his father, Frank ("Sunny"), who was born in 1892. When Sunny was a little tyke, he frequently rode over to Coble's ranch. Like most kids, he headed straight for the kitchen.

At the time, Horn had a little bell attached to a string, which he pulled when he needed to summon his nurse, Fannie Steele, for help. One time when he was in there, he heard a cowbell "clonk" in a bedroom nearby. The cook said, "Well, that's Tom Horn. He's got that fever that keeps coming back, and I tied a cowbell to him so I can hear him when he falls out of bed." So, Sunny and the cook went into the bedroom, found Tom "with the sweat just pouring off him, and got him back into bed," Larry said.

Chapter Ten

KILL HIM AND BE DONE WITH HIM

For a period things were quiet for Tom Horn. His activities early in 1899 are not known, although he required a period to recuperate from the fever. However, his involvement in one event in the late spring has been documented. It was the Wilcox train robbery of June 2, 1899. Authorities believe the robbery was engineered by the Hole-in-the-Wall Gang, a loosely knit group of outlaws who at times were led by Butch Cassidy. Cassidy did not participate in the Wilcox robbery but may very well have planned it.

At the time of the robbery, the Union Pacific's tracks ran north and east of present-day Rock River, Wyoming. (In 1900 the railroad embarked on a track-shortening project that moved the line to its present location. Today the location of the robbery is on privately owned land.)

The railroad moved large shipments of currency, gold, silver and other valuables on specific trains that were supposedly well-guarded secrets. However, information leaked out that high-value cargo, including unsigned bank notes and silver, would leave the U.P.'s headquarters at Omaha for points west. One historian, Nelson "Ed" Wren, believed that "Elzy" Lay, one of Butch Cassidy's associates, arrived in Medicine Bow the day before the robbery with word for his confederates that the evening train would be carrying the cargo in the express car.[1]

Three robbers (some accounts pointed to six men) stopped the train just east of a bridge around two o'clock on the rainy morning of June 2. After uncoupling the passenger cars behind the locomotive, tender, mail car, and express car, they ordered Engineer W.R. Jones to pull past the bridge for a moment. They then dynamited the bridge with charges they had already put in place to block the second section of the train from following them.

Union Pacific express car after being blown by the robbers at Wilcox and moved to Medicine Bow. (American Heritage Center, University of Wyoming)

The train pulled ahead about two miles. The robbers first ordered the mail car opened. They learned that any valuables on board were in the locked express car. When the expressman, Charles T. Woodcock, refused to open the express car, they blew the door open with powder. Woodcock was dazed from the blast and could not remember the combination to the safe or pretended that he could not. At that, the robbers blew the safe, using such an excessive amount of the "giant powder" that the car was destroyed. They escaped on horses they had hidden nearby with over fifty thousand dollars in loot.[2]

The bandits headed north toward Casper, crossed the North Platte River under the cover of darkness, and continued north toward the Big Horn Mountains. Stopping to rest overnight, they killed Converse County Sheriff Josiah Hazen when his posse discovered their horses and camp. During the shootout they lost their horses, but escaped on foot and reached the Big Horns. There they acquired fresh horses from "Black Billy" Hill, a local rancher known to be sympathetic to rustlers and others of their ilk.

Another posse, one that included railroad officials, U.S. Marshal Frank A. Hadsell, and others, followed the robbers but lost them west of the Big Horns near Kirby Creek because of rain. Investigations by subsequent groups failed to learn who the robbers were and where they headed. Joe LeFors, the lawman who later secured Tom Horn's "confession" to the murder of Willie Nickell, was probably one of the posse, as he stated in his autobiography.[3]

Tom Horn quietly investigated the robbery as the country simmered down. He apparently was working for the railroad, possibly with the Pinkerton's Agency through its role with Union Pacific.

At some time after the robbery Horn embarked on his investigation. He wrote his report to the division superintendent of the Union Pacific in Cheyenne on the identity of the three robbers who had headed north from Wilcox into the Big Horn Mountains:

> Iron Mountain, Wyo.
> January 15th, 1900

> E. C. Harris, Esq.[4]
> Cheyenne, Wyo.

> I have this to report in regard to my investigation in Johnson County:

> On January second I went to the house of old Bill Speck, and stayed all night with him. In the morning it was snowing and I stayed all day. Occasionally I would bring up the train robbery, and he never wanted to talk about it, so on the morning of the fourth when I was going to leave I told him that he had some information that I wanted and he must give it to me, or I would kill him and be done with him. Well, that was just [what] Speck was looking for, and he commenced to cry and said the rest of the rustlers would kill him if he told. I told him I was worse than they, because I would surely kill then and there if he did not tell me, as no man was within eight miles of us.

> Speck asked my protection from the rest of the rustlers, which of course I offered him, and then he told me as follows:

Horn continued his report by summarizing Speck's story:

The morning of the killing of Joe Hazen, George Currie came to Billy Hill's ranch on Red Fork of Powder River about one o'clock in the morning, and wanted to get some of his own horses that were at Hill's ranch in charge of Alec Ghent.[5] Currie had four horses there, but there were only two of them in the pasture, the rest being out on the range. Ghent had been looking for these other two horses for three weeks, but could not find them. Currie got his own two horses, and Hill gave him two. Currie told Hill, Speck and Ghent of the robbery, and said it was himself, Harve Ray and a stranger in Powder River country [who had committed it], but Currie would not give his name, saying only that the stranger came from the British possessions and that he could blow Christ off the Cross with dynamite.

Harve Ray did not come to Hill's ranch, as he had played out in camp after they lost their horses, so Ray and the stranger stayed at Al Smith's ranch, and Currie got a horse from Al Smith and rode up to Hill's to get a mount and some saddles. Ghent went out and got all of Hill's horses, and Currie took his own two, and bought two from Hill. Currie then went back to Al Smith's and got his two partners, and pulled out.

Another man named Loller was at the ranch of Hill working on a ditch, but did not come around.

Currie told Speck and Hill all about the robbery, and about losing their horses [after the robbery]. Said the reason they lost their horses was they had been riding all night, and stopped in the morning to get something to eat, and hobbled their horses, and after they ate they laid down and dropped off to sleep, and they heard the posse driving off their horses and woke up. Currie said they had been keeping a good lookout, and did not know anyone was following them. Currie said they exchanged some shots, but did not think anyone was hurt, as Currie and his men did not want to hit anyone. Currie said they had made a good, comfortable haul, and that they had come from the British Possessions and were going back there as the officers there could not catch a cold.

Horn continued his report, still summarizing what Speck had told him, in great detail:

> Currie said that he was married, and had a boy one year old, and that he had married Annie Ehrgood somewhere in Idaho. Currie said he had been on the British line for a year smuggling opium for some Chinamen, and that himself and Ray could make two hundred dollars in three nights when there was opium to smuggle, so advised all good rustlers to go there.
>
> Currie left Hill's ranch before daylight with the horses, and they have not heard anything of them since, although Currie said he would write Ghent.
>
> Speck was sure Currie had never written, or he would have heard of it. The same day Currie left Hill's ranch a man from Buffalo came to Hill and told them of the robbery, and they said nothing to him of Currie being there (this man was Johnny Rounds), and the next day the posse came in and camped at EK Mountain, and Speck went over and told them the robbers had been at Hill's ranch the night before and took some of his horses, while in reality they had been there 24 hours before the time they told the posse. Speck said the posse could not have been on the trail, as the robbers came by Al Smith's ranch, and Currie got a horse there and came on to Hill's, and then went back to Al Smith's and got his partners, so that they were not on the side of the Red Fork that the posse said they were trailing them on.
>
> Alec Ghent was at the ranch the night the robbers were there, but the night they told the officers the robbers were there Ghent had left and gone after a load of lumber.

Horn's report to the Union Pacific continued:

> This is about all of Speck's statement, and the most I drew out of him by questions put to him. I had him on the rack for five hours. He was crying at first, and then got calm and cool when he saw I was not going to kill him. Of course this information will be valueless to you, as you don't care to go to any

Billy Hill, who aided the robbers in their escape through the Big Horns. (Wyoming Division of Cultural Resources)

more expense in the matter, but I thought I would give it to you anyway. After Speck told me all he could I thought it best not to kill him, for he will tell me if any of them ever writes to Hill or Ghent.

In the last few days I have made arrangements to go to Johnson County again about the middle of March for the Cowman, for cattle are getting a good price now, and the Hole-in-the-Wall gang have been in hiding all summer, and there is no complaint of any stealing, which is new for that country. Cowmen think my being in that country keeps it down.

I came home right away after my talk with Speck, for I know there was nothing to learn there, and I was already out about six hundred dollars for my time and expenses.

If when I go back I learn anything more I will write you if you care for the information. I won't be in for some time, as it is snowing now, and I want to get in some horses as soon as the storm is over, so I can commence to feed them. Of the five Company horses I had two were sold at the VR ranch, and the money sent to you, so the foreman said. Those two I got from Hiatt. Of the three I bought one was lost, one I killed, and the best one of all I have here at Coble's ranch at Iron Mountain. I will bring him in when I come, or send him the first chance I have if you are in a hurry for him.

Enclosed you will find my bill of my expenses. Please deposit money to my credit at the Stock Growers National Bank if the bill and statement meet with your approval. If the bill does not meet with your idea of it, just change it to suit yourself, and it will be perfectly agreeable and satisfactory to me.

Yours truly,
Tom Horn[6]

Pinkerton's assistant superintendent in Denver, Frank Murray, wrote about Horn's letter to U.S. Marshal Frank Hadsell on June 7, 1900:

I enclose for you herewith copy of the Tom Horn letter of January 15th, 1900, that I spoke to you about yesterday in Cheyenne.

You will find on reading this that the name "Harve" was used by Speck in his talk with Tom Horn, but he said Harve Ray. There is a Harve Ray, who would now be a man about 30. He went to school with George Curry [*sic*] and was raised at Sundance; but Harve Logan might have been the man Speck was talking about just as well as Harvy Ray.

I find that we have no extra copy of this letter and therefore will thank you to return it when you are through with it.[7]

The *Buffalo Bulletin* had reported on January 18, 1900, that "Deputy United States Marshal Tom Horn" had been in Casper, "on the trail of the Wilcox train robbers. Describing him as "the famous detective," the article continued that Horn and another officer had murdered two rustlers in northwest Wyoming. Horn said that the robbers had gone to British Columbia. On February 8, the paper said Horn had been interviewed in Cheyenne and had said, "We know who they are and the Union Pacific will pursue them to the end."[8]

Other historians have asserted but without substantiation that Tom Horn was part of the posse in the Big Horns. One legend has it that he chased two robbers to a cave near Muddy Gap, where he killed one, Kid Curry (Harvey Logan), and then returned to Cheyenne to claim part of the reward. According to the story, the railroad paid the reward but learned later that Curry was killed long after his alleged assassination by Horn. As the legend goes, the railroad then decided to pay no rewards without a body, dead or alive.

The *Cheyenne Daily Leader* stated in an article published the day of Tom Horn's execution that he was a member of the posse. The *Leader's* version was that Horn had killed two prospectors by mistake and showed no remorse for his error.[9]

J. Elmer Brock wrote in 1937[10] that two of the leaders in the posse that pursued the Wilcox train robbers were Joe LeFors and Tom Horn. Brock's recollection of the episode (which took place while he was a teen) is most likely incorrect; his memory was probably clouded with the passage of almost forty years. Although LeFors may have been a part of the posse, Horn's involvement didn't come until later.

Neither LeFors nor Horn ever mentioned any association with each other before the Nickell killing. If they had worked together, LeFors probably would not have acknowledged it in his autobiography, *Wyoming Peace Officer*, since his goal in the Willie Nickell affair was to portray Horn as a vicious child killer. Moreover, Horn confirms that they had not worked together in his letter to LeFors of January 1, 1902: "Joe, you yourself know what my reputation is although we have never been out together."

Years after the Wilcox robbery, while at the Miller homestead in July 1901, Horn bragged to Jim Miller and the Miller boys that he had encountered the Wilcox robbers. He told the impressionable homesteaders, during his stay with the Millers early in the week that Willie Nickell was killed, that he alone had apprehended the thieves, and after a vicious knife and gunfight he had single-handedly made the arrest. The story was a product of Horn's imagination.

His association with dangerous characters was not.

Chapter Eleven

Don't Say Anything

A NASTY CHARACTER, AND mysterious one, too, was Robert D. Meldrum. Meldrum, a shadowy figure who straddled the nineteenth and twentieth centuries, was one of Tom Horn's closer friends.

More than just passing acquaintances, Horn and Meldrum were casual friends in an alliance forged by a common background as lawmen. The fact that they had joint escapades is evident from their correspondence.

Bob Meldrum was born in England in 1866 and immigrated to the United States, where his family settled in Buffalo, New York, in 1880. Little is known about his whereabouts before he arrived in the West.

He was imprisoned at the state penitentiary in Deer Lodge, Montana, from December 23, 1894, until August 18, 1896,[1] for the theft of a saddle in Billings. He had been a member of a gang of horse thieves around Forsyth, east of Billings. The *Billings Gazette* wrote on October 31, 1894, that law officers described him as "not considered overly bright...a tool of some gang of thieves located here."

He first showed up in the Baggs, Wyoming, area around 1899. He boasted of having worked with Tom Horn for a law enforcement agency, probably Pinkerton's. Meldrum found work in nearby Dixon as a harness-maker, a trade at which he had considerable skill. Meldrum worked for Charley Perkins, who also had a sawmill, saddlery, and general store west of town. Meldrum frequently received "wanted" posters in the mail, and noticed one day in 1900 at the post office that another Perkins employee, Noah Wilkerson, was wanted "dead or alive" in Texas.

One version of the episode is that after leaving the post office together, Meldrum let Wilkerson pull ahead and then drew his Colt's

*Bob Meldrum, circa
1903.* (Museum of
Northwest Colorado)

forty-four and shot Wilkerson in the back of the head. Supposedly "Bad Bob" then collected his reward and dropped out of sight.

However, a local paper[2] reported at the time that Wilkerson was armed and went for his gun, at which point Meldrum drew his own and shot Wilkerson in the mouth. A coroner's jury declared that Meldrum had shot in self-defense.

The same paper reported a week later that Wilkerson had been shot twice. One shot had entered between the shoulders and exited to the right of the mouth. The other shot creased the skin over his left eye. After another week the paper reported that Sheriff Kirk from Texas had arrived and identified Wilkerson as the sought-after "cold-blooded killer." He recommended that the State of Texas pay Meldrum the two hundred dollar reward.

In 1901, the year Willie Nickell was killed, Tom Horn wrote to Meldrum from the Iron Mountain Ranch, probably in late spring or summer:

> R. D. Meldrum, Esq.
> Baggs, Wyo.
> Dear Bob,
>
> I am going to Rawlins today and I will drop you a line from there. I think I am going to need your help to do some work shortly. There will be five dollars a day and expenses in it for you, and a visionary show[3] for something on the side. I will write you from Rawlins after I look around there a day or two. *Don't say anything to anyone* [emphasis Tom Horn's] about coming to me if I should send for you.
>
> I will certainly want you. I will send transportation for you on [the] stage.
>
> Look for another letter to follow this one in two or three days.
> Yours truly,
> Tom Horn[4]

Horn's mysterious "work" in Rawlins may have involved rustling. Jay Monaghan cited Horn as having fingered a county commissioner who was suspected of stealing cattle from the Swan Land and Cattle Company's holdings east of Rawlins. No date for the incident was shown.

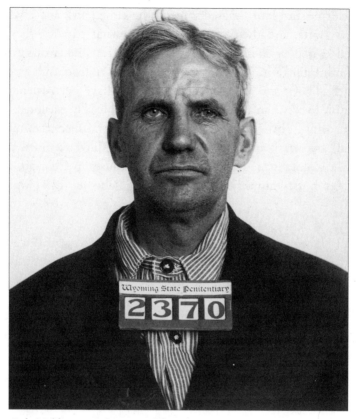

Bob Meldrum at the time of his imprisonment in Rawlins. (Wyoming Division of Cultural Resources)

Meldrum later visited Horn when he was in jail in 1902 and the two corresponded that year. Meldrum again wrote to Horn when he was in jail in Cheyenne before his hanging.

Meldrum led a colorful life on both sides of the law, sometimes serving as a deputy sheriff, but also reportedly killing up to a dozen men. He was charged with murdering "Chick" Bowen in 1912 and fled to Texas while awaiting a retrial after the first trial ended in a hung jury. However, he turned himself in and, found guilty of manslaughter, served a year in jail. He then became a trustee, which allowed him to serve out the rest of his sentence by working for local citizens. He later opened a harness shop in Rawlins. When it burned in 1926, he disappeared.

Meldrum and Horn shared some of the same Jekyll and Hyde personality traits, and their careers were somewhat parallel: they both worked as deputy sheriffs, they both worked for Pinkerton's Agency, they both built intimidating reputations using violence and threats of violence. They were acquaintances and may have been friends. But Meldrum lived to an old age. Tom Horn was legally executed before his forty-third birthday. Bob Meldrum simply vanished after his shop burned, and was variously reported to have killed six men in cold blood in Colorado, to have died of natural causes in Chicago, and to have been horsewhipped to death and dry-gulched north of Walcott.

Chapter Twelve

The General Welfare

AN OMINOUS KILLING in the northwestern Colorado Brown's Hole region startled residents in mid-1900. Even more sinister was the plot that lay behind it.

Two small cattlemen, Matt Rash and Isam Dart,[1] had been in Brown's Hole[2] in northwestern Colorado for a number of years. In July and October 1900 they were killed. Their previous actions, along with those of other small ranchers, had led to conflict and a conspiracy by three prominent ranchers to eliminate them. Tom Horn was their agent.

The prologue to their murders was the developing cattle business as the new century began.

By the mid-1890s the cattle business in Wyoming and Colorado was changing in major ways, in large part because consumer tastes had started to gravitate toward more tender and flavorful beef from breeds other than longhorns. And while longhorns are hardy and calve easily, they do not add weight as rapidly as other breeds.

Another major reason for the changes in the range business was an influx of homesteaders. The homesteaders, "nesters" or "grangers" as they were referred to disdainfully, proved up on claims to some of the best bottomlands. By doing so they decreased the availability of water for the herds of the dominant, larger ranchers who depended upon the availability of open range.

One major operator was Laramie's Ora Haley, who had enormous holdings both in northwest Colorado and southeast Wyoming, and who acted to adjust to the changing conditions.

Haley, born in Maine in 1845, had come to Wyoming at a young age and become a force in the Wyoming cattle business and in territorial politics.[3] Through his foreman, Hiram "Hi" Bernard, he brought in white-faced Herefords to improve the grades of beef to meet market demands.

Bernard, a Texan who had driven cows to northern reaches as a young man, observed that as cattle operations evolved, overhead increased. As the open range was fenced off by homesteaders, cattlemen were forced to lease land from the railroads or to purchase privately-owned land, to fence bull pastures to produce summer calves of uniform weight, and to raise hay for winter feed. Bernard purchased several large hay ranches for Haley in Colorado's Routt County area, which comprised Brown's Hole. Bernard's management was enormously profitable in spite of the depredations of locals. Bernard described the range and Haley's success. He commented:

> These ranches extended over a wide scope of the county, with both winter and summer ranges on all sides. It was [largely] open public domain, all choice range, and with few fences to hinder the movement of cattle for a distance of about 100 miles in all directions. That constituted a pretty layout, and easy to handle.
>
> It proved to be good. Haley made over a million dollars profit on his Routt County investment in less than ten years. And in that time he never saw the range end of the business but three times. He did not know a thing about it for he was not a range man.
>
> Haley was a smart and lucky financier. He came to Wyoming a bullwhacker, and started in the cow business at Laramie with three old dairy cows. He was smart enough to see opportunities and capitalize on them, lucky to find a sucker to handle a range cattle business better than he could, and he was wise enough to keep from meddling with the range end, where the payoff came from. That is a rare combination of human character.[4]

Conditions, however, were such that a range war was brewing in northwestern Colorado, just as one had raged in Wyoming.

But a difference existed in the situations between Wyoming and Colorado. In Wyoming, the cattlemen attempted to keep homesteaders and small ranchers from settling on lands they felt were exclusively theirs. In Brown's Hole, many homesteaders and small ranchers were already well established. Large outfits from other areas, squeezed from

Ora Haley. (American Heritage Center, University of Wyoming)

their traditional ranges or wishing to expand, discovered the little-used open range at Brown's Hole and began to move into the grasslands. Valuable land sat underused and they needed it.

The first mistake the Brown's Hole locals made was failing to acquire privately-owned ranches that were readily available along their eastern perimeter. Had they done so, they could have resisted further inroads by the large operators. Ranches owned by Ben Majors and one Sainsbury were acquired in 1894 by Ora Haley.

The second mistake was allowing the area to become known as a "safe haven" for outlaws. Hi Bernard remarked that "the reported presence of such characters helped to scare outside stockmen away from the gravy bowl. It was a 'no trespassing' sign, and it worked for a long time."[5] However, their sympathy for and assistance to outlaws inevitably created animosity.

Bernard added that the smaller outfits' third mistake was "they were range hogs, for they were controlling a greater amount of range

John C. Coble. (Wyoming Division of Cultural Resources)

than they used or could use. 'It must be kept that way'—one of Brown's Park's 'musts.' Well, time changes things, and it 'must' be a hell of a shock to some of them to see things now," he said.[6] Bernard's further observations, as reported by Frank Willis in his manuscript *Confidentially Told*, brought proof of Tom Horn's complicity in the murders that were to come.

Willis wrote that late in 1899 or early in 1900, Ora Haley ordered Bernard to meet him at Haley's Denver office. At the time Haley was fifty-five and married with four grown children living in Laramie. Three other cattlemen were present: Charles E. "Charley" Ayer[7], Wilfred W. "Wiff" Wilson, and John C. Coble.

Ayer, forty-three, was born in New York, married with five children and lived in the Four Mile area of Routt County, Colorado.

Wilson was born in Utah in 1857 and lived with his wife, three children, and mother-in-law near Baggs in southern Carbon County, Wyoming. Both Ayer and Wilson had significant livestock holdings in southern Wyoming and Brown's Hole.

John C. Coble was born in 1857 in Pennsylvania and was a partner of Frank Bosler in the prominent Iron Mountain Ranch Company of Bosler, Wyoming, north of Laramie.[8] Tom Horn was on Coble's payroll at the time of the meeting, having wrapped up his investigation of the Wilcox, Wyoming, train robbery. At the Denver meeting in Haley's office Ayer and Wilson bewailed the lawlessness that infested Brown's Hole, condemning "the place as an outlaw hangout and a threat to the Haley interests," Bernard said.[9] Both recounted their cattle losses and named Matt Rash and Jim McKnight as rustlers:

> Coble had like grievances in his part of the country, and he offered a solution to the problem that would wipe out the range menace permanently. He would contact a man whom he knew with the Pinkerton Detective Agency, a man that could be relied on to do the job, with no questions asked.
>
> Tom Horn was the man chosen by Coble.
>
> Coble continued that Horn was to be paid five hundred dollars for every known cattle thief he killed.[10]

Ora Haley was astute enough merely to nod his agreement to the arrangement, without making any verbal commitment. He told Bernard that he wanted Horn to know nothing of his involvement, fearing potential future blackmail. He did, however, order Bernard to provide Horn with horses and supplies from his Two Bar ranches in Brown's Hole.

This meeting seemingly was the first of several of a group of cattlemen whose goal was to eliminate opposition in Brown's Hole.

Corroboration of the Denver meeting emerged in a report by Harry Ratliff, the first supervisor of Routt National Forest. Ratliff wrote to the chief forester of the U.S. Forest Service[11] of a gathering of local ranchers held in Slater, Colorado, in 1908, to organize the Snake River Stock Growers Association. A proposed paragraph in the organization's legal documents referred to minutes of earlier meetings and mentioned an executive committee whose function was to rid the range of rustlers.

The president of the association called upon Al Reader, by this time a prominent Brown's Hole stockgrower, and possibly A. W. Salisbury, to review the paragraph in private. They agreed to delete it from official records, and Ratliff stated he burned the pages containing the incriminating language in a stove.

Ratliff verified that it was Ayer, Wilson, and Bernard who appointed an anonymous member of their group to hire a range rider to "rid the country of thieves." The name of the range rider was not specified.

Further corroboration of the Denver meeting came years later in 1959. J. Wilson Carey, manager of the Two Circle Bar outfit in the area, wrote[12] that he knew of an association of ranchers that met at the ranch where he worked. He said that he collected a hundred dollars in monthly dues from each member and turned it over to Ayer, who was the one who hired Tom Horn.

Horn, using the alias of "James Hicks," reached Brown's Hole in the early spring of 1900 and posed as a horse buyer or cowboy.

Despite persistent questions about whether Hicks and Horn were the same man, there is little doubt they were one and the same. Peter A. Burman provided verification in December 1944 when he recounted his own experiences in a letter to his son. Burman had driven a supply wagon from Rock Springs to Brown's Hole around the turn of the century:

> Yes, I knew Tom Horn personally when I was a young man. At the time I knew him he went by the name of Tom Hicks but it was Tom Horn alright.... As I remember him he was quiet and only talked when spoken to. In other words he wasn't a mixer or jovial fellow.... He killed two small cattlemen that I was personally acquainted with. Isom [*sic*] Dart a negro cowpuncher that was a superb horseman and Matt Rash a white man from Texas. These men had got their start rustling and I guess he was sent out there to get them which he did and how.... The reason I know Tom Hicks was Tom Horn was because a pal of mine Joe Davenport went down to Cheyenne after Tom Horn was arrested and seen him and said the Tom Hicks that we knew was the same man.[13]

An article in a local paper further documents Horn's early spring arrival in 1900. The *Craig Courier*[14] reported that a deputy sheriff shot Jim McKnight on April 4 as the officer was serving him with a court order prohibiting him from selling his property. McKnight was ending his marriage to Josey Bassett, who apparently wanted to ensure her fair share of their assets.

The Craig paper reported that Tom Horn rode to Vernal, Utah, for medical help for McKnight.

Matt Rash had arrived in Brown's Hole in the 1880s. He was well liked but carried a questionable reputation; he had been accused of stealing and altering the brand of a steer belonging to Nelson Morris in 1894.[15] He was also head of the Brown's Park Cattlemen's Association, an organization of smaller ranchers.

When Horn arrived in Brown's Hole using the alias James Hicks, he gained Matt Rash's confidence and worked for him for a period. It has frequently been written that Horn was along when Rash surprised Isam Dart, a well-known black itinerant cowhand from Texas, butchering a bull.

Bill Tittsworth was a turn-of-the-century cowboy who arrived from Missouri in Brown's Hole in 1899. He provided verbal documentation of events in Brown's Hole, which, while occasionally disparaged, provided insight to the era.

Tittsworth's recollection[16] too was that Horn gained Matt Rash's confidence and had operated under the alias of Hicks. He recalled Rash and Dart arguing over a bunch of cows the two had sold in town early in 1900. Dart believed that Rash had cheated him out of his share of the proceeds. In an argument, Dart had said, "You wouldn't do this, Matt, if I had my gun."

Bill Tittsworth further recalled that Rash and Dart had taken another herd of cows to Rock Springs to sell around the Fourth of July, starting with only five or six head. "When they got there I think they either had 17 or 21. These other cows, it just seemed like they were just attracted to these ones [laughing]."[17] These cattle may have been VD-branded cattle that were spoken of by others.

Rash received an unsigned letter while he was there telling him to sell out and leave the country or he would be killed. He discussed the threat with friends and decided to hang around, gather a few more cattle to sell, and then figure out what to do.

Tom Horn, in the meantime, had gathered evidence for his employers. Hi Bernard said that twenty-eight head of good heifers with the VD brand belonging to a man in Baggs had disappeared from the upper Little Snake River. Horn followed them and returned to fetch Bernard and Wiff Wilson to verify the results of his investigation. They picked up the trail and learned that two horsemen had driven the cattle to a camp in a small canyon near Beaver Basin. Bernard and Wilson then returned to their ranches.

Next Horn brought parts of two butchered cowhides he had found bearing the VD brand for the committee to inspect. He had found one at Jim McKnight's summer camp and one at Rash's. Bernard observed:

> Horn brought the pieces of cow hide for Wilson, Ayres [*sic*] and me to examine. We wet and stretched the pieces of hide, and found the VD brand on each piece. That looked like the boldest, most outrageous cattle-rustling job I had ever seen or heard of. Acting for the general welfare of all range users adjacent to Brown's Park, the appointed committee gave Horn the go-ahead signal, and cautioned him to be sure he got the guilty men only. Horn made a further investigation, and killed Matt Rash and Isam Dart.[18]

Yet another version of the incident surrounding the VD cattle and Tom Horn persists, one told by Ann Bassett of the prominent Brown's Hole family. She indicated that in June of 1899 a herd of young cattle branded VD had strayed in from the north and gotten into some young sheep owned by Tom Davenport. The VD brand had not been seen in the area previously and caught the attention of Matt Rash and Jim McKnight. Joe Davenport, Tom's brother, told a Mexican sheepherder who was tending the sheep to let him know if anyone asked about the cows. The herder later told him that Charley Ward had been there looking for the cattle.

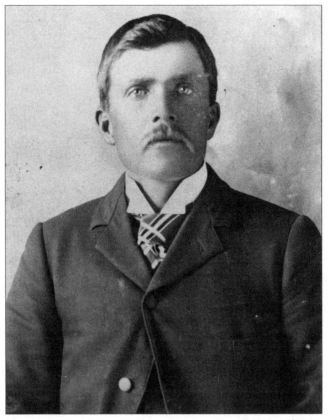

Matt Rash in Rock Springs. (Museum of Northwest Colorado)

Little is know about Ward except that he had a dubious reputation and had never owned anything more than a horse, saddle, and packhorse. His sudden interest in cattle aroused suspicion. Ann felt that Ward was in cahoots with Tom Horn and with him had stolen the cows.[19]

Ward and the cows suddenly disappeared. Ann Bassett contended that Tom Horn had gone to Rock Springs to find a buyer for the cows, and while he was gone Ward spirited them away. Horn had his own plot, she said: to sell the cows on his own and cheat Ward out of his share. With the cattle now gone, Horn implicated Rash and others, then killed him and Isam Dart. So Horn earned his fee but lost out on the money he would have made had he sold the cows. Ward's disappearance led to conjecture that Horn had killed him as well.

Matt Rash had been in Rock Springs on July 7. On his way back, Rash stopped in at Ann Bassett's place; local speculation was that the two were romantically involved and planning marriage. He continued on to his own place on Cold Spring Mountain.[20]

Late the next morning someone shot him in his fourteen-foot-square cabin while he was preparing to eat lunch. The killer shot him twice from the doorway, the first shot entering under the arm and the second in the back. Rash managed to crawl to his bunk where he died. Some accounts say that he had attempted to write a message in his own blood before he died.

On July 10 George Rife and Felix Meyers, then only fourteen, rode by. Meyers stopped and recognized from the stench that something was wrong. He entered the cabin and found Rash's body, by now badly decomposed. Outside lay Rash's horse, with a bullet through his forehead.

They summoned a small coroner's jury and conducted an inquest. Rash was buried next to his cabin.

Next, a letter dated July 8 from Denver written by Tom Horn arrived for Rash. Over the years a theory evolved that Horn had arranged for an accomplice to mail it, ostensibly placing him far from the scene and thereby exonerating him.

Meanwhile a new, even grimmer problem was developing in Iron Mountain, one that might provide Horn with his next job. John Coble wrote to Frank Bosler on July 16, 1900:

> The Iron Mountain, Wall Rock and Plumbago pastures are filled with sheep and look wooly. Our she cattle are in Iron Mountain and they are doing fine, like in a meadow. When the sheep men attempt to drive or handle our cattle I will at once have them arrested. But they are scared to death, are hiring all the six-shooters and badmen they can find. I want Horn back here; he will straighten them out by merely riding around.[21]

Rash's father and brother arrived from Acton, Texas, and exhumed the body for reburial. Tom Horn then showed up and claimed to the elder Rash that he and Matt were friends, and placed suspicion for the murder on Isam Dart.

About the time of the Rash episode, Tom Horn was cut on the neck in a knife fight just north of the Colorado-Wyoming state line. The *Craig Empire-Courier*[22] related an account by Bill Tittsworth (Tittsworth refers to Horn as Hicks):

> About two weeks after Matt Rash was killed (that would be about August 1900) Hicks rides into Baggs and puts his horse up in Bill Penland's stable. Then he heads for Roy Bailey's saloon and proceeds to get drunk. There had been two guys from Missouri around Baggs for some time, Nute [*sic*] and Ed Kelly. Nute liked to play around with a Colt 45; Ed was very handy with his fists. Ed was tending bar for Roy Bailey. Nute was tending sheep camp. Nute was in Baggs that day and there were some others in the saloon.
>
> Hicks comes in, don't nobody know Hicks. Hicks gets two or three shots of red eye and he thinks he is a fighting man from Powder River. The thought no more than hits him until Ed's fist connects with his jaw; that slams him up against the bar, then Ed grabs both his arms and pins him to the bar; Nute outs with his knife and slashes his throat; came very near finishing him. They get him over to the hotel and call in Dr. White who sews up his neck.
>
> Bob Meldrum was deputy sheriff and lived at Dixon. Someone got the word to him that Nute Kelly was on the warpath, so Meldrum comes right to Baggs and stands guard over Hicks until he can ride again. Hicks was riding a blue roan horse wearing Ora Haley's heart brand on his left hind leg.
>
> I rode into Baggs the next day after the fight. Meldrum was the first man I saw. He told me about the fight, and then he started to tell me what a hell-roaring bronc rider Hicks was. I asked some questions about Hicks, then Meldrum went deaf on me which was a habit of his when he didn't want to talk.[23]

Horn had lit out to the northeast, toward the Little Snake River and Wyoming, after Rash's killing. En route he unknowingly passed a wildlife photographer, A. G. Wallihan. Wallihan also owned a road-house nearby where Horn stopped.

Mr. and Mrs. A. G. Wallihan (Museum of Northwest Colorado)

Wallihan had moved to Colorado from Wisconsin, arriving in 1870 at age eleven. He later wrote:

> I know a lot more about the Tom Horn "war" because I saw that. Horn stopped here at my roadhouse on his way to Juniper Springs. He had got cut pretty bad in a fight with Newt Kelly in Baggs, and he thought that the springs might help him. He wasn't a bad-looking fellow, tall. He never looked at you. He always looked down. If you spoke to him he would look at you for a moment then his eyes would fall again....
>
> My wife had lived all her life on the frontier and she was not afraid of man, God or the devil, but she said that man Hicks is a bad man.

Wallihan had his camera set up in a deer blind he had built for his photographic work. As he was waiting for an opportunity to photograph deer at an adjacent crossing, he saw a man mounted on a buckskin horse ride up a ridge, pause, and look back. At the top of the ridge where he stopped, Wallihan got a good look at him. It was Tom Horn. Within a day or two Wallihan learned that Matt Rash had been murdered.[24]

Chapter Thirteen

MORE TROUBLE AHEAD

Y ET ANOTHER MAN was shot down in Brown's Hole in 1900. Isam Dart was born in Texas 1855[1] and arrived in Colorado in the 1870s or early 1880s. By one account,[2] he first bore the name Ned Huddleston, which may have been the name of the slave owner who owned his parents. He supposedly lost an ear in a knife fight with an Indian over the man's wife.

Dart was riding with the Tip Gault gang when the outlaws attempted to make off with horses they'd stolen from Margaret Anderson's outfit south of Saratoga, Wyoming, in 1875. A posse caught up with the thieves that evening as they sat around a campfire. The resulting shoot-out left all the thieves dead except Dart, who spent an uneasy night next to the body of one of the luckless thieves. He then gathered money belts and other loot from the bodies and took off on foot. He was wounded by a rancher when he attempted to steal a horse and later was found on the prairie by an accomplice who nursed him back to health.

He was an accomplished horse breaker and all-around top cowhand, superb at cutting out and roping cattle.

Dart ran for election as constable in Sweetwater County, Wyoming, in 1884. The position was to be in Coyote Creek Precinct, forty-five miles southwest of Rock Springs and a few miles north of Irish Canyon, an eastern access to Brown's Hole. Dart won the election with eight votes.[3]

Dart was not without sin. Three indictments for branding neat cattle in Sweetwater County were brought against him by the Territory of Wyoming in 1889, but were discharged.[4]

Dart was acquainted with one of the robbers of the Union Pacific train at Wilcox that took place north of Rock River, Wyoming, on June 2, 1899.

Isam Dart. (Wyoming Division of Cultural Resources)

D.G. Thomas, Sweetwater County Attorney, described in a letter to U.S. Marshal Frank Hadsell dated August 12, 1890, Dart's random encounter with one of the Wilcox robbers.[5] Dart and Angus McDougal happened across a man identified as Joe Curry who "virtually admitted" to Dart that he was one of the hold-up men. McDougal later offered to apprehend Curry, for a price.

Little did Dart know that Tom Horn would investigate the robbery, and that Horn's scrutiny of Brown's Hole a year later would lead to his own death.

Attorney Thomas wrote U.S. Marshal Frank Hadsell that Angus McDougal had arrived in town from roundups south of Rock Springs. He said that McDougal met a man "faged [*sic*] and worn out by hard riding." Thomas continued that Isam Dart was accompanying McDougal.

The man, however, apparently knew Dart. He asked Dart what he knew about "the condition" of the country. Dart replied that everyone knew the area was in an uproar over the recent robbery of the Union Pacific. The stranger told Dart that at the time of the robbery he was in British Columbia.

Dart persisted in talking about the robbery. The man inquired about McDougal and, on being told who he was, said, "don't tell, for God's sake don't tell any one you saw me." As Dart pursued the matter of the holdup, the man "virtually admitted that he was one of the parties, as he remarked, 'I had a hell of a time keeping away from the hounds... Dart, you must not give me away.'

"This man's name was Joe Curry, Joe Southerner, alias Tom McCarty, who used to work with Joe Hazen on the range."

He concluded by saying that Tom O'Day (of the botched 1897 Belle Fourche, South Dakota bank robbery) along with Charles Stevens (a.k.a. White River Charley)[6] and John Jinks (alias John Ray) "are in this neck of the woods."

Apparently Hadsell did not follow up on this golden opportunity

A fateful development for Isam Dart occurred two months after Matt Rash's murder. Boldly dropping his alias, on September 26, 1900, Tom Horn signed his own name to a complaint naming Dart as a horse thief.

Dart suspected that trouble was ahead for him after Matt Rash's murder. He holed up in a cabin with six other individuals: Sam and George Bassett, Louis Brown, Billy Rash, Larry Curtin and Elijah B. "Longhorn" Thompson, on his ranch on remote Cold Spring Mountain in Brown's Hole. The whole bunch had been friendly with Matt Rash and figured their names were on the list of those to be exterminated. They may have been right.

On the morning of October 4, 1900, Dart died of a single gunshot wound as he and the others filed out from the cabin toward a corral. In the cold and windy dawn, no one sighted the killer. They bolted for the cabin where they barricaded themselves until nightfall. The next day they found two thirty-thirty caliber shells at the base of the tree that had hidden the assassin. Tom Horn packed a thirty-thirty Winchester.

Several historic publications from the Brown's Park area add color and other perspectives to the events.

The October 17, 1900, *Steamboat Pilot*[7] reported the murder of Dart and stated that "a regular reign of terror prevails in Brown's Park since the murder of Matt Rash and Isam Dart." It also carried a brief article:

WARNED TO LEAVE

A special from Rock Springs says: There is more trouble ahead in Brown's Park, where Matt Rash, a cattleman, and Isham [*sic*] Dart, a colored cowman, were murdered by the lawless element which makes the park their headquarters. Yesterday a letter was found near the cabin of Dart containing a notification of speedy death for the Bassetts and Joe Davenport if they do not leave the county within sixty days. The men threatened are cattlemen who have refused to become friendly with the gang of cattle rustlers.

The November 14, 1900, *Pilot* reported that Rash's father's had arrived to disinter Matt's remains and ship them to Texas. It continued that people were speculating that the killer of Rash and Dart was one and the same person, and that he was not from the area, "saying there are so few men here it is an easy matter for each man to show where he was when Dart was shot." It also commented that A. G. Wallihan had seen a "lone horseman" riding east after Rash's death.

On December 5, 1900, the *Pilot* reported yet another shooting. Young George Banks of Lay, Colorado, had been shot at but not injured. An editorial of the same date presented an explosive theory: the complicity of the governors of Colorado, Wyoming, and Utah in the murders. It also raised the possibility of a second gunman:

> …And now for the tale that is whispered where death lurks so mysteriously: A little over a year ago the governors of three states [Utah, Wyoming, and Colorado] met to devise plans to clean out the Hole-in-the-Wall gang which has infested the country lying so conveniently near the corner of the three states. It is asserted that men who had the ear of the governors told them that certain settlers were the aiders, abettors and protectors of the outlaws. That they were themselves cattle rustlers and should be cleaned out. What the officials themselves did is not known, but they at least encouraged powerful interests which are antagonistic to the rustlers, if such they be, to employ a detective to enter that section. What his instructions were none may know. But his deadly work speaks for itself. In this remarkable story the assassin's name is even mentioned. According to the story he sat with Rash at his table and partook of his hospitality. He then murdered him like a dog. He was seen going from the place where Dart met his sudden fate a few weeks later.
>
> This man was spotted and a new one took his place. The first man openly boasted in Cheyenne, and his interview was published in the Denver papers that the "rustlers" would soon be cleaned out of Brown's Park and it would be a safe place in which to live. The second man is in the country now. He is evidently not as good a shot as the other. Twice he has tried and failed. There are said to be seven names on the death list carried by these men.

The second man under suspicion might have been Bob Meldrum, Tom Horn's fellow Pinkerton's operative. Meldrum was working in nearby Carbon County, Wyoming, at the time.

In February 1901 George Banks said that he had seen the gunman who had shot at him and chased him four miles. Then, in March a bullet hit his saddle below the horn. The horse spooked and ran, and Banks, frightened, let him have his head in order to escape. A. G. Wallihan added to the account, saying of Tom Horn:

> Lots of the men he was after used to stop here at my road-house. Longhorn Thompson had a ranch on Snake River joining the Two Bar outfit. He ate Thanksgiving dinner here with us at Lay and went home. He met Tom Horn in the willows on his own ranch, and jumped off into Snake River before Horn had time to shoot. Thompson moved to Craig after that and one night his wife heard a scraping at the window and she opened the curtain, and there stood Tom Horn. [The] Thompsons moved to Vernal, Utah, after that.... George Banks had a ranch right here at Lay. He was in Craig once putting up his horse in the barn and he heard some men talking outside in the corral, back of the barn. They were talking about killing Matt Rash. Then they stepped into the barn and saw that he had heard them. It was Hi Bernard... and Horn and another man. Banks let on he had not heard them, but a few days later when he went over a ridge there to look for his Jersey cow a bullet cut his shirt front and tore his vest. They wanted to get rid of him for fear he had heard them. Haley was an awful small man in lots of ways.[8]

Two years later, the *Craig Courier* issue of Saturday, January 18, 1902, reported on Tom Horn's arrest for the murder of Willie Nickell. It commented:

> ...The boy was murdered last July in cold blood, being shot from ambush in the same manner that Isam Dart of Brown's park was killed....
>
> ...The Cheyenne correspondents of the Denver papers state that Horn is suspected of being the murderer of Matt Rash and Isam Dart.
>
> Horn is well known to a number of Routt County stockmen and his name as been associated with Brown's park assassinations ever since the crimes were committed. He was Rash's employee

Joe LeFors as a member of the Tipton train robbery posse. The robbery occurred August 29, 1900, just north of Brown's Hole concurrent with the two murders there. LeFors became involved in the investigation of the Nickell killing a year later. (American Heritage Center, University of Wyoming)

Tom Horn's letter from jail to Bob Meldrum. (Wyoming Division of Cultural Resources)

for a short time and made several visits to Craig. While in this section he was known as Tom Hicks.

Tom Horn himself summarized his activities in Brown's Park in 1900, in the incriminating letters he wrote to Joe LeFors early in 1902. This correspondence led directly to his arrest and conviction.

Ironically and with perhaps a bit of humor, while in jail awaiting execution on April 18, 1903, Tom wrote a letter on Sheriff Ed Smalley's stationery to Bob Meldrum in Telluride:

> Dear Bob, Rec'd yours of the 10th today. It is the only word I have had of you since you were here. Snow slides are sure to be raising cain all over the San Juan. I will drop you another line in a few days. Yes, I am sure to get a new trial. I will come free then sure. I have not seen any one for a couple of months. We had a bad winter sure. All our fellows were in town a few days ago but I did not get to see any of them. Brown's Park was always a nice quiet place & I can't see what makes them cut up now. Harry Tracy gave the place a bad name. I guess one of the Hays was the first man Tracy every killed. Farnum had ought [to be] prominent now as he had the pleasure of arresting Tracy once in a snow-bank. I don't see any one and consequently have no news to write. I will see my lawyers in two or three weeks and will then write you through them.
>
> I am well and fat. Write whenever you can.
>
> Yours truly,
> Tom Horn[9]

Chapter Fourteen

KILLED TO GET THEM OFF THE RANGE

THE BROWN'S HOLE episodes evoked more vivid stories than any other incident in northwest Colorado, many about Tom Horn.

Carl Davidson, an old-timer who cowboyed along the Snake River at the turn of the century, had his own version of the Brown's Hole events.[1] He made the point that "none of the men were killed for rustling alone; they were killed to get them off the range."

Davidson also indicated that Ed Thomas had received a threatening notice similar to the one Matt Rash received early in 1900. Davidson's account was that Thomas left Brown's Hole in the spring of 1900. He repeated a story that Tom Horn had killed a man by the name of Walker, mistaking him for Thomas.

Walker lived in the Baggs area, was married, and had children. He worked with sheep, shearing in the spring and later "pulling" wool off dead sheep in the Red Desert. He disappeared in the spring of 1900. Later a skeleton found on the desert was identified as Walker by a ring he wore.

Davidson continued that Charley Ayer told him Tom Horn had killed Walker because he had arrived in Brown's Hole too late to kill Ed Thomas. Davidson's contention was that Horn saw Walker out on the desert, killed him, and then said he'd killed Thomas to collect the bounty on Thomas.

The recollections of William Daniel Tittsworth[2] provide a colorful account of the Tom Horn episodes in Brown's Hole. Tittsworth's recollections were transcribed from a recorded oral history session conducted by Chuck Stoddard in the late 1950s. Tittsworth, a turn-of-the-century cowboy, was born in Branson, Missouri, November 24, 1879. His words are worth knowing:

I went to Brown's Park in May 1899....

Well, I know that Tom Horn lived in Brown's Park.... He came in there under the name of Hicks. A fellow told me that knew, "There's a fellow around here by the name of Hicks, says he's a detective. Says he's posing as a horse buyer." Well, he got acquainted with Matt Rash and the Bassetts, and he made that his headquarters down there. It was in the fall [1899] and they brought the cattle off the mountain to winter down in the park.

Tittsworth's mentioning that Horn was in the area in the fall of 1899, if correct, points to the conspiracy being developed that year rather than in 1900, as has been commonly believed:

One day after they'd been up there some time, why they rode over to Isom Dart's corral. That was up on Cold Spring Mountain, about ten miles. When they got up to the corral there, old Isom was butchering a beef in the corral. Matt Rash thought it was one of his. He compelled old Isom to roll the hide over so he could see the brand. He was butchering a bull that belonged to Sam Spicer, a sheep man and cattleman, just down the...

That was the only one he could find that was isolated enough to take probably without creating too much suspicion. They had some words then and Isom got mad. He and Rash quarreled. They rehashed a lot of stuff that had been going on.

Isom shouldered up to him about the last time they took some cattle into town and sold them. Matt, the businessman, got the money but he didn't give Isom his share of it.

He told Rash, "You wouldn't do this, Matt, if I had my gun."

Hicks, Tom Horn, was there and he took the whole thing in. He had some business. Shortly after that Tom Horn left.

By this point Tom Horn had gained the information he needed. His precise movements after witnessing the confrontation between Rash and Dart are not known, but it appears that the dispute came to a head in the spring of 1900.

Tittsworth then recounted the story of the five or six cattle that had multiplied to become seventeen or twenty-one by the time they reached a fort in Rock Springs.

While they were in the fort there, Rash got a notice in the form of a letter, I think. It told him that he was to sell out while he was in town and leave the country, or he would be killed. He debated the thing over quite a while and talked to some friends of his. He decided that there wasn't anything to be done right away, so he'd go out and kind of round cattle up and sell them, then get out of the country.

He went out into the park the Saturday following the fourth of July. He got down to Bassetts in the park and stayed there all night. The next morning he went up on Cold Spring Mountain. Nothing was heard of Matt till Tuesday.

Tuesday, one of the Myers, and some of the other boys from over on Sparks Creek went up on the mountain there to look after some cattle or something and came to Rash's cabin. Here lay Rash in his cabin on the bunk, shot three times, apparently with a rifle, and blood all over the floor. There was $40 under the blanket on the bunk. He had out a little notebook and there was a little blood on the notebook. They never could figure out how, with the amount of blood on the floor and the distance that [he covered] that Rash could survive [as long as he did] with those three shots.

I've been in the cabin there and looked the thing over. The cabin is about 14 feet square, maybe, something like that...

It looked like Matt Rash was having him a lunch there, heard a noise, and partly turned to see what the noise was. The killer evidently at that time was right in the door, and as Matt turned he shot him and hit him under the arm here. The bullet went rings down and came down out on the opposite side. Then he fell down on the floor facing the killer, tried to get up and the killer shot him in the back here somewhere on one side that lodged back in the loin, I think. The other shot, I don't remember now where it went.

Anyway when he fell on the floor, he'd be about eight or ten feet from this bunk. There was a lot of blood next to the stove, and then just a trail from there to the bunk. He was carried over there, or got over there himself, which looks impossible with all them bullets that were in him. The fact was that he was in terrible shape.

Then they summoned the neighbors and they all went up there. The only thing they could do was they bandaged themselves and put handkerchiefs over their noses. They finally got him onto a blanket and they dug a hole, and just took him outside the door, rolled him in there and covered him up.

His horse was tied. The reins were hooked over a post or something about 30 or 40 yards from the house, and there was a bullet hole right in the horse's forehead and he was dead. There were two sage chickens on the saddle. Nobody messed up anything, nobody's around, why there was no evidence of who killed him or anything, but everybody suspected this Horn. At that time everybody seemed to think that Horn was just a cattle detective, but that was common talk....

Matt Rash's father came up there with his brother from Texas. Tom Horn came in over there to see the old man and his brother. He said, "There's been talk around that I killed Matt...Matt and I were good friends. We rode around all winter long." He denied having anything to do [with it] at all.

If the quotation of Horn's remark is accurate, it further points to his arriving in the fall of 1899. That being the case, his recuperation from yellow fever after returning to Wyoming following the Spanish-American War was apparently complete by mid-summer 1899:

> Some of the people there thought maybe that Isom had killed him. It was a kind of divided opinion, but there wasn't many of them thought that Isom had killed Matt.
>
> Later on I was down to Martin Guefanti's on Beaver Creek, rancher down there, an old timer. Larry Curtin came riding down there one after noon and said to Martin, "Somebody's killed Isom Dart, a Negro, and they're going to have the inquest tomorrow...." Larry had notified everybody in the park there and the next morning Martin and I went up to Isom Dart's cabin, which was situated up on the Cold Spring Mountain just north of the Mat Trail....

When we got up there, there lay Isom Dart in a wagon box outside the cabin. I think he had on a jacket. He had on one or two shirts and a heavy suit of underwear. He was shot just an inch to the right and an inch below the breastbone....

I remember Billy Bragg came out there and he was examining, like this was the shot. He took a little twig about the size of a small lead pencil. He ran it down in that bullet hole to see where that bullet went because he couldn't tell anything about it. I helped dig the grave with Eb Bassett, George [Bassett] and somebody else....

It seemed that they had found a shell, a cartridge from a rifle. I think it was a .30.30. They found that right south of the corral. [The corral was] 150 or 200 yards from the house.... They found this bullet along this fence that run south of the corral. That was the only thing they could find.... The killer could very well shoot right between the bars of the gate and kill Isom. He [Isom] was in plain sight....

Isom and George Bassett [had] met in the cabin that morning along about 8:00 o'clock and started out to the corral...Eb and Whitie were sitting out in front of the house watching them. They said they heard that shot and they both stopped. Then they said old Isom just pitched right forward on his face. George just whirled and ran to the cabin, and they said he made it in nothing flat....

After finding this shell they also found where a horse had been tied about 100 or 200 yards south of that in a grove of quaking aspens. There was a nice little spring and there were fresh horse tracks, about a number three horseshoe, going down the mountain for about ten miles or more.... The trail went off the mountain down onto Vermilion Creek and then it crossed over to Snake River.... Then [the posse] quit...; they wouldn't go any farther.

Four or five days after that, some fellow there had to go over to Snake River. He took this [same] trail up and there was that same horseshoe track running right across that trail. He followed that right over to Snake River.... Tom Horn rode into Ora Haley's cow camp that same day....

By the way, speaking about Isom Dart...Widow Warren had a pretty near brand new set of harness at her ranch on Beaver Creek. Isom Dart and one of his pals had been down in the park there and they went by the ranch that day. She was gone. When she came back this harness was all cut to pieces.

At this point the interviewer interrupted to ask, "What was the object of something like that?"

Tittsworth replied, "Just orneriness, probably had it in for her, mad about something."

⊁—⊱—⊰—⊱—⊰—⊱—⊰—⊰

Tittsworth's recollections have the ring of truth. While some latter-day historians in northwest Colorado feel he may have added color to his stories, the fact that he was a contemporary who "was there at the time"—plus the fact that his accounts correspond with those of others—lend them credibility.

Chapter Fifteen

HIS INTENTION WAS TO GET ME

A FTER THE MURDERS of Rash and Dart, Tom Horn evidently remained on the Pinkerton payroll in one way or another until late 1900 or early 1901.

He provided information on the Wild Bunch robbery of the Winnemucca, Nevada, bank that took place on September 19, 1900, and specifically on Harry Longabaugh, the Sundance Kid. Prior to that holdup, several men had robbed a store in Three Creek, Idaho, to obtain supplies and horses for the Winnemucca job. A man named Rowe was suspected of participating in the store robbery. George Nixon, an intermediary for the Pinkerton's Agency, wrote to J. C. Fraser at the Pinkerton office in Denver on March 4, 1901, regarding Rowe. In his letter, he quotes from an earlier letter he had received from Tom Horn:

> I have also received a letter from that other party [Tom Horn], from which I quote.
>
> "I have been away for two weeks after a bunch of stolen horses and have just got back.... About this man Rowe, *just as I told you* [emphasis added], there is or was on Snake River a man by the name of Rowe and he was a very bad and desperate man.... Rowe worked for Al Reader and also Ora Haley. Both these men say he is a bad man, but I know him myself and did not think him bad.
>
> "I am as sure as can be that it was Rowe that done that work [robbed the store], and not Cassidy, for the description will not fit Cassidy at all.
>
> "Cassidy would not have been broke so as to have held up a store before the bank robbery, as this man did." [1]

Tom Horn had been in communication with Nixon previously, and having worked for Haley in Brown's Hole would have been in a position to identify Sundance as the man known as "Rowe" while the two were employed there.

Al Reader, whose name was also mentioned in Horn's letter, was the son of Brown's Hole pioneer Noah Reader. Al became a prominent cattleman in the area and was aware of the conspiracy developed by Bernard, Haley, Wilson, and Ayer.

⸳⸳⸳⸳⸳⸳⸳⸳

The next incident involving Tom Horn, and the one that led to his fall, was the murder of Willie Nickell on July 18, 1901.

Kels Powers Nickell, Willie's father, had come to Wyoming in the mid-1870s with General George C. Crook's command. Crook's force was part of the ill-fated strategy that led to George Armstrong Custer's defeat at the Little Big Horn on June 25, 1876.

Nickell fought under Crook at the Battle of the Rosebud in southern Montana, north of Sheridan, Wyoming. Crook lost the battle, which forced his retreat to the south just days before Custer's annihilation.

Confederate Army deserters had murdered Kels' father, John DeSha Nickell, on February 7, 1863, eight years after Kels was born in 1855.[2] He was killed within earshot of the family on their farm in Licking River, Morgan County, Kentucky, by John Jackson Nickell, a second cousin, who also murdered Logan Wilson. Wilson was shot in his bed while recuperating from wounds. John Jackson Nickell was hanged for the two murders on September 2, 1864.

Kels's mother, Priscilla, and his five siblings remained on the farm in Kentucky for a period until the county circuit court sold it to satisfy a surety bond that the elder John Nickell had signed for a county elected official, whose name is unknown.

Kels remained in Kentucky, cutting timber that was assembled into rafts to be floated downstream to sawmills. He married Ann Brown of Greenup County, Kentucky, in 1873, but the marriage ended in divorce in 1877. One son was born of the marriage, John DeSha Nickell II, in 1874.

By 1875 Nickell had enlisted in the U.S. Cavalry. He was counted as part of the force at Fort Laramie, Wyoming, in the census of 1880.

Kels P. Nickell. (Wyoming Division of Cultural Resources)

After his discharge that year, he moved to Camp Carlin on the northwest outskirts of Cheyenne, and opened a blacksmith and farm machinery repair shop. He married Mary Mahoney, an Irish immigrant then sixteen, in Cheyenne on December 27, 1881. The daughter of a railway construction worker from Cork, Ireland, she had immigrated to the United States in 1868. Kels was ten years her senior.

Nickell took possession of his homestead claim in 1885 in the Iron Mountain region about forty miles northwest of Cheyenne. At the same time he filed for an additional 480 acres of government land, which could be acquired for $1.25 per acre. Over the course of years, he bought, sold, and filed desert claims (a common way to

Mary Nickell (left) and her three sisters. (Viola Nickell Bixler)

acquire arid government tracts by going through the motions of irrigating them) in the area.

The Laramie County Census of 1900, in which the Nickell family was enumerated at Iron Mountain on June 3, reflected the two parents and other members of the household:

Julia, born in 1883;[3]
Kels P., junior, born in 1884, whose occupation was a farm laborer;
Willie, born in 1887, also a farm laborer;
Katie, born in 1889;
Alfred (Freddie), born in 1891;[4]
Beatrice (Trixie), born in 1892;
Maggie, born in 1894;
Ida McKinley, a daughter born in 1896; and
Hiram Harlan, born in 1899.

Hiram G. Davidson[5] was the census taker who gathered the data. Ironically, he was to play a role in the events that followed Willie's murder and furnished testimony that led to the guilty verdict in Tom Horn's trial.

Kels Nickell had an explosive temper.[6] Testimony in the coroner's inquest that followed Willie's murder emphasized this point as much as any, and indicated that he was always in some kind of a "jangle." Tragically, his ill nature and frequent quarrels with neighbors—primarily Jim Miller—contributed to Willie's death.

At the same time, Nickell was a tireless worker. The homes he built both in Iron Mountain and later in Encampment, Wyoming, were located close to streams in order to provide running water, a rare convenience in rural country. The Iron Mountain home had water piped into it from North Chugwater Creek, a few feet to the south of the structure. The Nickell and Jim Miller families worked together to build a school located about halfway between their homes, near the north perimeter of Miller's land. The project seems to have been one of the few circumstances in which their interests coincided.

Kels and Mary Nickell sent their oldest son, Kels Jr., to a private school in Licking Green, Kentucky, before Willie was killed. They'd hoped to send all their children to private schools, to provide them with a better education than they could obtain in rural Wyoming.[7]

The scenario that led to repeated tragedy was the result of feuds in which Kels had become ensnarled as far back as 1890. On July 22 of that year, he tangled with John Coble and Coble's foreman, George Cross, at the western perimeter of Nickell's homestead, over some cattle. He knifed Coble, seriously wounding him in the abdomen.

As time elapsed, Nickell continued arguing with and making threats against many in the area.

The feud became acutely bitter between the Nickell clan and Jim Miller and his family, who lived about a mile south of Nickell. Kels and Willie Nickell sided against Jim Miller and his older boys, Gus and Victor. James Miller had established a homestead in the spring of 1883.[8] He was born in Galena, Illinois, in 1855 and was married to Dora Cora Lemon, who was born in 1864 in Greeley, Colorado. They had moved from Greeley in a covered wagon, where their oldest son, Charles Augustus "Gus," was born in 1882. They arrived at Iron Mountain about two years before the Nickells.

After building a log cabin where they lived the first winter, they established themselves by setting up a sawmill and raising a few head

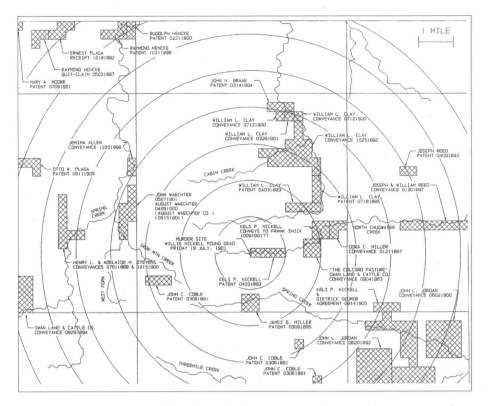

Locations of the Nickell, Miller and adjacent ranches. Chugwater lies approximately to the east. (Johan P. Bakker)

of stock. Miller sold logs and posts to neighbors, including John L. Jordan and John J. Underwood, whose names appeared in Tom Horn's last letter, written just before his hanging in 1903.

In 1900 the Miller household consisted of the parents Jim and Dora, nine children, and Miller's brother:[9]

> Charles Augustus (Gus), described as a farm laborer;
> Victor Henry, born in 1883, also a farm laborer;
> Eva Jane, born in 1885;
> Frank, born in 1887;
> Maude S., born in 1891;
> Raymond, born in 1893;
> Ina S., born in 1895;

Jim and Dora Miller. (Wyoming Division of Cultural Resources)

Robert L., born in 1897;

Ronald Andrew, born in 1899; and

Benjamin F., Jim's brother, who was born in 1858 and was a railroad laborer.

One daughter, Bertha May, born in May 1889, had died of diphtheria in 1898.[10]

The feud with Jim Miller and his boys reached a boiling point a year before Willie was shot. After the men in the family began carrying guns, a tragedy resulted on August 21, 1900, from the accidental discharge of a shotgun in Miller's spring wagon.[11] The shot hit fourteen-year-old Frank Miller in the head, killing him instantly, and severely injuring Maude.

Nettie L. (Mrs. John L.) Jordan, who lived with her family southeast of Miller and Nickell, wrote[12] of the incident in reminiscences presented in two speeches in the 1940s:

> In the foot hills back of our ranch lived two families the Millers and Nichols [*sic*] they quarreled all the time with each other. They also carried guns for each other, and one morning Mr. Miller took two of his children with him in the spring wagon, he was going to cut hay. The children were playing and the gun accidentally went off and shot both children. Mr. Miller brought them to me instead of taking them to their mother, who was sick in bed at the time. The little girl had one side of her face shot off, I bathed and dressed the wound as best I could, and dressed her in my clothes to send her to Wheatland to the hospital. Fortunately this happened about the time the train passed by our ranch on the way to Wheatland. We were just able to get the child on the train and as the train was leaving Mr. Miller said I think Frank is dead. I went back and there the little boy lay dead in the wagon.
>
> I was alone except [for] my [son] Frank. [He] was only 4 years old but I put him on a horse and sent him to the neighbors, with a note asking for help. John came and we brought the little boy in and prepared him for burial, we ordered the casket and planned the funeral services. Mr. Underwood and I conducted the services the next afternoon. There were about 30 friends present. We buried the little boy near his home.... his mother came to me and brought 4 little children and stayed until after the funeral. I was certainly a wreck by that time....
>
> Not long after that Willie Nichols was killed and there was great excitement again at our ranch. Sheriff Smalley[13] came to investigate the killing, he brought 8 men with him and for many days they came up in the morning and back at night. John had to take them up to the Nichols' ranch. They always arrived at mealtime. Tom Horn was arrested for the killing.... He was tried and found guilty and...paid the penalty. All this happened near our ranch. 7 miles.

Nettie Jordan. (Wyoming Stock Growers Association)

Early in 1900 Nickell began threatening that he would bring sheep and graze them wherever he wanted, even on neighbors' ranches.

The Iron Mountain country was off-limits to sheep in the eyes of most cattle ranchers. Cattlemen hated sheep because the conventional wisdom at the time was that sheep ruined the range for other livestock by grazing to the roots.

Frank Bosler, the son of the Frank Bosler with whom John C. Coble was in partnership, commented on the sheep versus cattle controversy in Iron Mountain. He said that one of the members of the Farthing family, early settlers in the area southeast of Iron Mountain, told him that there was a "deadline" north of which only cattle could be run. The deadline was on one of his east-west property lines. The

same line ran across the north perimeter of the King brothers' holdings on the west side of the Laramie Range, which runs north and south and includes the Iron Mountain country.[14] The King brothers were prominent sheep ranchers who respected the deadline. Kels Nickell's place lay well north of the deadline.

Tempers flared when a herder working for Nickell brought three thousand head of sheep into the area in May 1901. The herder, John Scroder, remained in the area working for Nickell.

Scroder heard someone prowling around his wagon on Tuesday night[15] before Willie's murder on Thursday morning. Tensions were high; Scroder was frightened and decided to quit at the end of the month.

A stranger had ridden through the country early Wednesday looking for a job. Not knowing at the time that Scroder planned to quit,

Nickell family around 1898 at the homestead, three years before the Nickell shootings. Willie is at the far right. Kels, Jr. is next to Willie. The tall young woman standing is Julia. The boy at left is Freddie. The woman seated at left center is Mary. (Viola Nickell Bixler)

Nickell declined to hire the man, and watched him ride away up the road that led west and then south toward the Iron Mountain depot. After Nickell learned that Scroder would be leaving, he sent Willie after the man to ask him to return to the ranch to discuss the job.

Following his father's instructions, Willie left home a few minutes before seven on Thursday morning, July 18. He rode his father's horse toward a gate about three-quarters of a mile west of the family home.

Mary Nickell's brother William Mahoney, who lived with the Nickell family, and John Apperson, a surveyor from Cheyenne, were at the Nickell home Wednesday evening. Together with Kels they left the Nickell house shortly before Willie left Thursday morning. They headed northeast about a mile and a quarter to survey part of Nickell's property.

Site of Nickell homestead as seen today. The road Willie Nickell took to the gate is at right. (Author's photo)

Around seven the men heard three shots from the area where Willie was headed. Nickell wondered aloud about who was shooting, recognizing that it could not be Freddie, his ten-year-old son, because Freddie used a smaller caliber gun than the weapon being fired.

It is possible that the weather was foggy near the gate as Willie approached it. Weather records in Cheyenne point to high humidity the previous evening, with a cooling wind from the southeast—conditions that would produce fog at the location of the murder, seven thousand feet above sea level. Rain had fallen in Cheyenne on July 16 and 17, and Kels Nickell testified to "sprinkles" in the area the day before the killing. The weekend after Willie's death rains were heavy enough to wash out the railroad tracks between Iron Mountain and Cheyenne, indicative of a lingering low-pressure system.

Foggy weather would lend credence to theories that Willie was shot in a case of mistaken identity. In testimony Kels Nickell stated that he believed that Willie had been shot by mistake, by someone whose intention was to kill him because of his irascible nature and his introduction of sheep into the area

Willie reached the gate around seven. He dismounted to open the wire gate. If he had been on his own horse he could have leaned over to open it from horseback,[16] but his father's horse was not been trained for this maneuver. After leading the horse through the gate, he turned to close it. At this point two shots rang out in quick succession and then, after a pause, a third. Two bullets hit him in the left side of his back and exited, one through the right abdomen and one through the sternum. Either would have been fatal.

He ran—surely stumbling—sixty-five feet toward his home to the east and fell facedown.

Someone, in all likelihood the killer, rolled his body over, pulled his shirt open and examined the exit wounds. Gravel and dirt clung to the blood on his face and the front of his shirt, which had drained from massive wounds.

His family was not concerned when he did not return home that evening, his father said, because it was possible he had gone on from Iron Mountain to the Diamond ranch (east of Nickell's place) in search of the prospective herder.

Four days earlier, on Sunday, July 14, Tom Horn had stopped at W. L. "Billy" Clay's ranch, about a mile north of the Nickell ranch. Clay was a prominent rancher, and Horn customarily stayed at his place when in the area.

❦

A few days before Horn's arrival at Clay's, he had been at the railroad depot in Cheyenne, according to Henry Daly. Daly had known Horn since the 1880s in Arizona. Daly said that when he met Horn at the depot, Horn "was on the lookout for a certain party and wished to be alone."[17]

On the Monday Horn rode out to patrol the area, returning for midday dinner at Clay's. He left in the afternoon, and, he said,[18] proceeded west of Nickell's land and then southeast toward Miller's. That night he arrived at Miller's around ten. Jim Miller invited him in to eat. He then bedded down in the tent outside where Gus and Victor slept.

The next morning he ate breakfast with the family and Glendolene Myrtle Kimmell, the teacher who boarded with Millers and taught at the Miller-Nickell school. After eating, he visited with her until shortly

Miller children in 1929. Back row, left to right: Andy, Eva, Ernie, Maude, Ray. Front, left to right: Gus, Victor, Robert. (Ruth Miller Ayers)

before she left for school a few minutes before nine o'clock. Then he and Jim Miller engaged in casual shooting practice at birds and tin cans.

A key question regarding Tom Horn's conviction pertained to his clothing and gear while at Miller's. In the inquest following Willie's murder, Jim Miller stated that Horn had no articles of clothing with him other than what he was wearing, a worn, blue-striped shirt, trousers, and a hat. He also carried a thirty-thirty smokeless powder rifle, canvas cartridge belt, and field glasses. No bedding or anything else was tied behind the saddle. Other witnesses at the inquest also stated he had no articles with him other than his Winchester and field glasses.

Around four Tuesday afternoon Horn saddled his horse and rode southwest toward Spring Creek. When he returned about forty-five minutes later he told Miller that Nickell's sheep were in his pasture. He spent the rest of his time talking with the schoolteacher.

Miller later spoke of Horn bragging that he had killed three men who were train robbers when he surprised them and that he had been in a knife fight with one of them before he shot him. Horn told him that he had killed another man in a fight about a year before and mentioned the murders of Lewis and Powell in 1895. Miller said, however, he could not recollect exactly what Horn had said about the latter two killings.

Tuesday evening, Horn again stayed at the Miller ranch.

On Wednesday, July 17, Horn left Miller's ranch about mid-morning, riding toward the southeast.

Tom Horn also had two conversations with Jim Miller and Billy McDonald, a neighbor. He wrote of them in his last letter to John Coble just before his execution. Horn wrote that Miller and McDonald approached him and said they had decided to eliminate the Nickells. They invited him to be the triggerman and said "Jordan and Underwood would pay me." He stated that he declined to participate in the plot.

A. F. Whitman, Billy McDonald, and their wives gathered for a visit at the Miller home later in the day Willie was killed. The Millers owned an organ, and after the evening meal they arranged an impromptu country dance. The dance lasted until late in the evening.

The McDonalds left to return to their home southeast of Millers around eleven-thirty that night. The Whitmans stayed overnight since some members of both families—the parents and children other than Gus and Victor—intended to go to Cheyenne the next day.

Friday morning Freddie Nickell left on horseback to herd cows near the gate. He found Willie's body and returned home, tearful and screaming, "Willie is murdered at the gate!"

After Freddie brought the news of Willie's death, Kels Nickell sent Will Mahoney for a wagon, and the men retrieved the body and sent word to Cheyenne of the killing. Nickell and Apperson, the surveyor, then returned to the gate where Willie was killed, to search for evidence. Livestock tracks through the open gate, however, had obliterated any sign of the events of the previous morning.

Mr. and Mrs. John J. Underwood. (Wyoming Division of Cultural Resources)

When Kels first reached the area where Willie lay, he noted that the boy's head lay on a flat rock about two inches in diameter that seemingly had been placed there to support it. However, the ground in the area is rough and rocky, and investigators could not find any such rock.[19]

After searching the area, Nickell summoned Joe Reed, a friend who lived to the northeast. The two went to the Miller-Nickell schoolhouse, where Nickell angrily questioned the teacher. Miss Kimmell refused to answer any questions at first, but relented when Nickell told her of Willie's killing. Joe Reed observed that "she didn't seem to answer the questions…. She showed a disposition not to answer the questions…."[20]

John L. Jordan. (Wyoming Stock Growers Association)

Deputy Sheriff Peter Warlaumont, Coroner Thomas Murray, and the court stenographer, Robert Morris, left Cheyenne Friday afternoon for Nickell's ranch. The first day of the coroner's inquest was Saturday, July 20, at Nickell's ranch. The panel consisted of T. J. Fisher, who was later clerk of the district court during Tom Horn's trial, Hiram G. Davidson, and George Gregory.

Willie's body was taken by train to Cheyenne on Sunday, July 21, for an autopsy. The coroner's inquest continued at the courthouse in Cheyenne on July 22. It then adjourned until early August.

Willie was buried in Cheyenne's Lakewood Cemetery on July 23, 1901.

Chapter Sixteen

Nobody's Family is Safe

A T THE INQUEST, the doctors who examined Willie Nickell's body indicated that the shots seemed to have come from a slightly higher location than where Willie was standing because they had followed a downward course.

Next District Attorney Walter Stoll questioned Jim Miller concerning the feud between the families. Miller said that as far as he knew Nickell's sheep were on his land, but that he could see no merit in trying to persuade Nickell to remove them; any such effort "was worse than useless…" and "would do no good." He added that he was still trying to avoid trouble with Nickell. He said that Tom Horn had not made any threats against Nickell.

But Miller elaborated on incidents that clarified the extent of his feud with Nickell and on encounters between Nickell and other Iron Mountainites.

In one revealing statement he said, "About a year ago I threatened to whip the oldest one, Kels…. He called me a liar and I jumped out of the buggy and took a little switch and started for him." He also added that one day on his way to Laramie in a wagon with Victor, Eva, and Maude he had tangled with Willie.

In that incident Willie and a Nickell hired hand, Harley Axford, both on horses, had caught up with the Miller family. Miller told Axford that Willie's father had once caught Victor and threatened him, saying "he was going to thump him."

When Willie rode up to the wagon, Miller struck at him with a switch. He stopped the team and told Victor to get out of the wagon and "lick him." Miller also threatened to shoot Willie's horse if he ran it over Victor.

Nickell ranch as it looked at the time of the shootings, from a painting by M.D. Houghton. (Author's photo, courtesy Gerry Walker)

He continued, apparently agitated, that he believed that there were "dozens" of times when Kels Nickell had threatened or whipped Victor from April 1900 until June of 1901:

"He had repeatedly threatened to strike him [Victor] with a whip he carried; he told him he would cut him all to pieces. He also told J.L. Jordan he would kill him or my kids if they went through his fence any more...."

He said that the enmity between the two fathers had affected the sons of both families. He had warned his sons Gus and Victor that they should carry guns and shoot Nickell if he pursued them. He added, however, that Willie Nickell was not of a "quarrelsome disposition."

Testimony by A. F. Whitman, a neighbor who lived west of the Miller and Nickell ranches and east of Coble's Bosler holdings, described the animosity. Whitman said that he had heard from neighbors that it would be "unwise" for Nickell to bring sheep into the country, but that he had never heard anyone speak of harming Nickell. Nickell, he said, had "a good deal of trouble" with people, and

Miller had expressed hatred for him and threatened to shoot if Nickell attacked him.

Willie was buried the next day, Tuesday, and the inquest panel adjourned until further notice.

In the meantime, Kels Nickell hired Italian sheepherder Vingenzo Biango to replace John Scroder.

On Saturday, August 3, 1901, Nickell's sheep again trespassed onto Miller's ranch, evidently driven there by the Italian under orders from Nickell. Around five-thirty the next morning Kels was shot while near a group of calves southeast of his home where he was milking a cow. He was wounded painfully but not severely. Two men had fired five shots from east of where Nickell was working. At least three hit him in both arms and the left hip. He stumbled back to the safety of the log home.

At the time, Will Mahoney and Harlan Nickell, Kels's brother who was visiting from Kentucky, were the only other adult males in Nickell's home. They were fearful to leave the house and risk being shot.

Julia Nickell Cook, Nickell's oldest daughter, had come from Carbon, Wyoming, south of Hanna, to be with the family during the period that followed Willie's shooting. Throwing caution to the wind, she rode horseback to the Reeds' place, arriving there around seven-thirty in the morning. Joe Reed, just finishing breakfast, agreed to accompany her back to the ranch.

Back at Nickell's ranch, Reed and Mahoney attended to Nickell's flesh wounds and then, together with Julia, helped him into a horse-drawn wagon and transported him to the Iron Mountain railroad depot. Mahoney accompanied Nickell on the train to Cheyenne for treatment. Nickell apparently recovered quickly as he was jailed on August 15 in Cheyenne for assault in a seemingly unrelated incident, and released after paying a fine and jail costs.[1]

Nickell had sent his rifle back to the ranch with Reed and Julia with instructions to give it to the herder. Later that day, Reed and Julia found sixty to eighty head of Nickell's sheep dead, shot and clubbed to death.

On August 6, the coroner's jury investigating Willie's death again traveled to the remote Iron Mountain area and reconvened at Nickell's homestead. They began with questions about the most recent shooting, trying to determine if it was connected to Willie's death.

Two of Nickell's small children testified they had seen two men to the southeast the morning Kels was shot. One man was larger than the other, they said, inferring that the smaller was younger. The children said the men walked away rapidly, then mounted and rode off to the south on a bay and gray horse. The color of the horses matched the horses Jim Miller owned, the children said.

Shortly after the August 6 coroner's session, Deputy Sheriff Peter Warlaumont and Joe LeFors, the deputy U.S. marshal who was now acting as a private detective for the county, proceeded to Iron Mountain. LeFors questioned Mary Nickell.

The two men, or perhaps LeFors acting alone, also visited the Miller ranch. LeFors interrogated the family at least once during two trips to the area[2] in Glendolene Kimmell's presence. She said later she sensed LeFors had something up his sleeve.[3]

Deputy Warlaumont arrested and jailed Jim, Gus, and Victor Miller on suspicion of Kels's shooting. After being interrogated, they were released, since their statements alibied their whereabouts at the time of the attack. According to Ruth Miller,[4] Glendolene Kimmell was responsible for gaining the Millers' release from jail. No one was charged with the shooting.

<hr/>

When the inquest reconvened in Cheyenne on August 8, the sheepherder who had originally brought the sheep to Nickell's ranch in May, John Scroder, added to the testimony about the enmity generated by Nickell's sheep. He also made clear his reasons for giving notice that he would be leaving before Willie was murdered: he was afraid.

Scroder had gone to work for Nickell on the previous May 9. He stated specifically that Nickell had told him to drive the sheep onto Miller's land, but cautioned him to stay off Two Bar ranges.

Scroder had been forewarned that Nickell and he were at risk. When he trailed the sheep from Loveland, Colorado, as he reached the western outskirts of Cheyenne he encountered a man who said that he did not believe Nickell "will live until 1902 if them sheep goes in there...."[5]

Joe LeFors in Miles City during the period before he became a deputy U.S. Marshal. He had been a contract brand inspector in northeast Wyoming for Montana livestock interests and reported to an inspector, W.D. Smith, in Miles City. (American Heritage Center, University of Wyoming)

Scroder said that one night the week Willie was killed he was lying in bed in his wagon when his dog started barking. He had no doubt he heard a man walking about. He figured that if anyone was outside with "legitimate" business, he would come to the wagon to speak with him. That episode, seemingly, was the reason he was quitting.

Vingenzo Biango (who at times was referred to as "Jim White"), the Italian sheepherder who replaced Scroder, next testified. Speaking through an interpreter, he related an incident occurring on Saturday, August 3, when he ran into two men and a woman. One was Jim Miller; the woman was Glendolene Kimmell. He said that Miller had shouted to him, "Get out of here, you son of a bitch. This is my own place.... The son of a bitch sent the sheep across to my house. I will fix the son of a bitch before daylight...."[6]

Biango also said that three men, "one large and two boys about eighteen or nineteen years old," were above him on a hilltop and that they fired at him "about thirty times." At that, he left and headed to Cheyenne:

> Attorney Stoll asked him, "Has anyone offered you any money to go out of town since you have been in town?"
>
> Biango replied, "About half past four or five o'clock at a corner here in the city a fellow on a bicycle said, 'Hello, Jim.' The young fellow said, 'You were the man that watched the sheep...?'
>
> "The young man pulled a pocket book out and said, 'If you want to get away from here I will give you five hundred dollars and buy you a ticket any place you want to go.' He showed a lot of bank bills...."

The man was never identified.

Dora Miller testified that she had gone to gather vegetables in a garden near their home the day before Kels Nickell was shot. She noticed that the sheep were almost in the garden. She further admitted that Jim Miller had threatened to kill Kels Nickell during the previous year.

Julia's[7] testimony at the inquest confirmed the duration and intensity of the Nickell-Miller animosity. She also revealed the circumstances leading to her father's shooting on Sunday morning, August 4:

STOLL. Have you heard of any anybody making threats against your father?

JULIA. Yes, sir.

STOLL. Who made those threats?

JULIA. A man by the name of Jim Miller.... He has been making threats around the country.... I heard Will McDonald tell Papa that once. Mrs. McDonald told me that [Miller] said he had laid out in the pasture to kill Papa time and again.... The last time we come to town I understood he bought a new gun for the purpose of killing Papa, [and] that he was not going to give him any chance....

STOLL. Your father also bought a gun when he was in town?

JULIA. Yes, sir.

Julia also testified that, after returning from the train depot on the day Kels was shot, she and Reed had followed the tracks of the gunmen's horses southeast, toward Miller's place.

Julia continued that the morning of Kels's shooting she and Reed had met Gus Miller on the road from Reed's. Miller did not seem surprised that her father had been shot:

STOLL. Did he seem to feel bad or say it was strange?

JULIA. No, sir.

STOLL. What did he say?

JULIA. I have forgotten the words he said; I know he was not surprised.

STOLL. Did he say it was too bad?

JULIA. He just said, "Is that so...?"

On August 6 the jury also questioned John (Jack) Martin, a blacksmith and deputy sheriff from Laramie. Martin said he had seen Tom Horn in Laramie on Friday, July 19. He said that he saw Horn after he had learned of Willie Nickell's murder through the newspapers. However, the newspapers first published the news of the killing on July 21.[8]

Site of the murder as seen in 1901–1902 from a rock outcropping three hundred yards northwest of the gate. Number 1 corresponds to a place where a killer might have hidden behind a smaller outcropping thirty yards from the gate, 2 is the location of the gate, 3 is the location where Willie fell. The photo appeared in local newspapers. (American Heritage Center, University of Wyoming)

Martin also stated that he did not believe Horn had killed Willie:

> STOLL. Is there anything you could tell us about this Nickell killing in any way, shape or manner, anything you have heard or anything you know or think of?
>
> MARTIN. No, sir, there is nothing I know. I am like everybody else. I have got my ideas but that would not do anyone any good.... I am satisfied that Horn had nothing to do with it. I don't think he did.
>
> STOLL. Why do you think that?
>
> MARTIN. Well, I think this because Tom Horn is a very smooth detective when he is sober. I don't think there is any better. If he was going over to do anything of that kind they would have never seen him....

Then the coroner asked, "Did Mr. Horn tell you that?"

Martin replied, "No, I say he is that kind of a man.... What makes me think that man [Horn] had nothing to do with it [is] because if he had done anything of that kind he would not have been around there the day before.... When it came out in the papers I think the papers said they accused Horn. I said Horn had nothing to do with this thing because he is not that big a fool as to go around a place and do a thing of that kind; he is too smart a man."

After Kels was shot, he sold out to the Two Bar and moved with his family to Cheyenne, where they lived in a house on East Twenty-third Street.[9]

Chapter Seventeen

HE WAS GOING TO KILL ME ON SIGHT

THE INQUEST continued intermittently for the next two months.
W. L. "Billy" Clay confirmed that Horn habitually stayed at
his place when he was in the vicinity, but that he (Clay) never
asked about Horn's business. He did note, that Horn was known as a
stock detective.

When it came to the subject of sheep Clay corroborated that no
one in the country liked the idea of their presence and that he himself
hated to see them because they "damage property." More troublesome
was Clay's worry that Nickell not only threatened to kill Miller and
others but that "Nickell has told several different parties that he was
going to kill me on sight...."

George Braae testified that he had overheard a conversation
between Nickell and a man named Joslin, in which Joslin told Nickell,
"Kels, I would gamble you wouldn't live to see 1902." Braae alleged
the remark was made in josh, but it carried a sinister undertone.

Kels Nickell had already been called. He had immediately proceeded to accuse the Millers of having murdered Willie:

> STOLL. Do you suspect anybody of having killed this boy?
> NICKELL. I do.
> STOLL. Who is it, or do you suspect?...
> NICKELL. I suspect the Millers,...Jim Miller, Gussie, and
> Victor Miller.

Nickell emphasized that he believed that the younger of the two
Miller boys, Victor, had fired the shots that killed Willie.

Victor had ridden up to the Reed ranch between ten and eleven
o'clock the morning Willie was killed, packing a Winchester. Nickell
acknowledged that he had ordered his sheep driven onto Miller's land.

Nickell added that he had met Tom Horn in May while in Cheyenne. They were in Kerrigan's saloon when Horn reassured him that he had no interest in the sheep matter and that his only purpose on his patrols was to ensure that no one was stealing the cattle of his employers, the Two Bar and John Coble. For that matter, neither the Two Bar or Coble cared about the sheep, he said.

The testimony of all three Miller men reflected the feud. Gus Miller acknowledged that the sons of both families had initiated "little" quarrels, but that the trouble was primarily between Victor and Willie. The matter had reached a head over a fence cutting the previous summer, resulting in an encounter at a gate owned by Nickell. He added that Nickell had caused his father to be arrested "two or three times," but did not go into particulars.

Jim Miller said that it was Horn who first told him the sheep were in his pasture, on the Tuesday after Horn's arrival. He acknowledged that both Victor and Gus always carried rifles and that he carried a revolver.

Stoll then moved the questioning to events preceding Willie's killing. Miller said that Horn arrived on Monday night about ten o'clock, ate something, and then went to bed in the tent where Victor and Gus slept south of the house. The next morning Horn ate breakfast with the family:

> STOLL. What did he do all day Tuesday?
> JIM MILLER. Up to about nine o'clock he talked to the schoolmarm.
> STOLL. Did he seem to make an impression on the schoolmarm?
> JIM MILLER. Yes, he seemed to make a very good impression.
> STOLL. Did he seem to try to make an impression?
> JIM MILLER. He did....

Stoll then returned the questioning to the sheep. Miller said that Horn was there primarily to take a look at the Two Bar's Colcord pasture. Later in the day the detective had ridden up a creek and returned, again telling Miller the sheep were in his pasture.

Stoll asked what Horn did the rest of the day, and what they had talked about:

JIM MILLER. He immediately went to the house and went to talking with the schoolmarm....

STOLL. Up to the time Horn left, tell what Horn said about his lying about in the hills or his watching....

JIM MILLER. He said he was paid to watch for the cattle business.... At one time we got to talking about Mr. Nickell being a kind of a mean man, and he said he had never catched him stealing anything; he did not think he stole a great deal....

STOLL. Did he say anything about his watching around in that locality...?

JIM MILLER. He said he had watched pretty near everybody in the neighborhood....

STOLL. Did he say anything about the way he looked upon Nickell bringing sheep into that country?

JIM MILLER. Yes, he looked at it as a very mean trick. I spoke about it. I says, "Coble has a pasture adjoining mine; he [Nickell] has filed on Coble's pasture and the next thing he will have them up there." Tom said, "No, [I don't] think he would do that because Nickell wants my friendship, and he would be afraid that would make me mad...."

Miller continued, "He [Nickell] also told J. L. Jordan he would kill him or my kids if they went through his fence any more...."

An alibi for the Millers later proved fatal to Horn. Witnesses, including sixteen-year-old Eva Miller, stated that on Thursday all the family members were at breakfast around 7:00 A.M. The rest of the day was occupied with normal chores and visiting with neighbors. She commented Horn had spent considerable time with the teacher.

Tom Horn had characteristically exaggerated and boasted while at the Millers, talking of his prowess with women in Cuba, his killings and mythical exploits against train robbers. Miller said he spoke of having killed a man within the last year and drew upon the murders of Lewis and Powell to embellish his stories.

Joe Reed was one of two brothers who were "about the only friends" Nickell had, according to Tom Horn. He had come from his ranch to the east to minister to the Nickell family after Kels was shot, having been summoned by Julia. He also confirmed the details of the encounter Julia and he had with Gus Miller on their way back to the Nickell homestead. Finally, he described their experience when they returned to the homestead after accompanying William Mahoney and Kels to the depot:

> STOLL. Have you ever heard Miller or any of his boys make any threats against Nickell?
>
> REED. Well, no I [personally] have not. I told you I lived there close to Nickell and Miller. As you know, they are in a jangle nearly all the time. I hear one talk and the other talk; I don't pay much attention.
>
> STOLL. A sort of growl?...
>
> REED. Yes, sir....
>
> REED. [Gus] came out and was riding a gray horse. When we met him I said, "Good morning, Gus..., seems there is lot of killing in the hills."
>
> He says, "Yes."
>
> I says, "Mr. Nickell was shot this morning."
>
> He said, "Is that so?"
>
> I said, "Yes, I heard he is shot and I guess he is pretty bad."
>
> He just said, "Hmm."
>
> STOLL. When you got to Nickell's house, you found Nickell suffering from the wound.
>
> REED. Yes, sir, he was lying on the bed.
>
> STOLL. What did Nickell tell you as to the shooting...?
>
> REED. The first thing said was, "Joe, they came very near getting me this morning." The women and children were jumping around there. Half the time I would be talking to him and he to me, and we [couldn't] understand each other. I asked him several questions, where he was and what he saw. He told us that he saw nobody, but the children saw two men running away. ...There was two sheep crippled. We wondered why the sheepherder left them. I thought they were sick.... We went a little further and I saw one dead. I got off and examined to see how it

had been killed. We got on our horses and went on, and found them strung here and there, some with their legs broke and some with their guts dragging on the prairie.... I asked Julia now, "What do you intend to do with these sheep?"

She said, "We will take them home."

I said, "We can't.... The men that done this meanness would shoot [me] if they saw me driving those sheep. They will say...[I have] a finger in those sheep too...."

Elizabeth Stein was one of four schoolteachers who spoke about the enmity that had been generated over the years. She taught at the Diamond, northeast of the Iron Mountain country. The Sunday that Kels was shot she and Louis Darman, a foreman of the Two Bar, had been invited to Miller's ranch, where they learned of the shooting.

She said that no one was surprised at the shooting of the elder Nickell, simply because the "general feeling" in the country was that whoever had shot Willie had intended to get Kels. She further said that with regard to the sheep, although most people generally felt it was unwise for Nickell to bring them, Glendolene Kimmell felt no one had a right to drive them onto Miller's property.

⁂

Diedrick George, a rancher who lived five miles east of Nickell, stated that he was at Nickell's shortly after Kels was shot Sunday morning. He verified that Mary Nickell was convinced that the Millers shot Kels and that the small children saw two men walking away from the location thirty minutes after it occurred. He also spoke about a secret organization that had been formed:

> STOLL. Do you know anything of an organization in that community, or a secret society?
>
> GEORGE. ...All I know, they have what they call a protective association in the Sybille country.[1]
>
> STOLL. What kind of protective association? Is it made up of ranchmen?
>
> GEORGE. Yes, made up of ranchmen.
>
> STOLL. When was it organized?
>
> GEORGE. I couldn't tell you. I believe Fitzmorris at the head

of the Sybille stream is president. He gave me a little book that gave all the men's names and each man's brand....

STOLL. Did Fitzmorris tell you the objects of the association?

GEORGE. No, sir.

STOLL. Are they stated in this book?

GEORGE. I think they are.

Then Coroner Murray assumed the questioning:

MURRAY. Is it not a fact that the ranchmen up in there don't want sheep running around in that country?

GEORGE. That is the way I understand it.

MURRAY. Was that the reason this organization was gotten up?

GEORGE. The organization was got up before sheep ever was talked of; ... the country was troubled with thieves.

MURRAY. You don't believe that people would care if they brought in sheep?

GEORGE. I don't think they would like it....

MURRAY. Did you ever hear Nickell say anything about the neighbors up there, threaten them? ...Didn't he talk to you about eating them out [of their grass]?

GEORGE. ...I understand he has to others....

MURRAY. Didn't he say there wouldn't be enough grass to feed a grasshopper after he got through with those fellows? ...Did he not say there wouldn't be enough grass around there to feed a goose when he got through with Jordan? ...He talked about killing people up there?

GEORGE. Not to me, [but] I passed Mr. Clay one time. He says, "...He was going to shoot you and me too."

The testimony returned to the events that occurred when Nickell's sheep were driven onto Miller's land:

MILLER. ...After breakfast I sat in the front room. Along about half past nine.... Gus came in and I noticed he looked kind of a little bit pale. "Something wrong?" I says, "How is the cows?"

He says, "All right." Then he says, "Nickell is shot."

Just then the schoolmarm came out of her room and my wife came up, and I think Victor came from out from the yard. I remember we were all there at that time.

I said, "I can't say I'm glad of it." I further said, "I prayed God his sins might be forgiven, [but] I believe the devil would get his own when he got him."

STOLL. You were not shedding any great buckets of tears?

MILLER. No, sir....

MILLER. I didn't think it was safe to go out without a gun; in fact I didn't go any place without a gun. I haven't been to the privy for two years without taking a pistol with me.... Mr. Nickell has swore he would kill me on sight—you understand that?

STOLL. I understand what you say. Did he tell you?

MILLER. No, but he told my boys and my neighbors....

William Edwards, an Iron Mountain resident, testified on August 13 that in the fall of 1900 he, his brother, and another man were working at Miller's ranch. He said that Miller "told us if Nickell ever whips his boys again he would kill him."

Deputy U.S. Marshal Joe LeFors testified briefly of his trip to Nickell's ranch with Peter Warlaumont a few days after Kels' shooting, and that it was raining at the time. He stated that when Freddie Nickell took him to the place where Kels had been shot, he could see only faint horse and human tracks. He offered no other new testimony with regard to the shootings.

But LeFors was not finished with the Tom Horn case.

Chapter Eighteen

OF COURSE, THEY HAD TROUBLE

GLENDOLENE MYRTLE KIMMELL had come to Wyoming to teach school early in 1901 from Hannibal, Missouri. Hannibal is near the location of Tom Horn's birthplace in Scotland County in the northeastern part of the state.

She was born on June 21, 1879, in Saint Louis. Her mother, Frances "Fannie" Ascenath Pierce Kimmell, was born in Hannibal in 1843. Frances was one of ten children in a socially prominent family. In July 1864 she married Elijah Lloyd Kimmell, whom she met in Saint Louis where he worked for a railroad. Elijah was born in Williams Center, Ohio, in 1842 and was a Civil War veteran.[1]

One of Frances's brothers, Glendolene's Uncle Edward Pierce, was a playmate of Samuel Clemens, better known as Mark Twain. The Pierce family home at 321 North Fifth Street in Hannibal was only a block from Clemens's boyhood home.

Glendolene had two siblings, John Pierce Kimmell, who was born in 1865 and died as a teenager in March 23, 1882, and Daisy Natalie Kimmell, who was born in 1870 and died June 27, 1872.

Elijah Kimmell died in 1881 in St. Louis. Glendolene, her brother, and mother then moved back to the family home in Hannibal. Both of Glendolene's parents and her siblings are buried in Hannibal.

Glendolene's name first appears in the Hannibal city directory in 1895 and 1897–1898. (Directories were not printed every year.)

Physically small in size in adulthood, she was estimated to be only four and one-half feet tall.[2]

She was one of a group of young women recruited to teach in the West at the turn of the century. On her way to Wyoming, she probably visited her uncle, Charles Pierce, who was working for a railroad and living in Jamestown, North Dakota.

Glendolene as a young teen. (Roberta Hagood)

Tom Horn's comments in his so-called confession that Glendolene was of mixed blood, possibly of Hawaiian or Polynesian ancestry, were incorrect. He added that she "spoke most every language on earth." She denied the ancestry and language comments and said, in the affidavit she filed as part of the appeals process that followed Horn's 1902 conviction, that if she spoke many languages she would not have been teaching school in Iron Mountain, Wyoming.

She authored a lengthy document in Denver in April 1904 that was printed in the appendix to Tom Horn's autobiography. In it she said that part of her reasoning for coming to the West and to teach at the Miller-Nickell school was that she had "been most strongly attracted by the frontier type. I was happy in the belief that I would meet with the embodiment of that type... [but] I was doomed to disappointment, for all the cattle men and cow boys I saw were like the hired hands 'back East.'"[3]

In contrast, her description of Horn is different: "...there stopped at the Miller ranch a man who embodied the characteristics, the experiences of the old frontiersman."[4]

Kimmell had been warned against going to the Miller-Nickell school because of the feud between the two families. However, she agreed to teach at the school and to board at Miller's ranch with her eyes wide open. She stated in the inquest into Willie Nickell's death that she felt the experience would give her a better understanding of human nature.

Her testimony in the coroner's inquest further reveals her feelings of disdain toward the homesteaders. She confirmed the events of July 15 to August 4 and provided her own assessment of why Kels Nickell and Jim Miller were inevitably bound to clash. She testified twice at the inquest: once preceding Horn's testimony and once after. The first part of her testimony covered the happenings at Miller's ranch when they learned that Kels had been shot on August 4:[5]

> KIMMELL. Well, Sunday morning I didn't leave my room until twenty minutes past nine. The occasion for my leaving then was that Gus Miller came into the front room just next to mine and announced to his father that Nickell had been shot....

STOLL. Up to that time, that is when you went into the room, upon hearing what Gus had said, you hadn't seen any of the Miller family that morning?

KIMMELL. Yes, I had seen Victor.

STOLL. Where and when had you seen him?

KIMMELL. I looked out of the window of my room about half past eight and saw him....

STOLL. Had you seen any other members of the family?

KIMMELL. I saw some of the little children playing about but none of the older members.

STOLL. Do you know anything about any of the older members being about the house previous to this time?

KIMMELL. I woke up the first time at five o'clock; everything in the house was still.... At seven o'clock I heard Mr. Miller in the front room just off of mine....

STOLL. How do you know it was Mr. Miller?

KIMMELL. He was passing back and forth, and singing....

STOLL. How do you know whether Mr. Miller and Mrs. Miller occupied the same room the night before?

KIMMELL. I don't know about that night.

STOLL. Is it their general habit to occupy separate rooms?

KIMMELL. Mr. Miller has a room by himself and Mrs. Miller has a room with some of the children.

Stoll reviewed the events of the Saturday previous to Kels's shooting, when Nickell's sheep reached the potato patch southeast of the Miller buildings. Kimmell confirmed that the Miller family had gone outside, strung out in single file, with Jim Miller and her in the lead. Stoll then returned the questioning to Sunday morning:

STOLL. What did Miller say when he heard of Nickell being shot?

KIMMELL. At first he said, "Well." Then he didn't say anything for some time. After the group had dispersed, after we had heard all that Gus knew about it and they had all gone from that room, excepting Mr. Miller and me, he raised his right hand up

Tom Horn and Glendolene Kimmell, from the painting, Iron Mountain Morning, *by L.D. Edgar, Cody, Wyoming.* (www.WesternHeritageStudio.com)

high and said, "I pray God to forgive him his sins, but I believe the devil will get his own...."

STOLL. He wasn't feeling very badly?

KIMMELL. When he first heard the news he was silent except [for] that remark, "Well...."

STOLL. Are you accustomed to any scenes of violence at all?

KIMMELL. No, not any shooting. I never saw anyone shot in my life; I never saw an animal shot.

STOLL. It was all new to you?

KIMMELL. It was new as far as actual experience was concerned. As you know perfectly, one can understand things and be familiar with things that one has not seen by reading and thinking about them.

STOLL. You are from Missouri. I didn't know whether you had been from sections where there were feuds?

KIMMELL. No.

STOLL. Do you take any special interest in this difficulty up there between Nickell and Miller?

KIMMELL. A great deal of interest in it.

STOLL. Why do you do that?

KIMMELL. Because of the knowledge it gives me of human nature and life.

STOLL. Is it a kind of a study?

KIMMELL. Exactly.

STOLL. To study human nature?

KIMMELL. It was when I first went out there. When the school was offered to me the trouble between the two families was fully explained to me. Those who had the giving of the school to me did not wish to give it to me on account of the trouble, but I insisted upon having it. From the very beginning, before any shooting occurred, I was interested in studying the relation of things there, but I kept this interest to myself. This is the first time I have mentioned it.

STOLL. Then the only interest you have is simply of its helping or adding to your knowledge of... human nature?

KIMMELL. Yes.

STOLL. Some people like to study those things. The more I
study them the less I admire human nature. Have you any interest as to the relative merits of Miller and Nickell to determine
which side was right and which side was wrong...?
KIMMELL. Yes.

Then Kimmell expounded on an amazing philosophy concerning
the men and their feud. Although not an expert witness, Kimmell
was allowed to give her opinion on why the combination of the families and the situation was like two trains heading down the tracks
toward each other: a crash was inevitable.

STOLL. What is your opinion?
KIMMELL. My opinion is this, that by a combination of circumstances rather strange, two men were thrown together
whose natures were respectively such that they could not get
along. Miller is unquestionably an obstinate man, and Nickell is
unquestionably a hotheaded man.... The difference is between
their respective interests, one being slower and obstinate, and
the other being quick and fiery. Now, if a man of a different
character than Miller...he would simply have ignored Nickell's
wrongdoing. On the contrary, if a man higher [different in tem-
perament than Nickell] had lived next to Miller he would have
ignored Miller's wrongdoings. The two men, being of the same
character and same plane of living, of course they had trouble.
STOLL. I can understand that, but you have not told what
your opinion was as to the merits of the controversy....
KIMMELL. ...They are both equally to blame. [In] the affair
of Saturday there is no question but that Nickell was in the
wrong, for he was responsible for the sheepherder being
there.... The land is not only deeded land, but a part of the
homestead....
STOLL. ...Did you come to any further conclusion, whether
Miller had a right to shoot Nickell?

Stoll had apparently concluded by this point in the testimony that
it was one of the Millers who had shot Nickell:

Well-known photograph of Glendolene. (American Heritage Center, University of Wyoming)

KIMMELL. Do you mean to shoot him at that time?

STOLL. That time or some other time?

KIMMELL. That is a matter of personal opinion. I can say that if I owned it legally, and had paid for it, and some man drove his sheep or took his stock on it, and I ordered him three times to take it off, I would use force. Because out there if you wait for the officers to come you will wait several days, or many hours....

STOLL. At the time you wouldn't have hesitated to shoot the man?

KIMMELL. ...I would have shot him....

STOLL. ...You stated Mr. Miller was singing on Sunday morning?

KIMMELL. Yes.

STOLL. Is he in the habit of singing a good deal?

KIMMELL. Yes, he is in the habit of passing back and forth when there is no one around for him to talk to. His knowledge of songs is not very extensive. I don't think he knows one through. He knows one line in three; he sang this morning one line of the same song over and over.

Then T. J. Fisher, a member of the three-man inquest panel, asked a few brief questions:

MR. FISHER. Is he [Miller] not a kind of a religious crank?

KIMMELL. Am I supposed to answer that question?

FISHER. Yes.

KIMMELL. My opinion, in fact my knowledge of him, is that is the case. He is a religious crank.

The young teacher's testimony in favor of the Millers immediately after the killing did not cast suspicion on Horn, but it did not clear him, either. Subsequent developments months later in the episode, primarily her blundering requests asking the governor to commute Horn's sentence to life imprisonment, raised major questions about the veracity of her testimony. But that did not come about until much later.

For now, Kimmell sympathized with Tom Horn yet defended the Millers. When Joe LeFors visited the area investigating the crime, she sensed that LeFors was not to be trusted. As Horn indicated in his "confession" to Joe LeFors, the teacher smelled a rat when LeFors was investigating the crimes. Her attempts, whatever they might have been, to warn the stock detective of LeFors's intentions were wasted effort, however.

If Horn had trusted the teacher's intuitive distrust of LeFors, he would not have sloughed off the schoolmarm's warning—an observation keenly made by T. Blake Kennedy years later.

Glendolene was never called to testify at the trial. After Tom Horn's conviction, her attempts to save him through his attorneys and her efforts with Governor Chatterton to gain clemency did more harm than good. Her efforts to save him seemingly were spurred by a sense of moral outrage—a man she believed innocent was going to the gallows.

In the period after his execution she was said to be in Denver, writing a book about Horn. Her writings appeared in an appendix to his autobiography. We will never know, but perhaps she spent the rest of her life grieving over what she thought was a grave injustice and the traumatic hanging of an innocent man. To her credit, though, she perceived better than any of Tom's closer contemporaries that he was out of step with his times, a symbolic victim "crushed between the grindstones of two civilizations."[6]

In the handwritten notes Mrs. John L. "Nettie" Jordan used in speeches in the 1940s, she wrote of the teacher, discreetly avoiding the use of her name:

> Willie Nickels was killed then every thing was upset around the Jordans. Sheriff Smalley and five other men come out on train had to be taken up to the Nickels Ranch and back in time for dinner with us. Next day another crew came and so on until Tom Horn was arrested. Then one day a woman came along. she asked if she could come in and then she wanted to go through the house. and at last she asked if I knew Tom Horn. I just shut up like a clam I did not tell her any thing I did say I was going to P.O. [post office] and would have to shut up my house. So she left, but came another day. I was very busy then and did not ask her in.[7]

Nettie's grandson observed that after her first encounter with Kimmell, Nettie never let her in the door again.

Chapter Nineteen

PRETTY PRONOUNCED THIEVES

Tom Horn was called to the stand on Friday, August 9, 1901, during the coroner's inquest into Willie Nickell's murder. District Attorney Stoll began his questioning:

STOLL. State your name, occupation and residence.[1]

HORN. My name is Tom Horn; I suppose my occupation is that of a detective, as near as I can get at it. When I am at home I reside at Mr. Coble's ranch in Albany County; that has been my home for a number of years.

STOLL. Mr. Horn, we understand that you have been up around this section of the country a good deal and have laid around the hills a good deal of the time and have had an opportunity to observe people, things etc. We would like know if there is anything you can tell us about the killing of Willie Nickell. If you saw anything or recollect around there at that time?

HORN: I was in the country just prior to the killing of that kid a day or two.

STOLL. Do you know what day he was killed?

HORN: No, I do not.

STOLL. It was Thursday the eighteenth of July?

HORN. Now, I will tell you I don't know about the dates, but I know on Monday of the week on which he was killed, on Monday morning, whatever date that was, I left Billy Clay's.... I went over to Miller's ranch.... I went to the head of a hay valley this Monday and went to Miller's ranch Monday night.

I was there all day Tuesday, and on Tuesday I went up [to the west] to the head of the creek that Miller lives on. Passed down to where Nickell [might have] had his sheep in Johnny Coble's pasture. I went up there and found they hadn't [the sheep had not gone into Coble's pasture] and my business was ended. I went back to the Miller's ranch and stayed there again that night. That was Tuesday night; I left there Wednesday morning.

STOLL. The kid was killed Thursday, did you say?

HORN. Yes, sir. I left there Wednesday morning; it was along before the middle of the forenoon after I got breakfast.

STOLL. Up to this time did you see any stranger in that locality, anybody riding along?

HORN. No, sir.

STOLL. Did you know Willie Nickell yourself?

HORN. I don't believe I ever saw him. I know Nick [Kels] very well himself but I don't think I ever saw any member of his family, only at a distance.

STOLL. Are you acquainted with the Miller family?

HORN. The family I do not know at all, only as I met them that night. I met Jim Miller before over on the [Laramie] Plains. I met him one evening, he and Whitman. Coble and myself got there in the springtime—the river was up pretty well—and went over to the Bosler Station to get a barrel of beer. We got it and came back. That was the first time I ever see him. He invited me to visit if I ever come through that part of the country. I happened to have a little business in there and I called....

STOLL. When you went away Wednesday, which way did you go?

HORN. I went down the river [toward the southeast] and up to what we call Colcord Place [a pasture owned by the Two Bar, one-half mile east of Nickell's land]. I thought maybe the sheep might be in there. I pulled across through the hills over on the head of the Sybille. This is the time [of year] you shift the cows outside.... I have been doing that except six or seven days. I was [going] in [to] Laramie to see Colonel Bill [*sic*].

The "Colonel Bill" Tom refers to here, and later in the testimony at his trial, was Colonel Edwin J. Bell, who was foreman of the Millbrook Ranch between Laramie and Centennial.

Edwin J. Bell came to Laramie in 1889 from Texas, where he had been known as Colonel Bell because of his leadership qualities. He was a son-in-law of George Morgan, who was connected with the Wyoming Hereford Ranch east of Cheyenne. By 1899 Colonel Bell had become foreman of the Millbrook spread, then owned by Dr. J. W. Harris, who also owned a ranch near Buffalo that figured in the Johnson County War in 1892.

Bell later became famous for his pioneering irrigation projects, which proved the feasibility of raising oats and other grains in the arid Wyoming climate. Tom Horn's reason for having the appointment with Colonel Bell on the Saturday after Willie Nickell was killed has never been documented, but one can speculate that he was the paymaster appointed by Coble to give the detective his cash at the end of the ten-day patrol. Coble had gone to the funeral of his mother in Pennsylvania, who had died while Horn was out on the range:

> STOLL. You were out among the hills Wednesday and Thursday?
>
> HORN. Yes, sir, and perhaps Friday; I went home Saturday morning because I had an appointment with Colonel Bell Saturday night of this same week. I come into the ranch Saturday forenoon, it must have been about ten o'clock.
>
> STOLL. The rest of Wednesday you were how far away from Miller's house, or Nickell's house, the rest of Wednesday?
>
> HORN. Perhaps eight or nine miles. I was in Henke's pasture and Allen's.
>
> STOLL. Did you see anybody that time, any stranger?
>
> HORN. No one at all.
>
> STOLL. Anybody riding around with firearms?
>
> HORN. I did not see a soul; the only man I saw was about Thursday evening. I guess it was Thursday evening, I saw John Braae coming down from Billy Clay's. I saw him riding down [north on] Mule Creek. I was on the hill above him; he was the only one I seen....
>
> STOLL. Did you see anybody around Nickell's ranch?
>
> HORN. I did not go past Nickell's ranch at all. I went through

Billy Clay's up to our north pasture. I was around there all day, until late in the evening…. I did not see a soul in there at all, no one. I went within a mile and a half of Nickell's ranch, closer than that when I came [in Monday night]…maybe half a mile.

STOLL. Thursday where were you?

HORN. I guess I was out on this divide between the head of the Chug and the Sybille.

STOLL. Were you on the Chug at all yourself?

HORN. Only directly on the divide, not on the stream.

STOLL. Did you see Jack Martin [a local rancher] anywhere Thursday?

HORN. The only time I seen Jack Martin for a couple of years was just in Laramie for a very few minutes last month some time.

Tom Horn's work—patrolling the ranges to determine if rustlers were depredating his employers' herds and halting any wrongdoing—required stealth. He was a master at it. Often no one would know he was conducting surveillance on a nearby range unless someone happened across the remnants of the small campfires he occasionally built.

It was, perhaps, Tom Horn's frequent invisibility during the key part of his patrol at the time of the Nickell murder that prevented him from being able to establish a solid alibi:

STOLL. On Thursday were you at any of those ranches [ranch houses]?

HORN. No, sir, I didn't dare go to a ranch when I am on that work.

STOLL. I thought you might have seen somebody working on the range.

HORN. I seen them working in the fields but I kept away from them. I did not want them to know that I was in the country at all.

STOLL. Where were you Friday?

HORN. Friday I was over around Fitzmorris's place and in above what the Two Bar called Hall Cabin.

STOLL. In the cabin?

HORN. Not the cabin but up in that country. Fitzmorris has been running Two Bar cattle and Coble's cattle.... [Fitzmorris was known to take liberties in determining whose stock he would handle. Rumor or perhaps common knowledge had it that he was a rustler.] I know I was in there Friday.... I went in there Thursday night. I crossed the Sybille above the Berner Place Thursday evening and slept on the divide Friday. I went down to Fitzmorris' place; I monkeyed around there all day.

STOLL. You did not go to his ranch?

HORN. Oh, no. I wanted to see if he was handling our cattle; if I showed up there he would not have done it.

STOLL. Up to Friday night the only person you seen to speak to was John Braae?

HORN. I did not speak to him; I seen him pass down below me several hundred yards.

STOLL. He did not see you?

HORN. No, he did not know I was in the country.

STOLL. You did not see anybody that attracted your attention in the shape of being armed and looking around?

HORN. I do not believe anyone was in there, or I would have seen them. I do not think there was anyone in there.

STOLL. Thursday how far were you all day from the Nickell's place?

HORN. I don't suppose all day Thursday at any time I was as much as a dozen miles from there. I don't think at any time I went up the divide. I think I was most of the day within seven or ten miles.

STOLL. Could you see Nickell's place?

HORN. You could not see his place until up within three hundred yards of it.

STOLL [Referring to a map]. Here is the place where the boy was shot; there is the fence running along there. Here is the road and there is the gate. Nickell's place is up here a distance of a mile and Miller's place is off in this direction. Here is the schoolhouse.

HORN. Yes, that is right.

STOLL. Do you recognize this country?

HORN. I recognize the country.

STOLL. How close to this country were you at any time Thursday?

HORN. The way that country lays I left Miller's and went in here [apparently pointing to the map].

STOLL. That is on Wednesday?

HORN. I went to the Colcord place. I went down in the cañón [canyon] from Miller's and turned up the cañón by the beaver dam. I didn't want to go by the schoolhouse. I went to the Colcord place. [On the way] I went along through Nickell's pasture into Billy Clay's pasture.

STOLL. Were you about in the same place Thursday?

HORN. ...The first day I didn't get over the divide. The first day I worked on Mule Creek and worked the Clay pasture and Henke pasture.

STOLL. You were on this divide on Thursday?

HORN. Not until Thursday evening.... I didn't start out in the morning until the cattle come to water.

STOLL. Long after sunrise?

HORN. Along about eight o'clock.

STOLL. While you were up on that ridge you didn't see anyone in this locality?

HORN. No, sir, all the time I was in there I didn't see one man riding or walking around.

STOLL. What time did you leave for Laramie City [Saturday]?

HORN. I don't know, perhaps two or three o'clock as near as I can judge, sometime after dinner. I remember I got in there and washed and changed clothes.

STOLL. At the ranch?

HORN. Yes, I should say about eleven o'clock.

When Tom Horn arrived back at the home ranch Saturday, he wanted to take a bath and change into clean clothes, and he was hungry. He had been subsisting on what little food he carried and perhaps a rabbit or two since leaving Miller's on Wednesday morning.

Stoll asked Horn to testify about the man who had ridden through the country, looking for work. The man had passed through Miller's ranch while Horn was there:

> HORN: I got into the Coble ranch on Saturday at eleven o'clock. I got my dinner. I hadn't anything to eat [for] three or four days, only what I carried on my saddle. You get hungry on that. After getting filled up again I went to Laramie:
>
> STOLL. You had been without anything to eat since Wednesday morning?
>
> HORN. Not a regular meal; I had a piece of bacon and bread on the saddle.
>
> STOLL. Roughed it in that way?
>
> HORN. That is the way I have to live. If I showed up at a ranch I couldn't do any good.
>
> STOLL. You showed up at the Miller ranch.
>
> HORN. That is different. I had been out then five or six days when I showed up at the Miller ranch.
>
> STOLL. Well, now, when did you go [back] out [to] that country?
>
> HORN. I have not been there since. I come home and went to Laramie, and went out on the other end of the Plains.
>
> STOLL. You have been working in another direction?
>
> HORN. Yes, entirely.
>
> STOLL. Do you know anything about any of the sheepherders that Nickell had?
>
> HORN. No, when I was there at Nickell's [Horn meant Miller's] ranch there was a fellow passed that Miller said was a sheepherder, but I didn't see his face, and don't know anything about him. I just saw his back as he was riding away.

This was an unidentified stranger who passed through, looking for work, the man whom Kels sent Willie to find the morning Willie was killed:

> STOLL. Were you at Nickell's sheep camp any night during this week before Willie Nickell was killed?

HORN. I rode by. The evening that I was at Miller's, I rode right by the ridge. I saw the wagon below but I didn't go to it. I also saw the sheep herd. I went up the creek and saw the sheep had not been up any further than they had a right to be; they hadn't done anything.

STOLL. You spoke about "our" field or pasture. Do you mean by that the field you have [a financial] interest in, or Coble?

HORN. Any property I am looking after I refer to as "ours," not because I am interested in it at all.

Horn had heard, of course, of the shooting of Kels Nickell earlier in the week he testified.

Walter Stoll commented on the fact that someone had killed a number of Nickell's sheep, and inquired if Horn might know who had made the attack on the herd. Horn's answer was to the point: "Just what I have heard. I don't know anything, Walter, not a thing in the world...." He added that he had heard of the ill will between Nickell and Miller and of their threats—"so much cursed," he said, "I don't think anything I would say would throw any light" on the matter. Horn continued:

HORN. I said to Miller, "There is sheep right in your door-yard, Miller."

He said, "The sons-of-bitches," or something of that kind. That is all the remark he made. In the spring when he was over on the Plains he cursed about them, the whole lot. I have heard Nick say he was going to do this and do that. It isn't never anything..., what they tell you. It don't amount to a great deal. Neither of them are reckoned a very high class of citizens, never have been.

STOLL. A source of a good deal of trouble and annoyance in that country?

HORN. Always have been since I have been in the country.... They go to the other neighbors with their troubles and tell what kind of ornery people they are. They are both the same kind of people. I may be mistaken entirely. Neither one has a good reputation; on the contrary they are reckoned as being the worst kind of people. As far as I understand it that is the standing they have.

Stoll now turned his questioning to the murder.

He asked why anyone should kill Willie Nickell unless it was because of the "difficulties" between the Nickells and Millers. Horn's reply was that he certainly did not know, adding that he did not know Willie and hardly knew the Millers either. "I saw this hereditary bad feeling," he said. He indicated that he had heard a month or so previously that Miller had whipped Willie, but added that while it was only hearsay information he felt it was probably reliable. He commented, "I didn't give Miller credit for having stuff in him to do anything" like murdering a boy.

When Stoll asked what he had heard of difficulties between Nickell and his other neighbors that amounted to anything, Horn knew only what Nickell had told him. Stoll then asked what Nickell had told him:

> HORN. He is not a man very choice in his language. To tell you what he told me I will have to use language he used.
>
> STOLL. You may tell it.
>
> HORN. He said, "Every damned son of a bitch has given me dirt, and I [i.e., my sheep] will eat them out of house and home." He said, "I will make their asses pop out of the saddle...." There was a good deal of growling when the sheep were taken into the country. He asked me how I felt about it.
>
> I said, "I have no feeling about it...." I told him why. Some seven or eight years ago when Al Bowie [foreman of the Two Bar, saw them] started to fence in the country, he exhausted all the influence we had to keep them from fencing it in.

Horn was referring to the way the large cattle interests tried, unsuccessfully, to prevent the settlers from fencing in the range as they staked homestead claims:

> HORN [continuing]. When we seen we couldn't do it, we just had to quit. We abandoned the country and have had no claim to it. When these sheep commenced to come in just at

that time it looked kind of comical to me. I said, "I will kind of get even, the sheep will drive these fellows out that drove me out of the country." Every time that Nickell and Miller meet they have a quarrel or a fight. The neighborhood rather expects it of them when they get together. Some two and a half months ago they had a school meeting down there. I guess Nickell went down and jumped on the whole outfit. He told me he did, and different people there told me he did. He said he "would eat them out of house and home and make them hump up like a sick dog"—such things as that. You asked me if I knew of anything that would cause trouble. Such things as that are a sort of trouble in a neighborhood....

STOLL. What time was it that Nickell had this talk with you last spring?

HORN. Last spring sometime. Just about the time he put the sheep in. The last time I talked with Nickell he had just put the sheep in there and come back to town. He told me, "I left them right in Jim Miller's yard.... I wonder how the son of a bitch feels about it now because I left them right in his door yard."

Next Stoll directed the questioning toward the possibility that Miller had placed a price on Nickell's head. Evidently, the prosecutor had learned of allegations that Miller had offered five hundred dollars to anyone for killing Nickell.

Horn replied that he had heard of Miller offering a five hundred-dollar diamond, but did not know if Miller actually owned such a diamond. He said Otto Plaga, the son of Raymond Henke, a prominent rancher and neighbor on the Sybille, had told him. Horn remarked that Miller may have only been boasting that he had the diamond to offer:

STOLL. When was it that Plaga told you this?

HORN. It was last fall as I remember, about November. It must have been the month of November; it was at the time he was working for Johnny Coble. The talk came up about the sheep and he made this expression. He is just about as unreliable as Miller or Nickell.

STOLL. You mean Plaga?

HORN. Yes, sir.

STOLL. You would not consider him a reliable man at all?

HORN. He is not considered that by anybody that knows him.

STOLL. As a matter of fact you do not know whether Miller said that?

HORN. I would not give credence to any statement the boy [Plaga] would make, or anybody else.

STOLL. You know John Apperson [the surveyor working with Nickell and William Mahoney, Nickell's brother-in-law, the morning Willie was killed]?

HORN. Old John, yes.

STOLL. Did you see him anywhere about Nickell's anytime while you were in that locality?

HORN. No, sir, I never saw him outside of town any time in my life.

STOLL. He was up there in that locality?

HORN. I understood he was there when the boy was killed.

STOLL. Is there anything else that you can say that will in any way throw light on this matter?

HORN. I could repeat a lot of stuff that Nickell has said, what he told me what he would do. He went into particulars about the grievances he had against different people in that country. The only thing that Nickell said about Miller was, "I left the sheep in his dooryard. I wonder what he will say about it." That is all he said about Miller. He told me how he was going to eat out John Durbin,[2] how he would ruin Billy Clay. He would bring his sheep within three hundred yards of Clay's house and Billy couldn't help himself. He told me he was going to fix Billy McDonald, "a damned ornery son of a bitch he was."

Tom Horn concluded his testimony by saying that the Reed brothers were apparently the only friends Nickell had in the area—but that Nickell had gone so far as to say he would leave them alone only until he needed their grass.

Two major ranchers, John Jordan and Billy Clay, Horn said, had hardly mentioned a word to him about Nickell's sheep. Only Clay, he added, had said two or three months ago that he intended to build a reservoir if Nickell did not "come in with his sheep and eat him out." He emphasized that he did not know of anything more he could add to help Stoll's investigation. He said that he had not paid much attention to Nickell's threats because he "always thought Nickell was harmless. If I did I would certainly tell you because neither one of them have ever been particular friends of mine…. They are a class of people I have no regard for." Neither Nickell nor Miller had any contact with the people Horn represented, he said, but added that at one time both homesteaders "were pretty pronounced thieves…."

Stoll took this opening to ask Horn more about the reputations of the two Iron Mountain ranchers and about suspected rustling activity. He also asked about Horn's methods of patrolling the range:

STOLL. [Are Nickell and Miller] supposed to have done a good deal of cattle rustling?

HORN. All the cattle they have, they started from Two Bar and Coble cattle. They come [arrived] there with nothing at all and they have built the herds of cattle they both [now] have. Nickell has sold his. They had three or four hundred each; they all come from the Two Bar herd. I rode those pastures [for] three or four years. If they didn't see me they would see some signs of me…. They have been honest within the last five or six years, but formerly they were not considered anything but rustlers, that is, by the larger stockmen. I know that each of them acquired his herd with nothing but a rope….

STOLL. In riding around this way do you lie [camp] out nights?

HORN. Yes, sir.

STOLL. Don't you have a blanket?

HORN. Only my saddle blanket.

STOLL. Don't you have a slicker?

HORN. No, never carry any.

STOLL. No overcoat?

HORN. No, just have a government blanket for a saddle blanket is all.

STOLL. You carry your bacon; do you have anything else, any coffee?

HORN. I do not use coffee when I am out. I take a little bread and a pound of bacon. Whenever I get hungry I shoot a jackrabbit and broil it. The living is not very good; the working months are short....

STOLL. How much of a bunch of cattle has Clay got?

HORN. He branded ninety-eight calves last year. You can judge from that.... I should say he had about four hundred.

STOLL. Clay was never considered one of these rustlers?

HORN. Never was. I never heard a suspicion of his ever being anything of the kind. Nor Johnny Jordan, or the Reed boys, or Billy McDonald. I never heard a suspicion of their stealing cattle.

STOLL. The last time you were anywhere near that vicinity was not later than Friday following the killing, or Saturday morning?

HORN. I worked clear across the Sybille when I started [toward] home. I started twenty-five miles from Miller's home. I started when in the Blue Grass country. I worked down through this Braae country and Henke pasture up on the Sybille and then up another fork of the Sybille to the Fitzmorris country.

STOLL. Wednesday you were not more than eight or ten miles from this locality after you left Miller's?

HORN. There was no time Wednesday that I was more than ten miles away.

STOLL. Thursday you were on that divide?

HORN. Thursday I got further away because Thursday evening I got over the head of the Sybille.

STOLL. That was not over fifteen miles?

HORN. No, sir.

STOLL. From that time you have not been in that locality?

HORN. I have not been there, in that locality, since the morning I left there....

The coroner then took up the questioning, probing Horn for information about the sentiments of other cattlemen in the area.

Horn maintained his composure, emphasizing that the major outfits in the area were against the introduction of sheep, but believed there was nothing they could do about it:

> CORONER. I am curious to know if a man that rides around like you do and hears the expressions of people, when a man brings sheep in the country, what the cattlemen think?
>
> HORN. Every cattleman I have heard talk, and I have heard a great many, small cattlemen, entirely disinterested, say it was not right, and say so in very strong terms. I know the sentiment and feeling of [the] cattlemen. They say if he had started in the sheep business it would be different. Being in the cattle business and deliberately selling his cattle and putting sheep in, than for no other reason than to spite the neighbors…,and to do them dirt and damage and ruin them if he could, and boast of it then — He would tell these people how he was going to do them up.
>
> CORONER. Did you hear any stockmen say how they would get the sheep out of there?
>
> HORN. No, sir, every one approached me to see how I felt about it. It was very easy for me. I was [financially] disinterested and [it] didn't make any difference to me.
>
> CORONER. It would be easy for you to give the sentiment of the stockmen?
>
> HORN. I know what the sentiment is. Their sentiment is that a man that would do as Nickell has, could only do so, being the kind of man Nickell is, troublesome and quarrelsome, turbulent man without character or principle.
>
> CORONER. Have you had any words with Nickell that if ever he caught you on his place there would be trouble? Did he ever say he would kill you?
>
> HORN. No, sir.
>
> CORONER. Did not he say that if he could get a gun first he would kill you?
>
> HORN. No, sir.
>
> CORONER. Didn't he say if you hunted deer or antelope there he would kill you?

HORN. No, sir. He must have told somebody else that.

CORONER. He testified [to] that here.

The coroner then bored into statements Horn allegedly made at the time of Fred Powell's murder inquest six years earlier. Horn, the coroner apparently thought, had had a run-in with Nickell over the detective's ranging through Nickell's ranch:

HORN. He simply lied. I have rode through there a number of years and he has not troubled me yet. I don't know why he should make a statement of that kind.

CORONER. Was not that statement made at the time you were before the grand jury? You were examined and the conversation took place in front of the courthouse here.

HORN. On what occasion was this?

CORONER. ...Mr. Nickell said it was on the occasion Mr. Powell was killed. You were called before the grand jury as a witness, and you sat on the steps in front of the courthouse.... This conversation was entered into in a friendly way?

HORN. He told me in a friendly way to keep out of the country?

CORONER. He said in substance he didn't want you to get off the road, and you could use his place as long as you kept in the road and didn't leave the road. It would be all right to go through his place—was this conversation ever had?

HORN. No, sir. I wouldn't allow fifteen of the worst men in the world to tell me that. I am at liberty to go where I please.... I wouldn't stand for anybody to tell me anything of that kind. If my business took me through that country I would go. He couldn't tell me that; he wouldn't tell me half before I would have got him to stop.

CORONER. He made that statement?

HORN. [That is] decidedly wrong.

CORONER. You say that you rarely visit those ranches?

HORN. Just this time of year when I am looking for calves.

The coroner ended his questioning and District Attorney Stoll resumed his probing. He dug into details about what Horn had observed, and who might have seen him. Perhaps he was looking for ways to substantiate Tom Horn's story—or to find holes in it.

STOLL. This Colcord Place is owned by the Two Bar outfit?

HORN. Yes, sir.

STOLL. When you speak of your employers you refer to the Two Bar as your employers?

HORN. They were up to the first of July. I refer to them in that manner.

STOLL. When was it that you said you were looking after Fitzmorris?

HORN. I went home Saturday. It was Friday I watched about his place.

STOLL. Were you watching about any other place there?

HORN. There is not another place in that country. It is the uttermost [farthest] ranch on that branch of the river.

STOLL. Who was at his place besides Fitzmorris?

HORN. There was a man of some kind there. They were haying; I did not go down to the ranch.

STOLL. There was no one outside of either the ranchmen or the people employed there?

HORN. No, sir.

STOLL. On Thursday whose place were you watching?

HORN. I was working [all] around there.

STOLL. Who did you see that day?

HORN. The only man I saw between the two ranches was John Braae; that was late in the evening. I know that he was coming down from Billy Clay's.

Chapter Twenty

A Confession?

WHERE WAS Tom Horn at the time of Willie Nickell's shooting, and where did he go? How did he get into the worst trouble he had ever known?

He had departed Miller's ranch mid-morning July 17, the day before Willie Nickell was killed. He headed southeast along Spring Creek and a canyon, through which it feeds, and then north to the Two Bar's Colcord pasture, roughly a half-mile east of Nickell's homestead.

Miller's ranch, a mile south-southwest of Nickell's, slopes toward the east and south, straddling Spring Creek and Sawmill Creek, which flow southeast. Nickell's homestead lay on North Chugwater Creek, a small tributary of Chugwater Creek. Spring Creek runs east and slightly north toward the town of Chugwater, flowing sometimes above ground and sometimes below the surface. Most of the terrain on Nickell's homestead slopes toward the east.

Horn's work necessitated secrecy, so that rustling could be more easily detected. Consequently only two witnesses[1] were able to confirm that they had seen him after he left Miller's. They were John Braae and Otto Plaga.

After inspecting the Colcord pasture he moved through the hills toward Mule Creek to the north, and northwest toward the headwaters of the Sybille. Mule Creek flows east and then north into the Sybille, north of William Clay's home.

Horn worked in a random pattern, not following any predetermined plan or map. Wednesday evening he was farther downstream (north) on Mule Creek, heading away from Clay's, farther yet from Nickell's and toward the ridge from which he saw John Braae. He was six or more miles from Nickell's. Although he thought Braae had not seen him, John Braae testified later that he'd seen Horn off his horse on top of a ridge to the northwest, studying something through his field glasses, looking north.

Under the cover of darkness—the moon was between the new and first quarter, and the weather was unsettled—he rode west, camping between Allen's and Waechter's ranches. The next morning, Thursday, he patrolled Mike Fitzmorris's pastures and then worked his way north toward Blue Grass Springs. He gradually worked back toward Fitzmorris's place on his way to Coble's headquarters north of Bosler junction.

Horn thought he was within eight or nine miles of Nickell's the morning of the crime, but qualified that by saying he was making an educated estimate.

Otto Plaga, a young local cowhand, stated[2] that he had seen Horn an hour after the killing—at a spot that was distant from the gate where Willie died. According to Plaga, Horn was moving slowly, his horse showed no signs of being pushed, and the distance was too far from the Nickell gate for Horn to have covered without exhausting his horse.

After he finished at Mike Fitzmorris's Thursday, he headed north four or five miles, and camped. The next morning he cut back and again worked the large Two Bar and Coble pastures adjacent to Fitzmorris's until mid-afternoon, and then camped overnight. Early Saturday, July 20, he started down to Coble's, west-northwest of the area he had been patrolling.

He arrived at Coble's in mid-morning, a fact that was attested to by a cowboy, W. S. Carpenter,[3] who was working in the stable, and by Mr. and Mrs. John Ryan. The Ryans had been hired by Coble and Duncan Clark, Coble's foreman, to keep house—cooking, cleaning, and laundering for the crew.

Horn cleaned up, changed his clothes, read his mail, and made a phone call to the Bosler station to send a telegram to Laramie. He ate, paid Ryan twenty-five cents for the wire, and left his laundry for them to do. He told Ryan he would pay for the laundry when he returned.

At Carpenter's suggestion, he drove John Coble's best horse into the corral and saddled him up. The horse, a bay named Pacer, was branded Lazy TY connected.[4] Horn pushed him hard on the ride into Laramie.

Coble had left on July 11 for his mother's funeral in Pennsylvania. Although Horn said he had an appointment with Bell in the evening, it could be that Bell, who may have been holding the funds to pay Horn for Coble, could not meet Tom and had left the money with another party. Horn was dressed in a good quality, brown wool suit.[5]

He deposited the horse and went on a ten-day drinking binge. Frank Stone drank with Tom on Sunday, July 21, and finally gave him a ride out of town in a wagon on July 30. It was time to sober up and go back to work. The next day, Stone accompanied him northward to within ten miles of Coble's Iron Mountain Ranch. Mr. and Mrs. Ryan saw him headed back to the ranch from the Bosler depot when they departed for Cheyenne that day.

Tom Horn's whereabouts from that point until August 7 or 8 are unknown. The prosecution attempted to link him with Kels Nickell's shooting on August 4, but Horn stated he was "a hundred miles" away on that Sunday morning. He wrote to John Coble[6] that he had been at Alex Sellers's ranch that day.

Sellers[7] was an Albany County rancher who owned a place in the northern part of the county in Antelope Basin. No part of northern Albany County, however, is more than one hundred miles from Nickell's ranch, so Sellers's ranch could not have been that far. However, Horn had admitted that he was not always good at estimating distances. (Sellers was never called to verify Horn's location during the trial, apparently because the defense team could not locate him.)

Horn stayed at Coble's ranch for a few days before he was summoned to testify at the inquest.

Shortly after Willie's murder the chairman of the Laramie County Commission, Sam Corson, had arranged for a deputy U.S. marshal, Joe LeFors, to investigate the Nickell murder. The county and state had each already offered a five hundred dollar reward for information leading to the arrest and conviction of Willie's murderer.

LeFors was born in Paris, Texas, on February 20, 1865. He arrived in Wyoming as part of a cattle drive in 1885 and went to work as a cowpuncher outside Buffalo.

LeFors was a minor player in the successful effort in 1897 to recover a large herd of stolen stock from the Hole-in-the-Wall area,

Joe LeFors around the time of the Tom Horn case. (American Heritage Center, University of Wyoming)

where rustlers generally felt unassailable by the law. He was later hired by the Montana livestock authorities as a contract livestock inspector for northeast Wyoming, working in and around Newcastle to apprehend stolen cattle and thieves and return them to Montana. He became acquainted with W.D. "Billy" Smith, a Montana brand inspector who was based in Miles City, north of Newcastle. Smith probably was LeFors's immediate superior.

LeFors married his first wife, sixteen-year-old Bessie M. Hannum in Newcastle, Wyoming, on August 5, 1896.[8] He played a minor role in the posse that pursued the three robbers of a train at Wilcox in

1899. The robbers eventually escaped into the Big Horn Mountains, and at least one reached southwest Wyoming, probably headed for Brown's Hole.

U.S. Marshal Frank A. Hadsell had appointed LeFors an office deputy on October 16, 1899.[9] LeFors contended that Hadsell had approached him to join his staff because of his work on the Wilcox posse.

Robbers again held up the Union Pacific on August 29, 1900, near Tipton, fifty miles west of Rawlins. LeFors participated in the posse that pursued the robbers to the Brown's Hole area south of Tipton, with a similar lack of success.

After his testimony on August 9, Tom Horn appeared at the rodeo during the frontier celebration in Cheyenne. According to the *Laramie Daily Boomerang* he won the multi-day steer roping competition at least once. His associates, Duncan Clark, Frank Stone, and Otto Plaga, also were rodeo event winners.

Horn stated that he talked with Joe LeFors twice about the Willie Nickell killing at one or more Cheyenne saloons during the festivities.

In September he took a load of horses by train to the Mountains and Plains Festival (a Denver rodeo and celebration), arriving early Sunday morning, September 29.[10]

He went on yet another drinking spree and tangled in a saloon with Denver's popular boxer "Young" Corbett, who broke Horn's left jaw. A Denver police surgeon treated Tom, binding up his head with plaster of Paris at five-thirty Monday morning. He was in St. Luke's Hospital for three weeks. In trial testimony, he said, "I got into trouble because a man called me a liar."[11]

Horn spent the next few months at Coble's ranch in Bosler, and in Cheyenne and Laramie. Late in December he took a load of beef to Omaha on the Union Pacific. Glendolene Kimmell spoke of his getting drunk in Omaha and losing his "outfit" there, and then returning to Cheyenne. He met with LeFors while in Cheyenne, where they again discussed the Nickell murder.

LeFors had John Coble take Horn a letter about a stock detective's job in Montana that he had received from W. D. "Billy" Smith, LeFors's old acquaintance:

Miles City, Montana
Dec. 28th 1901

Joe LeFors Esq.
Cheyenne

Friend Joe

I want a good man to do some secret work. And want a man that I can trust. And he will have to be a man not known in this country. The nature of this, there is a gang over on the Big Moon River that are stealing cattle and we purpose [propose] to fit the man out as a wolfer and let him go into that country [and wolf].

And if he is the right kind of man he can soon get in with the gang. He will have to be a man that can take care of himself in any kind of country.

The pay will be $125.00 per month and I believe a man can make good wages besides.

Joe if you know of anyone who you think will fill the place let me know. There will be several months work.

Yours Truly

W. D. Smith

P.S. Man will have to report in Helena.

Tom Horn, who was apparently idle at Coble's ranch, immediately responded:

Iron Mountain Ranch Company
Bosler Wyoming
Jan. 1st 1902

Joe LeFors Esq.
Cheyenne, Wyoming

Dear Joe

Recd yours from W. D. Smith Miles City Mont. by Johnny Coble today. I would like to take up that work and I feel sure I can give Mr. Smith satisfaction. I don't care how big or bad his men are or how many of them there are, I can handle them.

W.D. "Billy" Smith, the Montana livestock inspector who sent the letters at Joe LeFors's request about the nonexistent detective job. Photo taken while he was in Cheyenne for the trial. (American Heritage Center, University of Wyoming)

They can scarcely be any worse than the Brown's Hole Gang and I stopped cow stealing there in one summer. If Mr. Smith cares to give me the work I would like to meet them as soon as commencement so as to get into the country and get located before Summer.

The wages $125.00 per month will be all satisfactory to me. Put me in communication with Mr. Smith whom I know well by reputation and I can guarantee him the recommendation of every cow man in the State of Wyoming in this line of work.

You may write Mr. Smith for me that I can handle his work and do it with less expense in the shape of lawyer and witness fees than any man in the business.

Joe you yourself know what my reputation is although we have never been out together.

Yours truly

Tom Horn

P.S. Enclosed find enclosure of Mr. Smith.

Tom

Smith's own reputation was not entirely untarnished; he was known at one point as "the shooting sheriff."[12] Tom Horn would have known of Smith's reputation because of their similar work and mutual interest in ridding the county of thieves. Next Smith wrote:

Miles City, Montana
1/3–1902

Joe LeFors Esq.
Cheyenne Wyo.

Friend Joe

Yours of Dec. 31st rec'd. And I have today return male [mail] expect to get my orders to sed [send] for your man Tom Horn.

So you can expect a different answer within a week.

As ever yours

W. D. Smith

Smith mentions that Joe LeFors's communication to him, probably a telegram, was dated December 31. However, Tom Horn's response was not dated until January 1. By that time LeFors must have anticipated—indeed, he was banking on it—that Horn would jump at the opportunity to take up the kind of work being described. And, indeed, Horn did:

Iron Mountain Ranch Company
Bosler, Wyoming
Jan. 7, 1902

Joe LeFors Esq.
Cheyenne Wyo.

Friend Joe

Rec'd yours Jan. 6th today and contents noted.

Joe I am much obliged to you for the trouble your have taken for me in this matter and I will do my best to give satisfaction. I will get the men sure, for I have never yet let a cow thief get away from me unless he just got up a [and] jumped clean out of the country.

I will come to Cheyenne to get my pass as I can get one to Helena or any other from Cheyenne. I can go at any time after ten days. I will see you in Cheyenne when I come in. Again thanking you for your trouble.

I am yours truly

Tom Horn

Enclosed find letter of W.D.S.

Writing to LeFors on the same day as Horn, W.D. Smith clarified the details of hiring Horn:

Miles City Montana
1/7 – 1902

Joe LeFors Esq.
Cheyenne

Friend Joe

Mr. J. M. Boordman of Helena Montana has instructed me to have Tom Horn report at Helena soon as possible. The only thing now that stands in the way of him taking the job is this you say in your letter that Horn will be wanted down there next summer. And we do not want him to come at all unless he agrees to stay untell [until] we get through with him. He might complete the work in three months and it may take him a year or more. If Horn will come with that understanding, send him soon as possible. Have him report to W.G. Prewitt's [*sic*] office in Helena Montana. You give him a letter of introduction to Mr. Prewitt.[13] We will appreciate any thing you can do towards getting him transportation R-Ry. And if Horn needs any money please let him have it. And send your bill to me at Helena care

Pete Bergerson, the Cheyenne locksmith and gunsmith who modified the door at the U.S. marshal's office for Joe LeFors. This photo was taken when Pete was chief of police in Cheyenne. (Wyoming Division of Cultural Resources)

[of] W.G. Prewitt and I will guarantee you will be reimbursed. Wire me the day that Horn will arrive at Helena. As I want to meet him there and caution him to tell no one where he is going or who he expects to meet.

        Your friend

        W.D. Smith

On Saturday, January 11, 1902, Tom Horn headed to Laramie, started drinking, and caught the train to Cheyenne.

Horn stayed up all night carousing.[14] At some point he connected with LeFors. LeFors induced Horn to accompany him to the marshal's office on the second floor of the Commercial Block on Sixteenth Street. They arrived at 11:20 that morning. Witnesses Charles

Cheyenne's Sixteenth Street (now Lincolnway) near the turn of the century. The U.S. Marshal's office was behind the bay window above the first canopy shown at center. (Wyoming Division of Cultural Resources)

Ohnhaus, a stenographer, and Les Snow, a deputy sheriff, were already in place in an adjacent room. LeFors had arranged for Pete Bergerson, a locksmith and gunsmith, to put a lock on the door between the two rooms and to modify the door to make it easier for the two witnesses to see Horn and hear the conversation.

LeFors described the subsequent events in his autobiography.[15]

LeFors related how he had gone to the Nickell homestead with police officer Peter Warlaumont to investigate the two shootings and had found little. He continued:[16]

> *Faithful* [emphasis added] Sam Corson, the chairman of the Board of Commissioners of Laramie County, sent me word that he would like to see me privately and for me to arrange it so that it would be a secret. I met him in the U.S. Marshal's office that evening.
>
> Mr. Corson asked what I had found from the investigation I had made. I told him that there could be only one conclusion—

Charles J. Ohnhaus, the stenographer who recorded the conversation between Joe LeFors and Tom Horn. This photo was taken when he was clerk of the U.S. District Court in later life. (Wyoming Division of Cultural Resources)

that the killing was the result of a sheepmen's and cattlemen's war.

I told Corson, "Those killings are over the range [land]. Kels P. Nickell has the only sheep between the Iron Mountain country and the U.P.R.R., a distance of some sixty-five to seventy miles. And there can be but one interest involved and that is the open government range...."

I informed him also that there wasn't any doubt in my mind but that a few of the cattlemen were interested in keeping the sheep out, while they might not all sanction the methods being used. So to my mind the killing was all predicated on dollars and cents. Corson told me he was perfectly satisfied that my version was absolutely right....

I said that in order to determine who the guilty parties were one had only to ride the range, look at the cattle brands and see for himself who was immediately interested [financially]. The finger of guilt pointed to the few cattle companies who were using that particular range.

Corson then said that if he could get my chief [Frank Hadsell] in the U.S. marshal's office to consent to let me work on the case, what would I charge for running the murderer down.

I told him that I was under obligations to do all I could to land the assassin. But it would be much easier on me if I could get the consent of the higher-ups.... Corson said he would feel my chief out on the issue and let me know and advised me not to let my chief find out that we had had our talk saying, "I will get him to come to you with the proposition himself."

So the next day my chief came to me and asked what I thought about working on those killing and attempted-killing cases. I told him there would be no telling how long it would take to accomplish anything.

He finished by saying, "If you can bring those lawbreakers to justice you can get any position the state has to offer" [emphasis added].

At this time the feeling was running high and the demand was for justice. *I could scent a lot of politics coming into the case and I knew those Cheyenne politicians were for politics first and justice next* [emphasis added].

The fact that "killing and attempted killing cases" is used in the plural suggests that Corson, LeFors, and Hadsell all were speculating that Willie's killer was also the shooter who targeted Kels Nickell.

LeFors wrote that he became suspicious that Tom Horn was the guilty party after a conversation with George Prentice, a "boss" from the Coble-Bosler[17] cattle operation. He alleged that Prentice told him the powers there wanted to rid themselves of Horn because of his drinking and boasting "about the Nickell case."[18] Prentice, he said, told him that he was the payoff man who gave Horn his fee for the jobs previous to the Nickell shootings, specifically the Lewis and Powell killings.

Behind the locked door adjacent to the marshal's office, Stenographer Ohnhaus proceeded to record portions of the LeFors conversation with Tom Horn:

"Here is your letter of introduction to Mr. W.G. Preuitt, which reads as follows," and he proceeded to read it aloud. Then Horn said, "I want to go on the U.P. I know the route, and I don't know the others."

LeFors said, "It is about as near one way as the other, and you will get there about the same time."

After a couple of remarks Horn said, "Well, Joe, do you know anything about the nature of the work I will have to do up there?"

LEFORS. Tom, they are good people. I have worked for them five or six years. You will have to get right in among them, and gain their confidence, and show them you are all right.

HORN. I don't want to be making reports to anybody at any time. I will simply have one report to make, and that will be my final report. If a man has to make reports all the time, they will catch the wisest son of a bitch on earth. These people are not afraid of shooting, are they?

LEFORS. No, they are not afraid of shooting.

HORN. I shoot too much, I know; you know me when it comes to shooting. I will protect the people I am working for, but I have never got my employers into any trouble yet over anything I have done. A man can't be too careful because you don't want any God damn officers to know what you are doing.

LeFors evidently sensed at this point that he could lead Horn into the kind of incriminating statements that would accomplish his objective—to "cinch" Horn for the murder of Willie Nickell. His means was to toss out a compliment for Horn to digest—bait that was very effective:

LEFORS. Tom, I know you are good man for the place. You are the best man to cover up your trail I ever saw. In the Willie Nickell killing, I could never find your trail, and I pride myself on being a trailer.

HORN. No, God damn; I left no trail. The only way to cover up your trail is to go barefooted.

LEFORS. Where was your horse?

HORN. He was a God damn long ways off.

LEFORS. I would be afraid to leave my horse so far away; you might get cut off from him.

HORN. You don't take much chances. These people are unorganized, and anyway I depend on this gun of mine. The only thing I was ever afraid of was that I would be compelled to kill an officer or a man I didn't want to; but I would do everything to keep from being seen; but if he kept after me, I would certainly kill him.

LEFORS. I never knew why Willie Nickell was killed. Was it because he was one of the victims named, or was it compulsory?

HORN. I think it was this way: Suppose a man was in the big draw to the right of the gate—you know where it is—the draw that comes into the main creek below Nickell's house where Nickell was shot. Well, I suppose a man was in that, and the kid came riding up on him from this way, and suppose the kid started to run for the house, and the fellow headed him off at the gate and killed him to keep him from going to the house and raising a hell of a commotion. That is the way I think it occurred.

LEFORS. Tom, you had your boots on when you ran across there to cut the kid off, didn't you?

HORN. No, I was barefooted.

LEFORS. You didn't run across there barefooted?

HORN. Yes, I did.

LEFORS. How did you get your boots on after cutting your feet?

HORN. I generally have ten days to rest after a job of that kind. Joe, do you remember the little girl?

Tom Horn next meandered to the subject of Glendolene Kimmell. After explaining whom he meant—LeFors did not connect her with "little girl" immediately—Horn embarked on boasting of some prior knowledge of information heard at the inquest:

LEFORS. Who do you mean?

HORN. The schoolmarm. She was sure smooth people. She wrote me a letter as long as the governor's message, telling me in detail everything asked by Stoll, the prosecuting attorney. Stoll thought I was going to prove an alibi, but I fooled him. I had a man...keeping me in touch, before I showed up, with everything that was going on. I got this letter from the girl the same day I got my summons to appear before the coroner's inquest.

LEFORS. Did the schoolmarm tell everything she knew?

Then Horn, attempting to impress LeFors with his ability to keep his mouth shut and perhaps, in addition, his understanding of the teacher's feel for LeFors, hinted at Kimmell having tipped him off to LeFors's snooping:

HORN. Yes, she did. I would not tell an individual like her anything, not me. She told me to look out for you. She said, "Look out for Joe LeFors; he is not all right; look out for him; he is trying to find out something." I said, "What is there in this LeFors matter?" She said Miller didn't like him, and said he [Miller] would kill the God damn son of a bitch if God would spare him long enough. There is nothing to those Millers. They are ignorant old jays. They can't even appreciate a good joke. The first time I met the girl was just before the killing of the kid. Everything, you know, dates from the killing of the kid.

LEFORS. How many days was it before the killing of the kid?

HORN. Three or four days maybe. Damned if I want to remember the dates. She was there, and of course, we soon paired ourselves off.

LEFORS. What nationality was she?

HORN. She was one-quarter Jap, one-half Korean, and the other German. She talks almost every language on the earth.

LeFors apparently had a list of prepared questions which he now presented to Horn:

LEFORS. Tom, didn't Jim Dixon carry you grub?

HORN. No, no one carried me grub.

View east on Sixteenth Street. The county and prosecuting attorney's office was in the building now housing the Atlas Theater, diagonally across the street from the marshal's office. (Wyoming Division of Cultural Resources)

LEFORS. Tom, how can a man that weighs 204 pounds go without eating anything so long?

HORN. Well, I do. For some times I go for days without a mouthful. Sometimes I have a little bacon along.

LEFORS. You must get terribly hungry, Tom.

HORN. Yes, sometimes I get so hungry that I could kill my mother for some grub, but I never quit a job until I get my man.

LEFORS. What kind of a gun have you got?

HORN. I used a thirty-thirty Winchester.

LEFORS. Tom, do you think that will hold up as well as a thirty-forty?

HORN. No, but I like to get close to my man. The closer the better.

LEFORS. How far was Willie Nickell killed?

HORN. About three hundred yards. It was the best shot that I ever made and the dirtiest trick I ever done. I thought at one time he would get away.

LEFORS. How about the shells? Did you carry them away?

HORN. You bet your God damn life I did.

LEFORS. Tom, do you need any more money for this trip?

HORN. No. If I get a pass, I will not need any more money. If I have to buy a ticket, I must have a little more money; but today is Sunday, and I will have to wait until tomorrow.

LEFORS. Well, it is afternoon, and I will go home, and see you again this afternoon or this evening, when we can talk this matter over.

HORN. All right, I will be back. I want to know all about these people before I go up there.

LEFORS. Tom, let us go downstairs and get a drink. I could always see your work clear, but I want you to tell me why you killed the kid. Was it a mistake?

HORN. Well, I will tell you all about it when I come back from Montana. It is too new yet.

Horn and LeFors then left LeFors's office. Witness Les Snow was quoted as having seen the two in Harry Hynds's saloon immediately after the morning conversation. The conversation continued when they returned to the office later:

HORN. Joe, we have only been together about fifteen minutes, and I will bet there is some people saying, "What are those sons of bitches planning now, and who are they going to kill next?" We have come up here because there is no other place to go. If you go to the Inter Ocean [Hotel] to sit down and talk for a few minutes, some one comes in and says, "Let us have a drink," and before you know it you are standing up and talking, and my feet get so God damn tired it almost kills me. I am forty-four years, three months and twenty-seven days old, and if I get killed now I have the satisfaction of knowing I have lived about fifteen ordinary lives. I would like to have had somebody who saw my past and could picture it to the public. It would be the most God damn interesting reading in the country; and if we could describe to the author our feelings at different times it would be better still. The experience of my life, or the first man

I killed, was when I was only twenty-six years old. He was a coarse son of a bitch.

LEFORS. How much did you get for killing these fellows? In the Powell and Lewis case, you got six hundred dollars apiece. You killed Lewis in the corral with a six-shooter. I would like to have seen the expression on his face when you shot him.

HORN. He was the scaredest son of a bitch you ever saw. How did you come to know that, Joe?

LEFORS. I have known everything you have done, Tom, for a great many years. I know where you were paid this money.

HORN. Yes, I was paid this money on the train between Cheyenne and Denver.

LEFORS. Why did you put the rock under the kid's head after you killed him? That is one of your marks, isn't it?

HORN. Yes, that is the way I hang out my sign to collect money for a job of this kind.

LEFORS. Have you got your money yet for the killing of Nickell?

HORN. I got that before I did the job.

LEFORS. You got five hundred dollars for that. Why did you cut the price?

HORN. I got twenty-one hundred dollars.

LEFORS. How much is that a man?

HORN. That is for three dead men, and one man shot at five times. Killing men is my specialty. I look at it as a business proposition, and I think I have a corner on the market....

LeFors concluded, "Horn and I exchanged some stories and then left the marshal's office, with the understanding that he was to leave for Montana the next day."

Ohnhaus, the court stenographer, hurried and got everything typed Sunday night.

⋯⋯

Horn was arrested the next morning in the Inter Ocean Hotel.

Tom Horn suspected that he had been jobbed as soon as he was arrested. Ed Smalley related[19] the arrest and how Horn's demeanor

The Inter Ocean Hotel at the corner of Capitol Avenue and Sixteenth Street in Cheyenne, where Tom Horn was arrested January 13, 1902. The saloon was to the west of the canopy on the left. (Wyoming Division of Cultural Resources)

reflected his suspicion. After a little banter with Tom on the four-block walk to the jail, Smalley said:

> As we were walking along, I asked, "How much do you weigh, Tom?"
>
> "I weigh about two hundred pounds," he said.
>
> "How old are you, Tom, and what is your height?" I asked.
>
> "I'm forty-four years, forty-four months, forty-four days, forty-four hours, and forty-four seconds, and I'm six foot, one inch tall," he answered with his usual joking manner.
>
> After I locked his cell he asked to see LeFors. He smelled a rat, all right (it was Joe LeFors...who had secured Tom Horn's confession through a ruse). I telephoned LeFors, who was down at Walter Stoll's office.... LeFors said he didn't want to see Tom, but I suggested he might come and talk to him for a little. He did, but only a few minutes.
>
> Horn said to him, "They have got me in here for killing the kid."
>
> Joe said, "The hell they have."

In correspondence LeFors had with the editor of his autobiography, Agnes Wright Spring, he commented, "I got the letters [from W. D. Smith] for a good reason. And used them for a good purpose."[20]

More than sixty years after the Nickell killing, Thomas C. Allen wrote[21] that he had worked undercover for Joe LeFors in Cheyenne after the Horn trial and that Horn's confession was a set-up. Allen stated that LeFors and he were sitting in the lobby of the Inter Ocean when LeFors, recounting the Nickell-Horn incident, mentioned that he had written a letter to a brand inspector friend, W. D. Smith, up north. He asked the friend to write back asking if LeFors knew a good man who could act as a wolfer and put an end to a rustling problem in Montana. Smith's letter was the bait that lured Horn in from Coble's ranch to Cheyenne, and up to LeFors's office on the second floor of the Commercial Building on Sixteenth Street where the confession was extracted.

When Joe LeFors wrote his autobiography in the mid 1930s, he commented at the reaction his colleagues had to his questionable dealings in the Tom Horn case:

> Before the case was at an end nearly all the backing from the U.S. officers was withdrawn, and no officers of that department would give me the least support.[22]

Chapter Twenty-one

HUNG BEFORE I LEFT THE RANCH

A PRELIMINARY HEARING on the Nickell murder charge against Horn was held January 24. At that hearing, Judge Richard H. Scott ruled that the evidence was sufficient to require that Horn be held in the county jail without bail.

Scott had presided in the initial legal proceedings that followed the Johnson County Invasion of 1892, when he granted a change of venue to move the trial to Laramie. The proceedings ended with favorable results for the invaders: Johnson County said that it simply did not have the funds to pay for a long incarceration and drawn-out court battle. The invaders and hired guns were released.

Scott was no political neophyte. He may have perceived how the winds of change were shifting and projected that representatives of an emerging middle class would comprise much of the jury. And, such a jury would be predisposed to convict.

His own political ambitions were best known to himself, but he may have hoped that his work on the high-profile case could lead to a seat on the Wyoming Supreme Court, in that era a position elected by the citizens.

The news of Horn's arrest created a stir in Wyoming and was newsworthy in Colorado. Parties for, but primarily against, Tom Horn began to marshal their resources.

One letter in particular threw more mystery into the situation and reflected public sentiment. Bradford B. Davidson wrote Kels Nickell from Denver on January 15, 1902, two days after Horn's arrest. He said that:

> …Fred McDermott Nora's Bro' recalls the fact that Horn had a
> very small Half Breed…last summer with him on some occasion

213

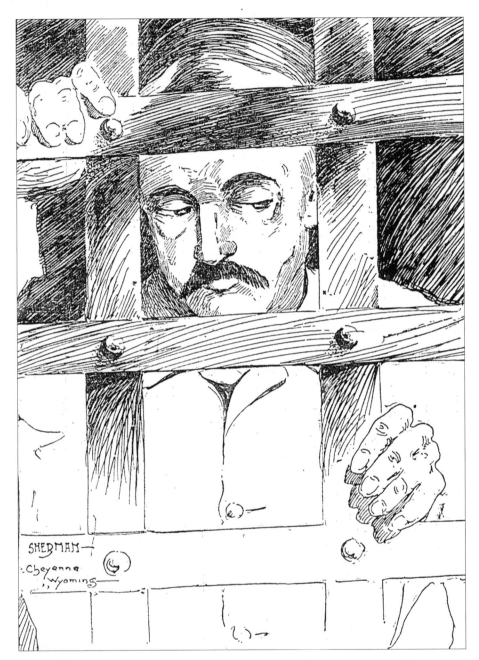

Sketch of Tom Horn in his cell in the Cheyenne jail. (*The Denver Post*: Denver Public Library)

with some horses around Rock River or Medicine Bow…and his [the half-breed] being very small all of which corresponds with the school teacher at your place last summer…that person was not there to teach school and was never there for that purpose—only as a blind to help to get rid of you and the sheep by any means necessary and the parties who hired him (Horn) knew it all the time.

…very likely he [the half-breed] is around where Miller is or up north where he came from. Horn & he & Miller in my mind did the dirty work, and others that you know as well as I [do] who furnished the money.[1]

Fred McDermott was sixteen years old at the time and living with his mother, Roxana McDermott, in Rock Creek Precinct.[2] Roxana was born in 1853 in Ohio, was married, and was a "boarding house keeper." Fred was a "range rider" whose father had been born in Canada.

"Nora" was Nora M. Davidson, Roxana McDermott's daughter, and Bradford B. Davidson's wife. She was living with her uncle, Frank Stuart, together with two daughters on Eighteenth Street in Cheyenne.[3] One of the children was named Roxanna, seemingly after her grandmother.

The description of the half-breed points toward the schoolteacher, although this person was referred to as a male. Fred McDermott may have seen whoever it was at a distance and mistakenly identified Horn's companion was male. Though this letter prompted much gossip and speculation, it didn't seem to lead further.

Hiram G. Davidson, Bradford's younger brother, lived at Iron Mountain and had conducted the 1900 Laramie County census in June for the Iron Mountain Precinct. He'd also served on the coroner's jury that investigated Willie Nickell's murder. He was born in 1860 in Oregon, was married with two children, and was a "farm laborer." Not a man of means, he rented the property where he lived and probably conducted the census to supplement a meager income.

Hiram Davidson and his father-in-law, Charles Edwards, also an Iron Mountain resident, testified for the prosecution in Tom Horn's murder trial. Ironically, Edwards's stepdaughter, Lilly Graham, came forward after the trial and signed an affidavit for the defense.

The trial was conducted from Friday, October 10, until Friday, October 24, 1902, at the old Laramie County District Courthouse at the corner of Ferguson (now Carey) and Nineteenth Street.

Cheyenne became carnival-like. Men made bets in saloons as to the outcome, with most anticipating an acquittal. Representatives of the press from as far as New York packed the courtroom. Attorneys called more than a hundred witnesses.

The team assembled to defend Tom Horn was a blue-ribbon assemblage of legal minds. Judge John W. Lacey from Indiana, whom President Chester Arthur had appointed as Wyoming Territory's first chief justice, headed the team. In 1889 he had been named general counsel for the Union Pacific and became part of Willis Van DeVenter's firm prior to the latter's appointment to the United States Supreme Court. Other members of the defense included Timothy F. Burke, Roderick Matson, Edward T. Clark, and T. Blake Kennedy. They were all Republicans.

In 1936 an attorney who was diametrically opposed to Lacey's conservative Republican views and frequently his opponent, John D. Clark, wrote in a testimonial memorial:[4]

> Memory is not long enough to reach beyond the time when Judge John W. Lacey was a familiar figure to me. In those early years of his Wyoming career he had already attained distinction. The half-century which has now passed has enlarged, not diminished, that eminence.
>
> In more than one respect his qualities were unique. Many great lawyers have been leaders of their communities and so it is not surprising that he long held that position in Cheyenne and in Wyoming.... His influence...was the reflection of his high repute as a lawyer....
>
> His reputation passed beyond the profession and permeated the business world, reaching even into those ranks of the population which have no interest in lawyers. It was of such a quality that he attained an authority the like of which I have never observed anywhere in the United States. "Getting an opinion from Judge Lacey" was more than a proposal to secure the best possible legal advice; in

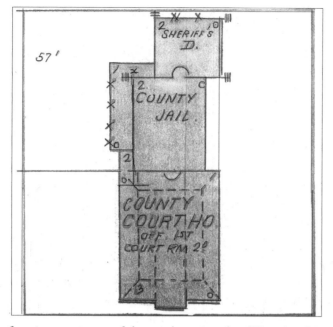

Diagram from insurance maps of the courthouse complex. (Wyoming Division of Cultural Resources)

the opinion of business men and laymen it was even more than the equivalent of securing a judgment from the Supreme Court of Wyoming. The Supreme Court might be wrong.

His ability was of the first rank in nearly every branch of the lawyer's work. His arguments upon the points of law, where his supreme power of rigid analysis had its fullest play, were always works of art and were seldom unsuccessful....

Certainly, some of Tom Horn's previous employers, well-heeled cattlemen, contributed financially to the Lacey team's effort. While Horn for many years had been an asset to them, he had become a liability from which they wanted to distance themselves, not wanting to be associated with any murder-for-hire schemes. They became a sort of silent conspirators in the effort to convict by their lack of testimony on his behalf.

Prosecuting Attorney Walter R. Stoll was an 1881 West Point graduate from Deckertown, New Jersey. After a brief assignment at

Fort McKinney, west of Buffalo, Wyoming, he arrived at Fort D. A. Russell in Cheyenne in 1882. He left the military to pursue the law and in 1886 he was elected Laramie County prosecuting attorney. He was a Democrat.

Young lawyers Clyde M. Watts and H. Waldo Moore made up the rest of the prosecuting team.

Stoll, facing reelection the month after the trial, knew that middle class public opinion could be an invaluable ally.

Yet another letter reached Kels Nickell fifteen days before the trial, mirroring public sentiment against Horn. J. F. White, who operated a general merchandise business in Rock River, mentioned "a few names that you should have struck off of the Tom Horn trial [illegible] men are under obligations to the Two Bar out fit and will do anything to clear Tom."[5] Among them were G. W. Whiteman and Amos Sarbaugh. White ended his letter by saying, "I hope you convict him." The letter had no effect, since both men were selected as jurors.

Jury selection was accomplished in remarkably short time. The *Cheyenne Daily Leader* enumerated the jurors:

> O. V. Sebern, ranchman of Wheatland [Sebern owned a 160-acre homestead about fifteen miles east of town]; Homer Payne, cowboy employed by the Two Bar[6]; F. F. Sinon, foreman of the White ranch on Little Horse Creek; H. W. Thomas, ranchman residing near LaGrange; T. R. Babbitt, ranchman near LaGrange; Amos Sarbaugh, foreman of the Two Bar Ranch; J. E. Barnes, a butcher in Cheyenne; G. W. Whiteman, a ranchman residing near Uva; Charles Stamm, a ranchman on the Wheatland flats; C. H. Tolson, a porter at the Union Pacific depot; H. W. Yoder, a Goshen Hole ranchman; and E. C. Metcalf, a blacksmith in Wheatland.

Yoder was the foreman.[7] Only Barnes, Sinon, and Tolson were from the Cheyenne area; the rest were from sectors of Laramie County that now make up Platte and Goshen counties.

T. Blake Kennedy attested to the demands placed upon the jury. After the trial he arranged to visit Homer Payne, the Two Bar cowboy

The jury. Left to right, upper row: Bailiff John Reed, O.V. Sebern, E.C. Metcalf, Foreman H.W. Yoder, Amos Sarbaugh, F.F. Sinon, Charles Stamm, Bailiff George Proctor. Lower row: James E. Barnes, Charles Tolson, Thomas R. Babbitt, Homer Payne, H.W. Thomas, George Wrightman. (Wyoming Division of Cultural Resources)

who served on the jury. Payne had worked with Horn and was friendly with him:

> I found Payne and got a rather comforting affidavit as to the things seen and heard by him while on the jury as to the seeming demands upon them by an enraged public to do their duty, but it was all lost motion so far as accomplishing results were concerned.[8]

A sloppy job of sequestering the jury did not help. And the *Denver Post*'s inflammatory coverage was bound to have had effects.

The prosecution's strategy was clear and well executed. The confession was the key element. Circumstantial evidence, which alone might not have been adequate to gain the conviction, was used as support. Testimony by three witnesses from Denver, Joe LeFors, a Laramie shoemaker, Frank Irwin of Laramie,[9] and others added to the weight.

For virtually every witness used by the defense, the prosecution effectively had a counter.

Doctors and ballistics experts gave exhaustive testimony about the wounds Willie Nickell had received. The defense attempted to prove that the size of the wounds was larger than a thirty-caliber weapon could inflict, but Stoll was able to build a credible case that Willie's wounds could have been caused by a thirty-caliber weapon, the type Tom Horn carried.

The prosecution had two interesting objectives. One was to establish that Horn had a history of taking matters into his own hands when he encountered a rustling situation. The other was to prove that he had been close enough to the crime to have committed it. Attorney Stoll questioned Horn:

> STOLL. You said your business was that of a stock detective. I will ask you to state whether or not, your business as a stock detective as you use that term did not include more than we understand by that term, merely a stock detective.
>
> HORN. It does. My understanding of the word stock detective, my position includes more.
>
> STOLL. It included so much, did it not, that your method [of] detecting the stealing of stock resulted in no necessity for

the trials by a jury, witnesses in court, attorney's fees or anything of that kind?

HORN. Ordinarily not.... You asked me in the first place if my work was more than that of the ordinary stock detective's work. I said it was.... I have got out where the stealing was going on.... I associate myself so directly with the neighborhood that stealing cannot go on without my being present; if they steal I will catch them in the act.... I can give you an illustration of what I have done in this country [with] which you are familiar, ...catching one of the most notorious cow gangs in the country, the Langhoff outfit. [They were,] I remember distinctly, engaged in the killing of cattle, calves.... I caught them directly in the act at nine o'clock at night and just gathered them in myself and took them off to jail. That was all there was; there was no expense to the county or the people that hired me....

STOLL. Since that time, you have not arrested anyone in that section of the country and brought him or her to Cheyenne for trial, or preferred any complaints against them?

HORN. No sir, I have [not]....

STOLL. ...You hadn't preferred any complaints or had people arrested since the Langhoffs were arrested?

HORN. ...I said it has not been necessary...when I would find a man stealing my calf, [or the calf of] people I represented, I would simply take the calf.... Such things as that stopped stealing.

STOLL. Go and take the calf and not have the party arrested, not have the party tried?

HORN. No sir.

Stoll induced Horn to speak of his lack of confidence in the legal system. Horn's disdain could not have played well in the scenario of a courtroom in which he was a defendant.

STOLL. And not submit the matter to the judgment of the courts at all, is that right?

HORN. My preliminary experience weaned me from that.

STOLL. ...I understand that you had not faith in courts or juries, is that correct?

Laramie County Courthouse, where the inquest and trial were held. This photo was taken a number of years before the Willie Nickell episode. (Wyoming Division of Cultural Resources)

HORN. No sir, I had more faith in getting the calf than in courts. [Laughter.]

STOLL. And because of that fact, your business has been the carrying on of the detecting of the cattle stealing in that way and not by any process of law?

HORN. ...When they know I am in the country; when cow thieves know I am in the country with nothing else to do, that I go at any hour of night or day—they realize that any time I might say "hello."

STOLL. Your presence you consider was necessary to prevent the continuation of this stealing?

HORN. ...[The] people that employed me considered my presence was necessary....

With Horn now having established his disregard for the legal system, the prosecutor asked Horn to confirm his earlier testimony in the inquest regarding his whereabouts the day of Nickell's murder.

Stoll's objective was to show that Horn had acknowledged that he had been close enough to the murder site to have been the killer:

STOLL. Now at the time, Mr. Horn, when you came to Miller's ranch from Coble's ranch, what was the object of your visit? Was it to see whether somebody had stolen calves, or was it to ride in among the people there, and inspire terror by your presence or actions, or what was it? Why did you go over to Miller's ranch?

HORN. I understood that Mr. Nickell had moved a bunch of sheep into that country, and I heard rumors of considerable kick and growl. I went in there to see if the sheep had been trespassing on any ground belonging to Mr. Coble. Also, I took a look at some Two Bar ground.

STOLL. Do I understand from your answer that you came over primarily to look over Nickell's sheep, and if you did anything else, that was a secondary consideration?

HORN. It would scarcely be that. I put two hours looking after Nickell's sheep, and the balance of the time, ten days, I put in looking over the pastures [of his employers].

STOLL. You stayed at Miller's Monday, Tuesday and Tuesday night, and left Wednesday morning at ten o'clock, or about ten o'clock; is that right?

HORN. I went there Monday night, and was there most of the day Tuesday, and left on Wednesday morning.

STOLL. Now, Mr. Horn, I will ask you to state whether or not in the coroner's inquest did I not say that on Wednesday, after leaving Miller's, "The rest of Wednesday, you were how far away from Miller's house or Nickell's...?" to which you replied, "Perhaps eight or nine miles."

HORN. I do not exactly recall the question and the answer, but I recall very distinctly where I was. I remember at the wind-up of the investigation, that your deductions from the investigation left you in no doubt as to where I was—and that I was nowhere near there.

STOLL. Now, in regard to where you were Thursday, in the coroner's inquest, do you remember this question being asked you,

"Thursday, how far were you all day from Nickell's place?"—to which you answered, "I do not suppose all day Thursday at any time I was as much as a dozen miles from there?"

HORN. I recall very distinctly having described the country I was in, and you asked me about the distance. I didn't know what the [exact] distance was then, and I don't know what it is now. But I say there was no misunderstanding between you and me as to my whereabouts.

To counter Stoll's contention that Horn was close enough to the murder scene to have committed the crime, the defense team produced several witnesses to testify about his movements

One of the witnesses was John Braae. He stated he saw Tom two-and-a-half miles north of Billy Clay's the evening before the killing. That would have placed him about eight miles northeast of the gate.

The defense called Otto Plaga. In critical statements he confirmed that he had seen Horn roughly twenty-five miles to the west of the gate an hour after Willie was killed:

LACEY. Do you remember where you were on the eighteenth of July 1901?

PLAGA. I was up in the hills, in the Fitzmorris country.

LACEY. How far is that from your ranch?

PLAGA. About eight miles.

LACEY. How far and in what direction is your place from the Nickell ranch?

PLAGA. West, about twenty-five miles.

LACEY. It is about twenty-five miles from your place to the Nickell ranch?

PLAGA. From the place where I seen Horn....

LACEY. Where did you see him?

PLAGA. I seen him up in that place, in a southwesterly direction from the Fitzmorris place.

LACEY. What was he doing? What kind of horse did he have?

PLAGA. He was just spooking along in his usual way, on that blackish brown "CAP" horse he used to ride. Just riding along at an easy trot.

Denver Post *drawing of Kels Nickell examining a diagram of locations during the trial.* (Denver Public Library)

LACEY. How did the horse seem as to whether he was fresh or tired?

PLAGA. He appeared very fresh. He didn't show wet or lather.

But Walter Stoll, in a pattern that proved highly effective, simply called witnesses to impugn Plaga's integrity. Two were Hiram Davidson and Charles Edwards.

Chapter Twenty-two

I Knew Perfectly Well What I Was Saying

OTTO PLAGA'S STATEMENTS for the defense might have supplied Horn with an effective alibi. But Tom Horn himself destroyed it. First Horn had testified during the inquest that Plaga was unreliable. Next Horn bragged that he believed that a good man on a good horse, who knew the country, could make the long ride.

One of the more astounding developments as the trial progressed was that Kels Nickell did an about-face and fingered Tom Horn as Willie's assassin and the shootist who had attempted to kill him. The fact that it came out in the *Denver Post* as the trial progressed did not help.

The overriding factor in Horn's damaging his own cause was his ego. Stoll discerned just how powerful yet frail it was and used it to induce Horn to make remarks that effectively destroyed his own defense. T. Blake Kennedy wrote of it in his memoirs.[1]

> Plaga gave me an affidavit to the effect that he had seen Horn on horseback at a point where it was practically impossible for him to be, had he been at the spot where the killing took place, which I thought was very valuable evidence; and it would have been except that Horn, when testifying himself upon the trial, not willing to subdue his passion for 'braggadocio' responded to a question that he supposed it would not be impossible for a man who was a good rider and knew the country to cover the ground between where the killing took place and where Plaga had testified he saw him.

Stoll next developed doubts concerning when Horn had actually arrived in Laramie after the murder. Frank Irwin made incriminating statements that he had seen Horn riding pell-mell into Laramie on Thursday. The defense tried to shake the effectiveness of Irwin's

Otto Plaga. (American Heritage Center, University of Wyoming)

statements with evidence of bad blood between Horn and Irwin as a result of suspicious cowhides Horn had spotted in Irwin's possession.

Frank Stone testified for the defense concerning Horn's boast of having run barefoot over the jagged terrain at the site of the murder, and further to a sweater that had been earlier introduced as evidence by the prosecution.

The prosecution had produced a navy blue sweater that a shoemaker in Laramie stated had been left at his shop by a man closely resembling Tom Horn. It was dirty and stained, and Stoll had attempted to prove that the stains were blood:

> LACEY. Are you acquainted with the defendant, Tom Horn?
> STONE. Yes, sir.
> LACEY. Did you see him in July 1901?
> STONE. Yes, sir, on the twenty-first of July, Sunday…. We roomed together that night.

LACEY. What was Tom's condition before he went to bed that night?

STONE. He was pretty well intoxicated. I had to put him to bed. He laid down on the floor, and I took off his clothes, and put him to bed.

LACEY. Did you take off his shoes and stockings?

STONE. Yes, sir.

LACEY. What did you notice about his feet, if anything?

STONE. I didn't notice anything.

LACEY. If his feet had been badly cut you would have noticed it?

STONE. Undoubtedly I would....

LACEY. Are you well enough acquainted with him to know the way he dressed and whether he had a sweater?

STONE. I seen him with a sweater a few times.

LACEY. What kind of a sweater was it?

STONE. Kind of a buckskin sweater.

LACEY. Who else have you seen wear that sweater?

STONE. Duncan Clark.

Stoll succeeded in impugning Frank Stone's integrity with statements by the justice of the peace, who stated that Frank had been arrested, fined, and jailed for drunkenness on Sunday, July 21. Stoll also insinuated that Stone had sworn to a false alibi when he said that Horn had been with him when the kid was killed:

STOLL. You took Tom out of Laramie to kind of straighten him up?

STONE. Yes, sir.

STOLL. He had been drinking quite heavily since you first saw him on the twenty-first?

STONE. Yes, sir.

STOLL. Let me ask, did you not in the office of the justice of the peace in Laramie state that you drank with Horn in Laramie on the nineteenth?

STONE. No sir. The justice of the peace asked me where I was when this murder was committed. I told him I was in the

Snowy Range. He went so far as to state what was in the Denver newspaper about me coming here to testify to a false alibi to clear Mr. Horn. Mr. Stoll, I know a great many men who try to break out of the penitentiary, but not to break in. I said I was a hundred miles away, and I would not swear to a false alibi or anything else.

STOLL. Do you state to the jury that you were not in Laramie and did not see Horn on the nineteenth?

STONE. Yes, sir. I did not.

Judge Scott seemed predisposed to rule in favor of the prosecution and against the defense when they raised objections. A prime example occurred during the grilling Lacey gave Kels Nickell. Lacey attempted without success to introduce the "alternative suspect" theory, which is critical to the defense in a crime of this nature:

LACEY. Did the boy [Willie] ever have trouble in that vicinity?

NICKELL. ...He had quite a little trouble with the Miller family.

LACEY. Which members of the Miller family?

NICKELL. Miller himself, but principally with the boys.

LACEY. Which boys?

NICKELL. Gussie and Victor....

LACEY. There had been trouble between you and Miller likewise?

NICKELL. Yes sir.

STOLL. Objection. Not proper matter at cross-examination.

JUDGE SCOTT. I think the objection is well taken, and will be sustained.

LACEY. We take exception to the objection being sustained....

LACEY. Do you know whether the Miller boys generally carried a gun?

STOLL. Objection. Not proper cross-examination.

JUDGE SCOTT. Sustained.

LACEY. Exception.

The Miller men were key figures for the prosecution. When Victor testified on cross-examination, Lacey was again thwarted in his effort to introduce an alternative suspect. One of Lacey's biggest failures during the trial proved to be his inability to introduce the alternative suspect theory on direct examination of a witness he had called himself. (Cross-examination is limited to matters introduced during direct examination; Stoll of course was smart enough not to allow that to happen.) Lacey attempted again to introduce an alternate suspect:

> LACEY. As a matter of fact, there is a good deal of trouble in the neighborhood between Nickell and his neighbors?
> STOLL. Objection.
> JUDGE SCOTT. Sustained.
> LACEY. We take exception. Personally you had trouble with Willie Nickell yourself?
> STOLL. Objection.
> JUDGE SCOTT. Sustained.
> LACEY. Exception. You had once in your father's presence a difficulty with him when you offered to fight him, and your father told you to fight him? And Willie tried to run you down with a horse, and your father pulled a pistol and told him if he did he would shoot the horse—that is a fact, is it not?
> STOLL. Objection.
> JUDGE SCOTT. Sustained.
> LACEY. Exception. That occasion you had such trouble with Willie was in June? State whether that trouble did not occur in June, immediately prior to the killing of Willie Nickell?
> STOLL. Objection.
> JUDGE SCOTT. Sustained.

A month before the trial, three individuals from Denver had contacted Joe LeFors: Frank Mulock, Roy Campbell and Robert Cousley. Frank Mulock's comments were the most damaging:

> STOLL. Tell the jury about the incident when you met Tom Horn in Denver during the carnival, the Mountains and Plains Festival.
> MULOCK. I was employed during Carnival Week by a ticket broker. I had a conversation with Horn with reference to a ticket

to Cheyenne. He invited me to go and have a drink. We went down to Seventeenth Street near the corner of Blake to the Scandinavian House. He had been drinking considerably. After we had finished this drink we turned around and a friend of mine said, "Hello, Frank, are you doing detective work for the Burlington yet?"

I said, "Not now."

Horn said to me, "Are you a detective?"

I said, "No, not at present."

He said, "I am a stock detective in Wyoming."

I said, "Is that so? If you are from Wyoming and a stock detective, I think you would go and get that reward for the man who killed Willie Nickell."

He said, "I am the main guy in that Nickell case.... I am the best shot in the United States. I can hit a ten-cent piece. That was the best Goddamn shot I ever made.... By George," he said, "that is the dirtiest trick I ever done. There is a lot of people mixed up in it in Cheyenne, and they had better keep their noses out of it...."

Later Lacey cross-examined Mulock:

LACEY. You say he had been pretty drunk?

MULOCK. Yes, sir....

LACEY. Do you testify he was talking in a bragging cowboy manner?

MULOCK. He was bragging....

LACEY. You say he was very drunk?

MULOCK. Yes, sir....

LACEY. Who did you first report this conversation to—what officer of Cheyenne?

MULOCK. I reported it to Mr. LeFors.

LACEY. That was after you saw the newspaper reports, saw some accounts of Tom being arrested?

MULOCK. Yes, sir.

Testimony by a police officer from Denver, Robert Stockton, who knew Mulock well, carried little weight for the defense. Stockton

Drawing of Horn in the Denver Post. (Denver Public Library)

stated that he had known Mulock for "ten or twelve years." When Lacey asked about Mulock's reputation for truth and veracity, Stockton said, simply, "It is very bad." Stoll, of course, objected that the answer was a matter of opinion, and Judge Scott once again sustained.

The defense attempted to introduce a copy of Mulock's arrest record, which showed over fifty arrests for infractions ranging from impersonating an officer, to assault, to attempted murder. Stoll was able to block it by insisting that only the original of the arrest record could be introduced.

During Lacey's interrogation in direct examination of Tom Horn, the defendant demonstrated remarkable consistency with the statements he had made during the inquest. Trial lawyers know that the mark of truthfulness is consistency in a person's statements over a period of time, but as matters progressed, it was to no avail:

LACEY. Now Mr. Horn, when did you leave Miller's ranch?

HORN. I left Wednesday morning.

LACEY. In riding about in your work, do you keep track clearly of the dates?

HORN. I do not keep track of the dates or days of the week. And I never would have kept track of them if I had not been arrested in connection with this murder.

LACEY. Do you remember about what time you left Miller's?

HORN. I remember it was after Miss Kimmell had left to teach school.

LACEY. You have spoken of your horse. State what horse you had.

HORN. I was riding a horse they call "CAP."

LACEY. What color?

HORN. Black.

LACEY. What firearms did you have?

HORN. A rifle.

LACEY. What kind of a rifle?

HORN. A thirty-thirty Winchester.

LACEY. Did you have anything else on your saddle?

HORN. Field glasses.

LACEY. What else?

HORN. Nothing else.

LACEY. State what you had, if anything, in the way of a sweater with you.

HORN. I never had a sweater. Sweaters are worn in the wintertime; this was in the middle of summer.

LACEY. Now, when you left the Miller ranch on the morning of Wednesday the seventeenth of July, where did you go?

HORN. I left the Miller ranch and turned right up the creek.

LACEY. Was it toward Nickell's ranch or away from it?

HORN. Directly away from it.

LACEY. Then where did you go?

HORN. Then I swung around [south, and then east and north] and crossed the South Chug east of Nickell's ranch.

LACEY. What was there, if anything, that you were looking after?

HORN. There was a piece of land there, just a small piece of meadow [the Colcord Place], that belongs to the Two Bar. I looked to see if Mr. Nickell had any sheep in there.

LACEY. What did you find?

HORN. There was not a sign of sheep there.

LACEY. There being none there, what direction did you go?

HORN. I headed back home towards the Laramie Plains. In fact I had started back home towards the Laramie Plains when I left Millers. I left Miller's with the intention of going through the Two Bar's meadow, and then home.

LACEY. Which direction from Nickell's house? Which direction with reference to the gate at which Willie Nickell was killed, same direction or opposite direction?

HORN. I was not going at any time toward this gate where Willie Nickell was killed.

LACEY. About how far were you from Mr. Nickell's house?

HORN. Perhaps from a mile and a quarter. I can't say as to miles, just making a guess. I crossed the South Chug a mile and a half below Mr. Nickell's house. I know the gate very well where the boy was killed; it is estimated about a mile above Mr. Nickell's house [to the west].

LACEY. Pretty near the opposite direction from where you were?

HORN. Yes, sir.

LACEY. Where did you go from the Two Bar's place across from the Nickell pasture?

HORN. I worked through Mr. Clay's pasture, to the north.... Saturday morning, the twentieth, I went home to the ranch.

LACEY. Do you remember what time it was you got there?

HORN. The middle of the forenoon.

LACEY. Who was there at the ranch when you got there?

HORN. Jack Ryan and his wife were in the house. Carpenter[2] was at the stable. When I got in, I went to the house and got my mail. After reading my mail, I wanted to go to

Laramie right away. I had planned originally to go to Laramie on Saturday evening, but after getting my mail I wanted to go right away.

The Ryans corroborated Tom's testimony, confirming that he had arrived at the ranch on Saturday, changed his clothes, made the telephone call, and paid them for the call.

Horn's testimony continued:

> HORN. I went out and I asked Carpenter what horses were there. The horses that were there were all little old sticks of ranch horses like I didn't care to ride. Mr. Coble's private horse was there, and I knew Mr. Coble had gone east. The horse was a big, fat, snorty horse, and Carpenter told me it was the only horse there that was any good. So, I went out and drove him into the corral.[3]
>
> LACEY. When you got that horse up and started, you went where?
>
> HORN. To Laramie.
>
> LACEY. What day of the week was it that you got to Laramie?
>
> HORN. It was on Saturday, the twentieth, the same day I got into the ranch.
>
> LACEY. From the time you reached Laramie on the twentieth, until you left there the thirtieth with Frank Stone, state whether you left town at all.
>
> HORN. No, sir.

The single most compelling part of the prosecution's case, of course, was the so-called confession. The approach taken by the defense to counter Stoll's use of the conversation was to attempt to prove it was nothing but a drunken josh and a contest between two braggarts:

> LACEY. Now, Mr. LeFors has said some things that you said to him when you had that talk with him that was overheard by Les Snow and Charlie Ohnhaus.
>
> HORN. We were just joshing one another, throwing bouquets at one another, you might call it.

LACEY. What intention, if any, did you have, in anyway in the world, to seriously admit that you had killed Willie Nickell?

HORN. I never had anything to do with the killing of Willie Nickell. I never had any cause to kill him. And I never killed him. LeFors was joshing me about it, and I did not object.

LACEY. State whether in that conversation you intended to admit that you really did kill him as a serious proposition, or in any other way than the mere joshing?

HORN. There was nothing serious about the talk at all. It was all a josh.

Next Horn denied that he had any conversation with Mulock, Campbell, or Cousley. Lacey's objective, now that he had introduced testimony about Horn's drunken condition while in Denver, was to show that Horn could not have even had a conversation with the three witnesses Stoll had presented:

LACEY. You have heard these men from Denver testify as to some talk you had during the first week in October, as they put it, the Festival week in Denver? What have you to say about that? Was that a true statement of anything you said to them, or was it not?

HORN. There could not have been any truth to it at all. Not one word of truth could there have been to it.

LACEY. Where were you the first week of October, 1901?

HORN. I was in the hospital in Denver, St. Luke's Hospital.

LACEY. What was it that caused you to be there?

HORN. I lost a fight.

LACEY. Lost in such a way you were injured, in what way?

HORN. I had my jaw broken to the extent that I had to go to the hospital.

LACEY. How long were you in the hospital?

HORN. Twenty or twenty-one days.

LACEY. Was there any opportunity in the world for you the next day to go uptown and tell Mr. Mulock, as he states, that you had been talking too freely the night before?

HORN. The next day it was impossible for me to communicate with anybody except by writing. I could not speak a word.

He also said on the witness stand that I was making some arrangements trying to buy a ticket. I had no reason to buy a ticket as I had a pass with a rail carload of horses.

LACEY. Was Sunday night the only night you were drinking in Denver?

HORN. It was.

Lacey's team brought the Denver police surgeon to testify in Horn's behalf. He confirmed that he had treated Horn for the broken jaw early Monday morning. Stoll, however, cleverly generated confusion in the minds of the jurymen over exactly when the festival had started, thereby creating doubts that Horn had not talked to the three men.

Another development was the introduction of the sweater. More noteworthy was how Horn incriminated himself in his remark about it:

LACEY. Something has been said here about a sweater, here, a navy blue sweater. Was that sweater yours?

HORN. No, sir. The jailer brought me a letter written to the sheriff. That letter says, "Tom Horn left a sweater with me which I send to him by express." I asked the jailer who this man was that was sending this sweater. I didn't know anything about the sweater. He told me it came from some shoemaker in Laramie. There was some conversation about the sweater. It occurred to me they were jobbing me about it.

LACEY. When the sweater actually came, what did you say?

HORN. When it actually came the sheriff and jailer brought the sweater in. I says, "I suppose it is that sweater they wrote me about." I got it out; it was an old dirty sweater. I said. "All sweaters look alike to me. But, if that is mine, you had better have it washed." I never saw it before, nor never seen it since....

Walter Stoll, having taken note of Horn's ego, proceeded to spur the witness into denying that he was too drunk to remember what he had said, thereby destroying the defense Lacey had attempted to build. Horn doubtless sensed that he was up against a skilled adversary, but believed he could handle him. (The *Cheyenne Daily Leader* reported that Horn said he was more afraid of Stoll than he was of the evidence.)[4]

STOLL. What did you do Saturday morning after you got up?

HORN. I went straight into Coble's ranch. I changed clothes. I wrote some letters. I sent off a telegram and attended to the little business I had to, done several things. I went out in the pasture and got a horse, also.

STOLL. You changed the clothes you had on this trip, having been sleeping out around as you had; they were more or less dirty? You thought you would go to Laramie and wanted a change of apparel. Is that not right?

HORN. I do change clothes sometimes. [Laughter]

STOLL. What time did you leave Coble's ranch to go to Laramie?

HORN. I got my noon dinner first, and left right away.

STOLL. So that you got into Laramie at what time?

HORN. I got there as soon as I could ride there.

STOLL. You know to a certainty that you did not go into Laramie either on the eighteenth or the nineteenth?

HORN. I was not there until the afternoon of Saturday, the twentieth.

STOLL. You didn't have tied on back of your saddle either on any of these days any bundle of clothing of any kind?

HORN. No. I remember to a certainty. And I didn't have a dark sweater. In fact, the only one I have had for three or four years is a yellow, buckskin, tan-colored kind of sweater. I have not worn that. Duncan Clark has been wearing it.

STOLL. On September 28, you left Cheyenne for Denver, and were there to take in the festivities of the carnival, the Mountains and Plains Festival? Is that not correct?

HORN. Yes sir.

STOLL. Is it a fact that you met these gentlemen that testified here as to conversations they had with you in the Scandinavian?

HORN. It is a fact that I never met, or spoke, or saw them, or heard of them, not on any occasion in the world.

STOLL. You never said any of those things testified to by Mr. Mulock?

HORN. I did not. I wish to say to the jury that at the time

Duncan Clark, who, it was said, had the buckskin-colored sweater belonging to Tom Horn. (Wyoming Division of Cultural Resources)

those gentlemen say I spoke to them, I was laid up in the doctor's care, and my head was in plaster of Paris. The only way I had to communicate was to write. I couldn't speak, even to the doctor. I had to write. He bound up my head and said, "Don't attempt to talk any more."

STOLL. State to the jury what the facts are. Did you have any conversation with them at all, at any time whatever?

HORN. I had no conversation with them at any time.

Regardless of whether Horn had lied here about whether he had talked with the three witnesses, Stoll wanted to strike home the detective's continuing assertions that he knew perfectly well what he was saying whether he had been drinking or not. Now was the time to strike a fatal blow to Lacey's attempt to weaken the confession:

STOLL. Were you in any condition to remember whether you had these conversations with these men or not?

HORN. I remember everything that occurred to me in my life.

STOLL. You have never been so much under the influence of liquor so as not to remember what you said?

HORN. Not if I could talk.

STOLL. So that you have a clear recollection of things that have occurred to you?

HORN. On this particular occasion I have a very distinct recollection. I have reason to have a very distinct recollection….

STOLL. You had sent him [LeFors] a telegram on January eleventh, 1902 that you would be down that night?

HORN. I presume it was January eleventh.

STOLL. At the time you sent the telegram you were fully cognizant of the fact that you had been asked for a job in Montana?

HORN. Yes, sir.

STOLL. And you were going to have an interview with Mr. LeFors concerning that job? This was a bona fide job, and the people were bona fide people?

HORN. As far as I knew….

STOLL. In that conversation did you say, "I don't want to be making reports to anybody at any time. I will have only one report to make, and that will be at the finish. If a man is compelled to make reports all the time, they will catch the wisest son of a bitch in the world?"

HORN. I think I made that remark. I don't know as that is the exact language, and those oaths being used, but in all probability I used them. I am given in a natural way to profanity.

STOLL. You will admit to using that language at that time?

HORN. If I did not use that, I used something very similar to it.

STOLL. You knew at the time perfectly well what you were saying?

HORN. I did.

STOLL. Did you say, "If a fellow goes to shooting, they won't get scared?"

HORN. I did.

STOLL. You do not claim that you were so intoxicated that you did not know what you said?

HORN. I know to a certainty what I was saying. I had not been to bed the night before. I had been up visiting, drinking, having a good time. But I knew perfectly well what I was saying.

Horn's defense team produced a series of witnesses who testified that he had, in fact, arrived in Laramie on Saturday, and that he was thoroughly intoxicated by the next morning. Stoll once again produced counter witnesses who testified to an apparent sobriety:

STOLL. When Joe LeFors said, "No, they are not afraid of shooting," did you say, "That is all right? I don't want them to get scared if I get to shooting. I will protect the people I am working for. When it comes to shooting, you know me." You used that language?

HORN. I did. Every time that LeFors and I have ever met, the conversation has generally been about shooting someone or killing someone. I do not remember having talked with Mr. LeFors about anything other than somebody he had killed, or somebody I had killed.

And so it went. As Stoll recapped the conversation Tom had with Joe LeFors, he succeeded in gaining Tom's acknowledgment to every statement he had made, one by one—except for one: "About three hundred yards. It was the best shot that I ever made and the dirtiest trick I ever done." With respect to that remark, Horn said that if it was in Ohnhaus's notes he believed he must have made it. But he consistently maintained that he could never determine why he was being tied to Willie's murder. His conversations with LeFors, he said, were more about how LeFors had offered to split the reward if Tom would throw in with him and help convict a party "in the country:"

I told him that I didn't see why anyone should connect me with the killing of Willie Nickell, because after the officers had made an investigation they found I was not there. We had been talking for two or three hours that night and Joe LeFors says, "Tom, if you will throw in with me we can cinch that damned

outfit out there." I did not know the details of the killing. I did
not know he was on that road to Iron Mountain. I supposed the
circumstances of killing the boy were that he was prowling
around the hills, and run onto somebody else. I didn't know
what the facts were in the case. The talk I had with LeFors had
never been for the matter of developing any legitimate information, it was to job somebody.

STOLL. Now, you remember that conversation was used, do
you? You were in a condition to understand it then?

HORN. I was. But I didn't happen to have a stenographer to
take it down.

STOLL. You say you had three conversations with Mr.
LeFors relating to the Willie Nickell killing?

HORN. That many, I say. The principal one, I think,
occurred at the Tivoli, the second day of Frontier Days, 1901.

STOLL. In these conversations, each of them had as the subject the killing of Willie Nickell? Was that the matter that was
discussed?

HORN. It was not so much the subject of the killing of
Willie Nickell, as it consisted of his asking me to go in with
him, and furnish evidence from the country, to convict somebody out in the country.

STOLL. Anybody in the country?

HORN. One particular party. The talk was generally to get
me to go in with him, and we would make a thousand-dollar
reward, and we would cut it up between us. There was a party
in the country, he said, and with my assistance, he could convict
[the party] of the murder of Willie Nickell. The question of the
killing of Willie Nickell was not discussed so much, as com-
pared to how we could job this man, fix it up so as to convict
him. He could handle the sheriff and prosecuting attorney here
in town. But, it would be necessary to have some witnesses from
the country to convict this party, and he thought I could furnish
those witnesses.

STOLL. Whatever may have been said, the matter talked
about was the killing of Willie Nickell, was it not?

Horn stuck to his guns, not allowing Stoll to deflect the testimony away from Horn's adamant contention that LeFors was not after anything other than the money at stake. Horn held his own in this small segment of the testimony, but it did no good in swaying the jury's disposition to convict:

> HORN. It was the thousand-dollar reward. He told me what a bad man he was, and I told him what a bad man I was. I don't think there was any other conversation that occurred between us, except that something was mentioned about this crime, and something about someone he had killed, and some others I had killed.
>
> STOLL. Now, instead of referring to any facts in this particular case, there had been nothing in your past that could be used as the basis of any assertions about killings?
>
> HORN. There was certainly not. I never killed a man in my life.
>
> STOLL. I will ask you if this language was used. "How much did you get for killing these fellows? In the Powell and Lewis case, you got six hundred dollars apiece. You killed Lewis in the corral with a six-shooter. I would like to have seen the expression on his face when you shot him." To which you replied, "He was the scaredest son of a bitch you ever saw." Was that language used?
>
> HORN. I think that language was used. If he would have asked me if I killed him with a double-barreled gun or gatling gun, I would have said "yes." But, anybody that investigated or knew anything about the killing of that man Lewis knows I was summoned before the Grand Jury here, and it was established that I was in Bates Hole in Natrona County at the time the killing occurred.

To counter Horn's position that the substance of the conversation was essentially fiction, Stoll introduced matters of fact. He artfully wove matters of fact into his questioning and gained Horn's acknowledgment that the matters to which he referred had actually happened. The murders of William Lewis and Fred Powell—and the public's belief that Horn was their killer, even if not true—had the effect of weakening the detective's assertions that his conversation with LeFors was largely two braggarts blowing and blustering.

> STOLL. Several times you stated that all these things you referred to here were more or less fiction. However, with regard to language, there was something referred to that was a fact. For instance, Lewis and Powell were known to have been killed.
>
> HORN. The killing of Lewis was a fact, certainly, but he was a man that I never knew or saw at no time in my life.
>
> STOLL. The killing of Powell was a fact?
>
> HORN. Powell had also been killed.
>
> STOLL. So that when you referred to those matters you referred to something that was well known?
>
> HORN. They were shot, certainly.
>
> STOLL. But it was not a fact that you got six hundred dollars apiece for shooting them?
>
> HORN. Oh no. Even if he had asked me if I got seventeen thousand dollars, I would have told him "yes."
>
> STOLL. If you got fifty dollars apiece you would have told him the same?
>
> HORN. Yes, or a dollar twenty-five [Laughter].

Next Stoll moved the questioning back to details about the Willie Nickell killing and the crime scene:

> STOLL. Then was this language used, "Why did you put the rock under the kid's head after you killed him? That is one of your marks, isn't it?"
>
> To which you replied, "Yes, that is the way I hang out my sign to collect my money for a job of this kind."
>
> HORN. I think it was used. But then I realized when he made that remark, about there being a stone under the boy's head, that I never heard of that before either. It occurred to me that he knew a great deal more about the details of the killing than I did. That was news to me that there was a rock under his head. But we were just joshing, and even had he said, "Why didn't you lay him on a cot, or hang him up on a tree" I would have given him the same answer.

STOLL. You had quite a distinct idea of what had happened in that killing, did you not?

HORN. Not so much as I had the idea that he knew more about the killing than I did, and I had better be careful how I talked.

STOLL. Did he say, "Did you ever have any trouble collecting your money?" To which you replied, "No, when I do a job of this kind, they knew they had to pay me. I would kill a man if he tried to beat me out of ten cents?"

HORN. I think I did. But I never killed anybody, or contracted to kill anybody.

STOLL. You want to say to this jury, you would not kill anybody?

HORN. I would not talk to this jury as I did to a man like Joe LeFors.

STOLL. You wanted LeFors to understand you would kill a man if he tried to cheat you out of ten cents after you done a job of this kind?

HORN. He knew different. LeFors is very much the same kind of man for talk as I am.

STOLL. Was this language used, "You got five hundred dollars for that. Why did you cut the price?" To which you replied, "I got twenty-one hundred dollars?"

HORN. I think it was. As to the twenty-one hundred dollars, I might have said twenty-five hundred dollars or fifteen hundred dollars.

STOLL. Was this language used, "How much is that to a man?" To which you replied, "That is for three dead men and one man shot at five times. Killing men is my specialty. I look at it as a business proposition, and I think I have a corner on the market?"

HORN. I think it was.

STOLL. I will ask you if the three dead men referred to there were not Powell and Lewis and Willie Nickell?

HORN. I think they were.

STOLL. And the one man shot at five times was Kels Nickell?

HORN. I think so.

On redirect Lacey attempted to repair the damage that Stoll had inflicted:

LACEY. When these insinuations were made against you for killing Willie Nickell and other people, why didn't you deny them?

HORN. Nobody except LeFors ever insinuated that I done the killing. I was always of a rather generous disposition. I would rather lie than disappoint him. When he said I done the killing, I told it all to him like [as if] I had.

LACEY. All the men that you ever did kill actually existed only in these friendly talks with Joe and other people like that?

HORN. As far as actual killing is concerned, I never killed a man in my life, or a boy either.

Chapter Twenty-three

GUILTY!

A S THE PROCEEDINGS drew to a close in Horn's murder trial, the defense introduced evidence showing that only Victor Miller could have committed the crime—a footprint of a size six or seven shoe near the body. Of all who possibly could have been near the site, only young Victor could have worn that size shoe. Tom Horn's shoe was considerably larger, of course.

By the time Joe LeFors testified, even in the face of intense cross-examination by Tom Horn's lawyer, most of the jurymen had largely made up their minds.

LeFors acknowledged in direct examination by Walter Stoll that his conversation with Tom Horn had occurred in the morning, starting around eleven o'clock, and that it had "perhaps" continued in the early afternoon. He stated that Horn's condition was "sober and rational."

When John Lacey commenced cross-examination, he tried to have LeFors acknowledge that part of the stories he told were yarns. LeFors feigned ignorance of the term "tall yarns" and tried to emphasize that most of the information he had given Tom in their banter was factual, such as accounts of the skirmishes he'd had while working in Weston County. He finally did admit that he had woven a tale when he had told Tom about having moved bands of sheep without the consent of the owner. He added that he heard the story about Horn killing a Mexican lieutenant, being imprisoned, and escaping. Lacey did not pursue that vein, probably because it was not pertinent.

When the subject turned to the Nickell murder, LeFors generally became vague. As Lacey probed to verify what Horn had said about the location from which the killer had fired the shots, LeFors acknowledged that Horn's comment was that he had been in the "draw to the right [south] of the gate":

Freddie Nickell and Julia Nickell Cook at the trial. (Wyoming Division of Cultural Resources)

LACEY. ...Well, now in stating how he supposed that the way the killing of Willie Nickell happened, he said, "Suppose there was a man in the draw, in the big draw to the right of the gate, the draw that runs down to the main creek, near Nickell's house." Is that what he said?

LEFORS. Yes, sir....

As soon as Lacey became specific, asking for examples about whether Willie had run in "a southern direction," LeFors said his impression was that Horn meant the boy had run to the south. At the same time, he hedged, saying, "That was the way I understood it, from the way he was pointing off the paper he had." It was not, however, what Horn had actually said. LeFors explained, "Not from that [Horn's oral explanation], Judge. He had a piece of paper, and he was marking on it. From his marks I thought that was the way it occurred."

Turning to the assertion that Horn had run barefoot across the country, LeFors was similarly hesitant, and acknowledged he was not very familiar with the area:

> LACEY. When asked the question, "You had your boots on?" he said he was barefoot. Why did you say, "You had your boots on?"
>
> LEFORS. It would look kind of unnatural for a man to pull his boots off when in a hurry to do a job.
>
> LACEY. What was there about that particular country that it looks like a man must have had his boots on?
>
> LEFORS. There is nothing particular about it. I have never been over that country except for twice.
>
> LACEY. You don't know it very thoroughly?
>
> LEFORS. Not very thoroughly. I have only been over it a couple of times.

Lacey then tried to gain a firm assertion that both Horn and LeFors were spinning tales, with LeFors leading Horn on. LeFors again was vague, and the effort was ineffectual:

> LACEY. You were asked the question, "You don't know which of you told the biggest yarns." Is that correct? To that did you answer, "That would be problematical?"
>
> LEFORS. I think I did.
>
> LACEY. Were you not asked this further question, "And so what you said about killing people was not true?" And to that didn't you answer, "I was just leading him on?"
>
> LEFORS. I might have done that. I don't know as to that. I don't remember.

Walter Stoll then began redirect. He asked LeFors if he and Horn had had any conversations about the killing before January. LeFors

Prosecutor Stoll, "The Hero of the Hour," from the Post.
(Denver Public Library)

acknowledged that they had met, but only twice in the summer during Frontier Days and said that it was always Horn who brought up the subject of the murder. When it came to LeFors's attempts to induce the detective to throw in with him, finger the party in the country, and split the reward, he retorted, "Never had any such conversation as that at no time."

Lacey had another opportunity to question LeFors. He asked whether the deputy marshal had told Horn that he already had evidence that would convict Jim and Victor Miller. LeFors denied he had said anything of the sort. Lacey then turned to LeFors's interest in the reward money, Frank Mulock, and LeFors's relationship with District and Prosecuting Attorney Walter Stoll:

LACEY. You have taken a good deal of interest in the case?

LEFORS. I have taken an interest in this way—the defendant wanted to talk with me.

LACEY. I did not say how. I say you have taken an interest in the case?

LEFORS. Yes.

LACEY. You have taken an interest in this case, considerable interest?

LEFORS. Well, I have been in the case at different times. I have been asked by the prosecuting attorney in the case—

LACEY. You went to Denver and interviewed those witnesses?

LEFORS. Well, no—

LACEY. Didn't you go to Denver?

LEFORS. Two of the witnesses I never saw.

LACEY. You went to Denver to see one of them?

LEFORS. I don't believe I did.

LACEY. Did you interview one in Denver?

LEFORS. I never interviewed him in Denver. Two of them I never seen before.

LACEY. Do you not remember seeing either of them?

LEFORS. Only here in Cheyenne.

LACEY. When?

LEFORS. After this case started. I met Mr. Mulock and this other gentleman. I forget his name.

Lacey's attempt to prove that LeFors was operating out of his jurisdiction as a U.S. marshal went unheeded by the jury, but it probably did not matter:

LACEY. The truth is, you are a U.S. marshal, and that has no connection whatever under the state laws with the prosecution of state offenses?

LEFORS. No legal connection.... I have been asked to go into the case by the prosecuting attorney. At different times I have went ahead and did such work as he told me to, to the best of my ability. I have done things under his instructions. That is my explanation.

Both sides began delivering their closing arguments on October 22. Attorney H. Waldo Moore stated for the prosecution that Horn had killed Lewis and Powell, statements objected to by the defense and sustained by the judge, who cautioned Moore to confine himself to matters covered in the prosecution's case. Moore further disparaged the already confusing testimony of the expert witnesses who had testified on the gunshot wounds.

Timothy F. Burke for the defense began by emphasizing that the prosecution had presented primarily weak, circumstantial evidence. He argued that Stoll had never demonstrated that Horn had a motive to commit the murder. He added that the testimony of the Denver witnesses was perjured, and he pointed to the fact that they had parroted the same language in their versions of Horn's remarks that had appeared in newspaper reports of the confession. He hammered on the fact that Horn was in the hospital with a broken jaw when the alleged conversations had taken place.

He continued by deriding Frank Irwin's testimony that Horn had ridden into Laramie on July 18 as being simply motivated by bad blood and Irwin's desire for vengeance.

John W. Lacey followed Burke for the defense. He started by covering testimony by firearms experts and doctors about Willie's wounds. Some had said that the wounds were too large to have been caused by a thirty-caliber weapon. Other experts had testified that the wounds could indeed have been made by a thirty-caliber gun. He emphasized that for Stoll to disparage the testimony of the five doctors who doubted the wounds had been caused by a thirty-caliber weapon, was to brand them as liars.

He emphasized that the footprint found near the murder scene was too small to be Horn's and that it could only be Victor Miller's. He then stated that someone in the Miller family had known that Willie would be headed for the gate early on July 18.[1]

Lacey's strongest argument was that the "confession" was the result of Horn's having consumed too much alcohol and that it should be construed only as a drunkard's boasts.

Walter Stoll closed the arguments for the prosecution the morning of October 22. He pointed to Horn's statement that Willie's killer

*Judge Scott delivering his instructions to the Horn jury.
From* the Denver Post. (Denver Public Library)

had murdered him to keep him from running home and "raising a hell of a commotion" as Horn's motive. He introduced the myth—though widely accepted—of young Billy Powell's remark, "That's the man that killed Daddy," and called it a turning point in Horn's thinking. He said it was at that point that Horn decided no kid would ever again finger him.

He argued that LeFors should be believed rather than Horn. He said that Frank Irwin should be considered a hero because he had the courage not to be "afraid of a coward" like Tom Horn.

He characterized Horn's defense of the confession as the "last straw of a drowning man," grasping for a way to destroy the value of the conversation.

The most effective component of Stoll's remarks were reminding the jury that if they stood for conviction, Horn could still request a new trial, appeal to the Supreme Court and finally appeal to the governor.

Excerpted from newspaper reports[2] and the defense's appeal to the Supreme Court[3], some of Stoll's remarks were highly inflammatory—yet effective:

> Gentlemen of the jury, you do not have the ordinary man here to deal with; you have the criminal, a man of criminal mind and criminal instincts; an extraordinary man....
>
> You need not fear imbruing your hands in the blood of this defendant; after you is [sic] is the Court, then the Supreme Court, and then the Governor....
>
> The people are very much in earnest in this case, they have furnished the money necessary for the prosecution; the officers have done their duty and now the people demand a verdict at your hands....
>
> You do not wish to be placed in the position and suffer the regrets which a jury trying a case in this Court at one time have suffered, where the nine who desired conviction yielded to the wishes of the three and acquitted the defendant, who shortly thereafter killed a whole family of six persons, some of which jurors you are undoubtedly acquainted with and have heard them express their regrets....

The jury retired at 11:25 A.M., and after five votes, only the jury foreman, H.W. Yoder, and Homer Payne, the Two Bar cowboy, held out for acquittal. Payne was the last to change his vote. At 4:30 P.M., Yoder announced that the jury had reached a verdict.

Guilty of murder in the first degree, the foreman announced. Death by hanging was set for January 9, 1903.

Chapter Twenty-four

He Talked too Much

QUESTIONS REMAIN unanswered to this day in the trial and conviction of Tom Horn.

During Horn's trial, H.M. Hasker wrote to John Coble on October 18, 1902, that Edward Richter, who could be reached at his Cottage Club residence in Denver, could testify that the character of two witnesses for the prosecution, Roy Campbell and Frank Mulock, was "very bad." Hasker also said that his object in writing was "friendship for Tom Horn."[1]

J. M. Kuykendall, president of the Denver Omnibus and Cab Company, also wrote to Coble on October 18, 1902. He said he had received a telephone call from the sporting editor of the *Denver Post*. The editor told Kuykendall that Horn's adversary in the fight that resulted in Horn's broken jaw, Johnny Corbett, would testify that Horn had never told Corbett that he had killed Nickell.[2]

W. E. "Ed" Finfrock wrote from Albany County on October 25, the day after the guilty verdict was rendered, to Otto Plaga. Plaga was the witness who stated he saw Horn twenty miles from the site of the murder an hour after it occurred.

Finfrock wrote that he had read a newspaper account about a witness by the name of Faulkner. Faulkner, the report said, swore on the stand that:

> I [Finfrock] said that you [Plaga] could not be believed under oath. I hardly know this man Faulkner, and I don't think your name was ever mentioned by me to him. If so, I never said any such thing for I do not know of your ever telling me anything but the truth.... If you wish I will make a sworn statement to this effect. I have told the reporter of the [Laramie] *Republican* to publish such a denial and send you a copy...."[3]

Faulkner had testified but had said that he could not state whether Plaga's reputation was good, but only that he had heard from a man who worked for Ora Haley that it was not good.

On November 15, 1902, Lilly C. Graham of Cheyenne filed an affidavit[4] in Horn's behalf.

Graham was the stepdaughter of Charles Edwards, who lived near the Iron Mountain Station and who had testified against Horn. She swore to the feuds that had developed between Nickell and Miller:

> I was visiting my mother and step-father there [at Iron Mountain], two years ago, just after Franklin Miller was accidentally shot...when his father, Jim Miller, came to the Edwards home on his way to Cheyenne...He stated the object of his going to Cheyenne was to have Kels Nickell prosecuted or bound over to keep the peace.... He said, "...I will never rest until that boy's death...is avenged and if the law does not do it, I will."
>
> I know that there was exceedingly hard feelings existing between Jim Miller & Kels Nickell & they were reputed to have carried guns with which to shoot in case of opportunity or trouble arising between them.... Jim Miller attributed the death of his boy to the actions and conduct of Kels Nickell....

Otto Plaga wrote from Sybille to T. Blake Kennedy on January 31, 1903, sending the letter from Finfrock. He indicated that George Proctor, who had been a bailiff in Horn's trial, had been snooping around on a matter of alleged theft of U.S. horses:

> I think they are trying to get me into trouble of some kind, I know. I wish you would let me know just what to do if they come again, as I think they will, as Proctor said he was coming back here again...he is trying to make out that U.S. horses have been stolen from Cheyenne, and they are trying to make out that I have got the horses out here.[5]

John W. Lacey, Horn's chief counsel, received a letter dated October 29, 1902:

The Tivoli in Cheyenne. (Wyoming Division of Cultural Resources)

There is a man employed at the Tivoli saloon, named Elton Perry, who says *a juror told him before the trial was over* [emphasis added] that "Horn ought to be hung as high as they could hang him." It was signed, "Not a friend of Horn."[6]

For years people have speculated that the Horn jury was tampered with. Bill Babbitt was a great-nephew of juror Thomas R. Babbitt who had first-hand recollections of the parties involved in the Horn episode[7]. He observed, "My father always thought that money was passed to the jury. Dad said that my Uncle Tom was so dishonest you couldn't believe him if he said 'good morning.'"

Another juror is suspect. Orien V. Sebern, who had arrived in Wyoming around 1883, homesteaded on 160 acres fifteen miles east of Wheatland. The county assessor's rolls showed that Sebern owned only a few cattle and horses, with a value of $340. In 1905 he sold his property to the Swan Land and Cattle Company for $2,100 and moved to southwest Idaho.

Sebern reappeared there on the jury of the conspiracy trial that followed the murder of former Governor Frank Steunenberg in December

1905. After the conviction of Steunenberg's assassin, the governors of Idaho and Colorado spirited three leaders of the Western Federation of Miners to Idaho for trial. Sebern attempted to be excused from jury duty, pleading that he had to attend to his farm. Both the prosecution and defense had exhausted their peremptory objections, and the judge impaneled him.

Notwithstanding Sebern's vote to convict Tom Horn, he was, according to commentary in union-biased publications, an influential juror when the panel ultimately voted for acquittal in the Idaho trial.[8] Middle-class anti-mining baron sentiment was evidently a factor in the outcome of the trial, just as anti-cattle baron sentiment was reflected in the Horn verdict.

Charles A. Siringo, the famous "cowboy detective" employed by Pinkerton's, was on friendly terms with a defense lawyer, Peter Breen. They met in the lobby of the Idanha Hotel in Boise during the trial.

J. Anthony Lukas[9] described the incident:

> Breen ventured a prediction: "It will either be an acquittal or hung jury."
>
> How did he know? Siringo asked.
>
> Because one of the jurors "could be depended on," Breen replied.
>
> They walked together over toward the courthouse to find out for themselves. As they strolled across a grassy park, they saw the jury marching away from the courthouse, apparently having rendered their verdict.
>
> "Charlie," said Breen, "do you see the tall man in the lead?"
>
> Yes, said Siringo, he did.
>
> "Enough said."
>
> Siringo doesn't give us the juror's name, only that he was "the former resident of Cheyenne, Wyoming, who was on the jury which convicted stock detective Tom Horn.[10]

One of Clarence Darrow's former partners, Edgar Lee Masters who was not on the best of terms with him, wrote later that Darrow who had been the chief defense counsel had bribed the jury.

In a striking parallel between the Horn and Haywood cases, speculation ran rampant about the Pinkerton's agents in the Horn case.

First, Joe LeFors said that there were Pinkerton men following Horn around in Cheyenne after the Nickell murder. This theory was that the Pinkerton's agents had bribed one or more of Horn's jurors to vote for conviction, thus eliminating the risk that Horn would implicate them in murder-for-hire conspiracies.

Another parallel exists between the Horn and Haywood cases. The jury in the latter was afraid of the consequences of a conviction. Pinkerton's Denver manager and one-time Tom Horn boss James McParland stated that Sebern had frightened the Haywood jury and had told them that they and their families would meet a terrible fate if they brought in a conviction. In the Horn case it was generally believed that the jurors and their families were intimidated or threatened.

But the bottom line is that Horn was convicted because of what and whom he represented: big business and the cattle barons. The general population had grown tired of the arrogance the cattlemen exhibited toward settlers in the lynching of Cattle Kate and others, in the Johnson County War, and now this. Haywood's acquittal came about for the same reason, except that it was the mining barons whom he opposed. With both juries made up of the working class, in retrospect it should come as no surprise how each trial ended.

The lawyer who conducted the defense in the retrial of Tom Horn in 1993, Joseph W. Moch, wrote:

> The community was tired of the big ranchers taking the law into their own hands, and the Johnson County Invaders were not yet forgotten. There was a community cry for action against the bigger cattle interests. The conviction of Tom Horn would be the perfect opportunity to satisfy the cry for justice.... Tom Horn became sort of a sacrificial lamb to community politics for past wrongdoings, not only Horn's but of others' as well. After his sacrificial death, the slate would be wiped clean." [11]

Newspaper coverage of the trial affected its outcome. Although Judge Scott ordered the jurors not to read newspapers, suspicions that they did persist. Scott was not obliged to refrain from reading the

Drawing in the Post. (Denver Public Library)

newspapers and as an elected judge may very well have been influenced to favor the prosecution.

Horn, himself, in his last sentence of his autobiography, said, "And I think that since my coming here the yellow journal reporters are better equipped to write my history than am I, myself." [12]

John Coble emphasized that the newspapers' compulsion to sell copies and beat their competitors by stooping to mistruths affected the outcome of the trial. In the appendix to Horn's autobiography, Coble said that he had resisted all efforts to be interviewed, as "a private citizen protecting his individual interests and the interests of others entrusted to his charge from the rapacity of maudlin and not over-scrupulous newsmongers." [13] He also attacked the public officials who played a role in the trial. He commented on:

> …men in positions of trust, puffed up with their "little brief authority," who have besmirched their trust and stooped to odious means for their selfish ends…. Wyoming politicians play the game of justice with human souls for pawns, and, I may add, with Cowardice as referee. [14]

On October 7, 1902, *The Denver Post*[15] carried a headline, "A Black Life Awaits A Fair Trial." In the body of the article it stated that Horn was "blissfully contemptuous" of the impending trial, and that "The [Hiram G.] Davidsons have moved from the mountain district into the city, but the fear of Tom Horn and the greater fear of what may follow, has sealed their lips."

The same issue stated that Horn had murdered Lewis and Powell, and that during the grand jury investigation of one murder, Powell's son called to his mother, "Oh mamma, take me, quick! That's the man that shot papa!" However Billy Powell most likely had not been present at the ranch when Powell was shot. It continued that Horn decided he would not repeat the mistake of letting children tell tales. Consequently, when Willie Nickell spotted him in ambush to murder his father, "it was good-bye for Willie Nickell."

Attempting to besmirch Horn's reputation, the *Post* printed a story about his father the day after the trial started.

> October 11, 1902—This may be true—but it isn't the whole truth. According to the records of the states of Illinois and Missouri, Tom Horn Sr. had a record that discounts that of Tom Jr., and whether or not he trained the son in the way he went or left it to others, the fact remains that father Horn lived in Missouri until he was forced to leave the country and take refuge in British Columbia, and that he did not die until Tom was well under way as an Indian scout and had a killing or two already laid by to his account.
>
> Tom Horn Sr. was a much cleverer rascal than the son; he belonged to a family of forgers, swindlers and blackmailers, and with a brother-in-law, Tolver [or Toliver] P. Craig, got control at one time of the famous—or infamous—Scotland County Gang of Missouri, a gang so much more clever and far reaching in its organization and manipulation than the Powder Springs Gang [loosely connected to the Wild Bunch].... The old man made a point of handling other people's stock after the fashion of a wealthy ranchman living on his income...; he went into politics for the power it gave him over other people...; he went

into a banking business on other people's money—and all three of these trades he combined under a beautiful forging, counterfeiting and blackmailing scheme that paid very well so long as the settler of Illinois and Missouri were new to the game....

If Tom Horn Sr. turned Tom Jr. over to the Mexicans and Indians at the tender age of 12 or 14, it was because even he foresaw that swindling as a fine art was doomed in Missouri....

Virtually all of the purported "facts" were the creations of the reporter's imagination, though, no doubt, the older Tom Horn's reputation was muddy.

The October 13 issue carried a report that Stoll had information to the effect that Horn had told Matt Rash's father that he had killed him while in Rock Springs. The account said that Horn walked into a saloon with a well-known resident of the town. The resident, a friend of Horn's introduced him to the elder Rash. Horn said, "Yes I am Tom Horn. I have just come from the Brown's Park country, where I put Matt Rash where he won't do any more rustling. Have one on me."

Polly Pry was a *Denver Post* columnist who provided observations on various participants. On October 14 she wrote, "Tom Horn—with his cruel nose, his wide, snaky, treacherous eyes, his loose-lipped, sensual mouth, his slanting, misshapen head, and his degenerate's ears,..." sat listening to the testimony "...with a face as unmoved as any man in the room." She added that he "chewed contentedly on a big piece of tobacco." She described Stoll as being "capable of holding his own with anything put up against him."

Another article in the same issue stated that Duncan Clark had left Coble's employ because of differences between the two over the Horn situation. Coble, in the appendix to Horn's book, denied that was the case and said the report was a lie.

Midway through the trial, on October 18, the *Post* reported that the previous night A. F. Whitman of Iron Mountain told its reporter that a meeting had been held at his house where it was proposed that Kels Nickell be lynched because of his feuding with people in the country and because he had been stealing and butchering cattle. Whitman asked at the meeting if there was any evidence other than hearsay and was told there was none. At that he said he "would not stand for hanging a man on hearsay evidence…. This saved Nickell's life." The article continued that a close friend of Horn's had said, "if we had a few more Tom Horns in Albany and Laramie counties there would have been fewer cattle thieves and the country would have been better off…. And a group of cattlemen standing by [during the conversation with the reporter] nodded assent."

On the same date Polly Pry wrote that Kels Nickell had told her that it was Tom Horn who had shot him. She said Nickell was sitting at her table, and she whispered:

> Is that the man who shot at you?
>
> "Yes," he said, "that is the man. He murdered my boy, and he tried to murder me!"
>
> And the secret was a secret no longer.
>
> Then we went outside, and he walked through the sunlit streets to the hotel with me, while he told me a tale that turns one sick with horror—a tale of a cold-blooded, heartless monster, who, for a few paltry pieces of silver, had slain his beloved son and deliberately tried to murder him.

On October 18, reporter J. Emerson Smith indicated that a court official had told him that Horn's testimony about his conversation with LeFors "weakened the case of the defense to an almost fatal extent." The comment was accurate, but if any of the jurors saw the paper, before they retired for deliberations, it could have inflicted more damage.

Polly Pry, on the same date, launched her most vicious attack:

> …He has not hesitated to eat a man's bread and murder him in cold blood…. Witness the brutal murder of Matt Rash.
>
> He is a coward!
>
> Never in all the long list of his crimes has there been one where his victim has had a show for his life. He has been that lowest of low assassins—the man who shoots from ambush….
>
> Now, who hired him…? Horn is the inhuman wretch who did the deed—but where is the fiend who planned it, the man who put up the money?

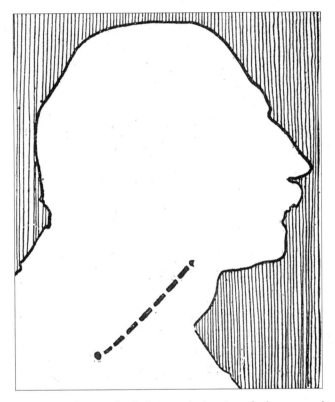

A diagram of Horn's head, showing the location of a huge scar which appeared in the Post *during the trial.* (Denver Public Library)

...The conviction of Tom Horn should be followed by the arrest, the prosecution, the conviction and the punishment of the men who instigated his crimes.

Is this what Tom Horn's backers fear?

If not, why this costly array of talent, this reckless waste of money, this frantic anxiety over the fate of a poisonous reptile who should be shown the same mercy accorded a deadly rattlesnake?

On October 23, the day before the verdict was rendered, the *Post* carried a story called "The Bumps of Horn." The subheadline read, "A Phrenologist Says He Is a Very Bad Specimen of Humanity." The article started by indicating that phrenology[16] had not been introduced as evidence but that a Cheyenne woman, Carrie Thronensen, had made of study of the "subtle art" and psychology.

Thronensen, described as a wealthy widow, had studied drawings and photographs of Horn, the article continued, and persuaded Judge Scott to allow her to sit in the first row of the spectators. The story concluded:

> ...The lady is quite certain that Horn's skull is that of a natural-born criminal, and that the formation indicates that if he is acquitted and again given his freedom that it is quite possible that he would kill more men. The slope of the forehead and the formation of the ears shows, in her opinion, an abnormal criminal development.
>
> Horn bore this inspection with great fortitude, as well he might, since he knows nothing of it until the publication today in *The Post*.

The next article in the column covered "Kels Nickell and His Enemy, Miller."

It stated that Nickell's life and fortunes had undergone great changes over twenty years, that he had started only seventeen miles from Cheyenne, where he was "well-fixed for those days" before locating to Iron Mountain, where he had secured a good ranch:

> ...Until he became the target of the spite and venom of his neighbors, whose ill will he had somehow incurred.
>
> Today he is living in a humble home here [in Cheyenne]. His hundreds of acres of ranch land are gone; his cattle and horses are also disposed of, and his 14-year-old son has been cruelly murdered.
>
> Miller, on the other hand, is today the possessor of two large ranches...one of which was formerly owned by Nickell. Now he is looked upon as a well-to-do ranchman with moderate means.

Theories abound on what really happened; a favorite implicates the Miller family. The Miller family men have for generations been known as accomplished outdoorsmen. A friend of the author who lived for years adjacent to the original Miller and Nickell homesteads said that the Millers could move through the timber only twenty yards away from where he was, and he'd never know they were there.

Post *drawing of John Coble.* (Denver Public Library)

This is one theory. When Nickell's sheep trespassed onto Miller's land, Jim Miller indicated that this was the last straw. He instructed Gus and Victor to creep up on the Nickell home the night before Willie was murdered. They learned that two adult males, Will Mahoney (Mary Nickell's brother) and John Apperson, a surveyor from Cheyenne, were there. They also heard Kels instruct Willie to take Kels's horse and, in the morning, ride west toward Iron Mountain to find the stranger who had been looking for work.

The Miller boys returned home and warned their father that two more adult males were at the Nickell home. But Victor and/or Gus made his own plans.

Why did the defense not call character witnesses to testify about Tom Horn's service to his country in the Apache wars and in Cuba? That had worked effectively in the Reno trial. Perhaps the defense was not aware of the case, and Horn had not volunteered that information because of embarrassment.

Why did the defense not call John Coble, Horn's employer and friend, at least as a character witness? Was it because he paid their fee? Why did the prosecution not call him, in an attempt to establish a murder-for-hire motive? Why did Coble commit suicide years after Tom's execution? Was more weighing on his mind and conscience than ill health and financial reverses?

Why was no attempt made by either the prosecution or the defense to determine why Horn went to see Colonel E.J. Bell after his ten-day patrol through the Iron Mountain and Sybille country? Was Bell so closely allied with Coble and others in the ranks of the elite that they made sure he was not called?

Why did Judge Richard H. Scott overrule so many of the defense team's objections to testimony that was damaging Horn? Most importantly, why did the judge permit no "alternative suspect" testimony that alluded to the "Miller-Nickell War," as Tom Horn described it?

What about the discrepancy between Horn's stating he had carried a thirty-thirty rifle, and later that he had burned five forty-five-ninety empty cartridges after the shooting of Kels on August 4, 1901? Horn would not have used the latter caliber because of its rainbow trajectory, but only the state-of-the-art thirty-thirty.

Where were Horn's backers when he needed them most? That rhetorical question needs no answer; they disappeared to keep from being implicated themselves. They had hired him to rid the country of rustlers, he performed the job well, and was well paid for it. As Larry Jordan[17] pointed out so perceptively, in the end they let him down to save their own hides. And to their credit, part of Horn's job description was that he did his work in a manner that avoided court and legal battles. He, in a way, had failed them first.

Bill Babbitt's aunt Jennie Tupper worked for John W. Lacey for fifty-eight years, many of those as his private secretary. Bill stated that with the exception of only one occasion, "Aunt Jennie would never talk about the Tom Horn case, even in the closed circles of our family." Why?

The occasion when Tupper broke her silence on the Tom Horn case was in the 1930s. Bill, a cousin, and Aunt Jennie were listening to a radio broadcast from Denver's KOA station on Wyoming history that covered the Tom Horn affair. She said when it ended, "You know, boys, Tom Horn never killed Willie Nickell."

Even without answers to these questions, it appears Tom Horn's legal defense team also was, plainly and simply, overconfident and undermotivated. Stoll had more to lose, in part because he faced reelection the next month. "Politics first and justice next."

The defense unquestionably walked a greased tightrope by representing a client who was an embarrassment to his former employers.

The attorney who headed the defense in the 1993 retrial of Tom Horn was Joseph W. Moch, a nationally known trial lawyer. He stated that Horn's team conducted the worst defense he had ever studied. They failed to prepare Horn for the manner in which the prosecution would be conducted and failed to advise him that when on the stand he should answer questions as briefly as possible. Perhaps they had poor client control, because the more he talked the tighter the noose was drawn. Reading between the lines of the transcript, it appears that his confidence that he would be acquitted was perceived as defiance.

Moch also commented that it appears no one took charge of the defense. It was like a team with no coach.

There is no question that Horn convicted himself with his own testimony. His lawyers said he wanted to go on the stand, perhaps because he felt he could present a strong case for himself. The October 25, 1902, issue of the *Denver Post* reported that some felt:

> He talked too much when he was on the stand...and even one of his own attorneys said last night:
> "Tom made a fool of himself when on the stand the afternoon that Stoll cross-examined him. He talked too much, and that was always his trouble....

"He had read that evidence so often, when in jail, that he came to believe that he had really made some of the statements which he admitted.

"But he wanted to go on the stand and he went."

More than one paper commented on the mistake made by allowing Horn to testify. The *Boulder Camera* commented in a front-page article on October 25 that "An attorney for the defense was heard to remark: 'We made a mistake by putting Horn on the stand to testify....'"[18]

The *Cheyenne Leader* tended to walk a middle ground in its coverage until the last part of the trial. In the October 23 issue it commented that "Stoll's argument was a "masterpiece of forensic oratory...his graphic portrayal of the crime was a terrible arraignment, overwhelmingly strong."[19] The article appeared while the jury was in deliberations.

Four days later, after the verdict was returned, the paper reported that an Elizabeth Sims, one of Horn's "sweethearts," had said the previous year that he had confessed but she was not brought to testify because of her reputation."[20]

Whether Stoll deliberately played up to the newspaper reporters and the crowd at the trial is not known. He seemed to have a flair for the dramatic, and the journalists of the day were more flagrant in their sensationalizing then than now.

The grandson of a rancher who employed Tom Horn told the author, "I was privy to the names on Tom Horn's list [to investigate]. Kels Nickell was not one of them."

T. Blake Kennedy, who more than any other lawyer on the defense team left no legal stone unturned in his efforts to save Tom, developed a feel for what the stock detective was really like. His judgment that "the world is better off without the likes of Tom Horn" does not address the issue of whether the man really murdered Willie Nickell.

Years of hindsight provide another perspective on the political and social context of the episode.

TYPES OF HORN'S FRIENDS.

Post *drawing that appeared during the trial.* (Denver Public Library)

With the advantage of retrospect, Cheyenne newspaperman John Charles Thompson, who was the only reporter allowed to view the entire execution to the point where Horn's body was cut down, wrote:

> He was hanged not because the murder of the boy was fastened upon him "beyond peradventure of a reasonable doubt," but on "general principle" that he "had it coming."
>
> ...Before a shred of testimony was offered he was a doomed man; public opinion had convicted him and intended to have him hanged.... The jury returned the verdict...despite the testimony of a physician who performed an autopsy on the Nickell boy that the bullet which killed him was of much greater caliber than those of Horn's gun....[21]

Chapter Twenty-five

How Is the Horn Case?

THE DEFENSE TEAM immediately set in motion a process to try to save Horn. Three days after the verdict, it filed a motion for a new trial, which Judge Scott denied. A supplemental motion for a new trial stated that there was irregularity in the proceedings of the jury, specifically, misconduct, undue influences, and pressure by third parties upon the jury that damaged Horn's case.

Homer Payne signed an affidavit on October 30 stating that during the jury deliberations one juror parroted Walter Stoll's remark, saying if they made a mistake Tom Horn always had recourse for a new trial or, should that fail, the Supreme Court would grant a new trial. Payne also said that as the jurors passed in and out of the courtroom and the Inter Ocean Hotel, bystanders pointed at him and others. He and other jurors heard remarks that he was a friend of Horn's and a "Two Bar man" and would hang the jury. He commented that he overheard bystanders remark that he had been "bought or fixed."

Greta Rohde, the head waitress at the Inter Ocean dining room, swore in an affidavit on November 3 that she had heard various people direct remarks to the jury from an adjoining table. The essence of their comments was that three men on the jury were "particular friends" of Horn's, and they would not vote to convict.

J. Emerson Smith was a reporter for the *Denver Post* who covered the entire proceedings. He signed an affidavit on November 5 before the clerk of the U.S. District Court in Colorado to the effect that he had taken his meals at the Inter Ocean and heard remarks in the dining room and at its entrances that two of the jurors were friends of Horn's and would hang the jury. He specifically said they were Homer Payne and H. W. Yoder. He added that "said conversation at a table adjacent to that occupied by the jury was in such a loud tone that the jury easily could have overheard it.... It was not an infrequent occurrence to hear remarks of the same general nature...made in the rotunda of the hotel...."[1] He also stated that Bailiff John Rees protested to the manager of the hotel about a conversation that Rees heard made by people at an adjacent table.

In spite of all the efforts by the defense, Stoll continued to prevail by matching the affidavits with some of his own. One, by J. Emerson Smith, stated that Homer Payne told Smith that he found it difficult to vote against a man he knew and who was a friend, but in the end he had to do his duty.

On September 30, 1903, the Wyoming Supreme Court denied the appeal filed on behalf of Tom Horn by his defense counsel. The eighty-six page decision, the longest yet in Wyoming, was written by Justice Charles N. Potter. Chief Justice Samuel T. Corn and Justice Jesse Knight concurred.[2]

A cloud already hung over Justice Corn from an earlier cattlemen-homesteader confrontation. In 1899 Corn had served as the presiding judge at the tainted coroner's inquest that followed the lynching of Jim Averill and "Cattle Kate" Ellen Watson in Carbon County. The upshot of that proceeding was the release of cattlemen who had lynched the two after the key witness to the lynching mysteriously disappeared. Corn, like Judge Scott, shifted his legal decisions to side with the voters in the Horn affair.

In the appeal to the Supreme Court, Horn's lawyers argued strenuously on a number of points.

The principal argument was that the evidence was not sufficient to convict. They contended that the only evidence was the confession, which they argued should be considered suspect. They argued that other circumstantial evidence did not connect Horn conclusively to the crime.

The Supreme Court, of course, stated that its function was not to set aside a verdict reached by a jury, but only to determine if the conduct of the district court was satisfactory. The justices stated that it is the jury who decides if evidence is sufficient, because the jury is the entity in the best position to do so.

As to the question of whether Horn's so-called confession was truthful and whether he was drunk, the Court pointed out that Horn himself had said that he had been drinking but that he was not impaired. The justices augmented that point by noting the jury had determined he was not so drunk as to warrant disbelieving what he said.

The defense argued that the testimony by the three Denver witnesses about Horn's remarks was inadmissible and not believable, and that Horn's jaw was broken and he could not talk. The Court's position was that their testimony was admissible, and they could not judge whether the testimony was believable or not. Again, that was for the jury to decide. Further, the defense had not objected to it.

In the appeal, the defense referred to an instruction it had requested Judge Scott to give the jury—that confessions by a defendant not in custody are a doubtful species of evidence and should be acted upon with great caution. Scott had refused to issue the instruction. The Court's position was that Horn had admitted making his remarks, they had not been misinterpreted, and the jury determined that he was not so intoxicated that his remarks were inadmissible.

The Court commented about defense efforts to introduce an alternative suspect. It ruled that Stoll's objections to efforts by the defense to introduce testimony in cross-examination about Nickell's neighborhood feuds were proper. The Court noted that the mere casting of suspicion on another party was not adequate. It said that rulings in other states indicated that testimony about threats made by third parties was classified as hearsay and therefore not admissible.

To the defense's contention that testimony about Horn's possible involvement in the Kels Nickell shooting should not have been allowed, the Court ruled that evidence about another crime is allowed if it shows the defendant had the moral capacity to commit it.

Walter Stoll's contention was that Horn's motive was summarized in his statement that the kid was killed because the murderer wanted to prevent him from getting home and raising a commotion. The Court considered that to be adequate.

Stoll said in his closing statements that the defense arguments were improper. They were cited in the Court's decision:

"If the defense felt the remarks were inappropriate it should have objected in a proper manner at the time they were made." The Court pointed out that the defense only made a quiet comment to the judge that it felt the remarks were objectionable.

Finally, the defense introduced points about the jury. Essentially, they pointed to what they believed were third parties acting in prejudicial, hostile ways, actually influencing the jury, and speaking to the jurors individually and as a group. Specifically, it alleged that remarks had been directed toward the jury as they left the courtroom and in the Inter Ocean, including the dining room. However, the prosecution introduced an affidavit that one juror, Tolson, sat across from Homer Payne during meals and did not hear any inappropriate or hostile remarks. The bailiffs also swore that they ensured that no remarks were made to the jury at meals or any other time.

After the Supreme Court's decision the prosecution and defense generated statements from various parties supporting each side's own case.

The defense's effort was for naught.

After the Wyoming Supreme Court rejected his appeal, with his fate weighing on him, Tom wrote an impassioned plea to Charles Ohnhaus, the stenographer who recorded the confession:

Cheyenne, Wyo., October 3, 1903

Chas. J. Ohnhaus, Esq.,
Cheyenne, Wyo.

Sir:

I was informed by the sheriffs and my lawyers that the Supreme Court has refused to grant me a new trial, and that I am to be hanged November 20th.

Now, sir, I am going to make an appeal to you to act on my behalf, and it certainly is not much I ask—only that you make an affidavit to the facts in this supposed confession of mine.

You and I and Snow and LeFors and Stoll all know that you changed your stenographic notes, at the instigation of someone, from what was actually said, to what you wanted me to say. In speaking of this money that was paid to me by George Prentice and that Hi Kelly [a prominent southeast Wyoming cattleman] had given me two $100 bills and a $50 bill.

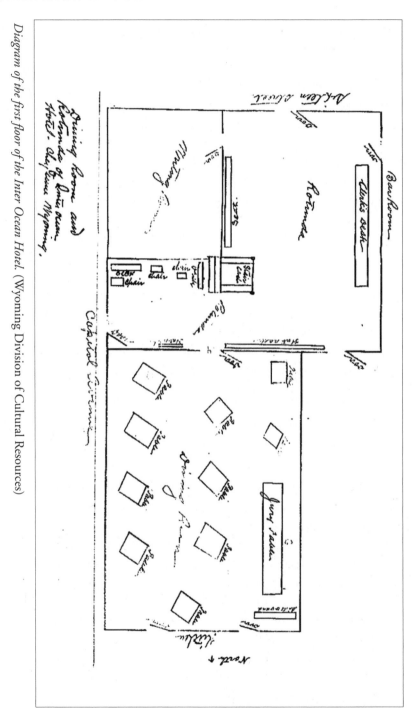

Diagram of the first floor of the Inter Ocean Hotel. (Wyoming Division of Cultural Resources)

Why was that cut out of your notes?

On first entering the Marshal's office LeFors showed me his rifle, and we had some conversation about the sights on the rifle, which he said were aperture sights, and he explained to me how they were used. Why was that cut out of your notes?

You said in your notes that I said that I ran across there bare-footed, when, as a matter of fact, I told LeFors that if he ever wanted to cover his trail to go bare-footed. In speaking of the rock under the boy's head, he asked me if it was a sign, and I said I supposed it was. I never said I put it there, nor did I intimate that I put it there. I did not say, "That is the sign I put out to collect my money."

You put that in at the instigation of someone.

You put in your report that I said: "That was the best shot I ever made, and the dirtiest trick I ever did." You and I, and the others I have mentioned, know that was made up by Stoll or LeFors, and put in the notes by you.

You said in your notes that I was paid a certain sum for killing three men and shooting another one, and every word of that also was manufactured....[3]

Ohnhaus never replied or went to visit Horn.

The same day Horn wrote to John Coble about the Supreme Court decision:

Oct. 3rd, 1903

Dear Johnny,

Judge Burke & Lacy [*sic*] made a gallant fight and lost. I knew in my own mind that they would loose [*sic*] from the time that I first came to trial. I don't know what can be done now and from what the lawyers told me I guess I am in the last ditch but *quién sabe*. I wrote a letter to Chas. J. Ohnhaus today and asked him to come up and tell the truth and that would clear me but although the letter was as strong as I could make it, I have no faith in his telling the truth.

That conversation in the marshal's office was all changed to meet the requirements and Ohnhaus would hardly go back on it now. I don't know why (illegible) would be to try and get the Governor to cut the sentence down to life imprisonment and wait for Snow or Ohnhaus to get around to tell the truth. They will tell it some time but I can't benefit by it much if they tell it all after I am hanged.

I know if there is any thing on earth you can do for me you will do it and anyhow come down and see me if you will be permitted to do so.

It may be, and probably is a fact, that the governor is swayed by the sentiments of the people and if so, he would probably fear that he would be injuring his political career to interfere.

I can't say that I am stuck on being hung or even on going to the pen for life, only if I could get the sentence commuted to life I could make so many good ropes and hackamores.

Write to Proctor and ask him if he will let you come to see me.

Burke & Lacy were badly worked up when they came to see me this morning and I would judge from the looks that they thought there was no hope for me. It will be 48 days yet according to my notch stick before the Hangman gets around. Nov. 20th was the day set.

Anyhow Johnny write me a good long letter. Who is Foreman on the Ranch, who is the cowboys and so on? How is Kate and the rest of the push?

If you can get permission to see me come down.

Kindest regards to all.

Yours truly,

Tom Horn

I have a history of my life written up to the time I came to Wyo and I will finish it up and I want to turn it over to you for maybe by printing it some money can be made out of it. It will only take about two weeks to finish it now. I have already got 400 pages the same as this written. Write soon.

Yours, TH

The final step was to appeal to the acting governor.

On October 29, 1903, the *Cheyenne Daily Leader* reported that Horn had written a novel. The paper corrected itself in the article stating that it was in fact an autobiography that Horn had penned, containing about five hundred pages in four notebooks. Adding that the book had been completed the previous week, it said:

> The work has been presented by Horn to his friend, John C. Coble of Bosler, Wyo., who has loaned it to a friend in this city. No one is permitted to see the work, but it is understood that Mr. Coble contemplates having the book published later, the proceeds to go to Horn, if he escapes the hangman's noose, or to be used in the interests of his father, if the execution is carried out. Horn's father is now a fugitive from justice from the state of Missouri and is living in British Columbia.[4]

In June 1903, with Horn's appeal pending review by the Supreme Court, Joe LeFors resigned from the U.S. Marshal's Service. He signed over his reward in a document typed on the letterhead of the United States Marshal's Office in Cheyenne on June 12, 1903:

> To whom it may concern:
>
> I having this day assigned to Mr. Frank A. Hadsell, of Rawlins, Wyoming, all my right, title, interest and claim in and to all rewards offered by the State of Wyoming and the county of Laramie for information leading to the arrest and conviction of the person or persons who killed and murdered William Nickel [*sic*] on or about July 18, 1901, in the vicinity of Iron Mountain, Wyoming, and having authorized said Frank A. Hadsell to collect the amount of said rewards:
>
> I do hereby authorize said Frank A. Hadsell to pay over to Leslie E. Snow of Cheyenne, Wyoming, an amount equal to eight per cent of the total amount collected as such reward.[5]

LeFors quietly decamped the United States. Bessie LeFors, his wife, received a letter from him written on July 15, 1903, from Cape Gracias a Dios, Nicaragua. The letter stated that he had made arrangements with U.S. Consul W.P. Henley for $100 from his salary to be sent to her by Henley's office each month.

Hadsell referred to the letter in correspondence he wrote to Henley, stating that LeFors was employed by:

> ...A large mining and cattle company, the name of which I do not know, his work being in the interior, out of reach of mails, except at long intervals.
>
> As Mrs. LeFors has not heard from you she requested me to write asking if you had made a remittance. She is in need of money and is worrying fearing a possible loss of the drafts.
>
> Mr. LeFors claims that he has received no communications from here, either from Mrs. LeFors or others. There have been several letters written to him.[6]

LeFors wrote Hadsell a six-page letter on September 21, 1903, from Somoto Grande, Segovia, Nicaragua. Across the top of the letter he wrote and underlined, "Personal." In it he described the ordeal of a forty-one-day, four hundred-mile trip up the Coco River in a small boat paddled by Indians. He described the hot, humid climate, insects worse than he had ever experienced in the United States, native foods, the cattle industry, and the opportunities in mining.

But it appears there was something greater on his mind, which he revealed in the last few sentences. "Write me the news, Frank. I do not see anything at all here, not one paper since I left the States. How is the Horn case?"

Chapter Twenty-six

LAW AND JUSTICE?

THE LAST AVENUE to save Horn from the gallows was a petition to the acting governor, Fenimore Chatterton, to commute the sentence from death to life imprisonment.

Fenimore E. Chatterton was born July 21, 1860, and came to Wyoming in 1878. A native of Vermont, he was raised in Washington, where his father was a government attorney. The family moved in 1878 to Chicago and then Grinnell, Iowa. While still in his teens, Chatterton accepted an offer to become the bookkeeper for John Hugus, the post trader at Fort Steele, east of Rawlins.

Chatterton obtained a license to practice law and entered the profession in Carbon County. Early in his career he developed a political instinct and attempted to align himself with those whose association would, he felt, be to his benefit. While that instinct served him well for a period, it was not without consequences in the aftermath of the Tom Horn affair.

Early in Chatterton's career, his Carbon County law partner, David Craig, parted company with him because he felt Chatterton had been unduly sympathetic to and in the pocket of the cattlemen accused in the lynching of Cattle Kate/Ellen Watson. Craig suspected that Chatterton had accepted a bribe but did not come out and make that accusation.[1]

Chatterton became Wyoming's secretary of state, the state's second-ranked elected official, under Governor DeForest Richards in January 1899.

Chatterton succeeded Richards as governor in April 1903 after the latter died in office. When the Supreme Court sustained the judgment of the lower court and set the November 20 date for Horn's hanging, the Governor was besieged with appeals for commutation.

Chatterton said he learned of a plot that would go into effect if he commuted Horn's death sentence to life imprisonment., He believed Horn's friends planned to free the detective during the train ride to the penitentiary in Rawlins. With a relay of horses in place, Horn would be able to reach the Mexican border and the sanctuary of his earlier years. Chatterton speculated that Horn's former employers were afraid that he might implicate them and wanted him out of the country.[2]

The governor received letters from St. Louis, Omaha, Chicago and Denver threatening his own assassination if he did not commute the sentence.

Horn signed a written statement to Chatterton, accusing LeFors, Stoll, and Ohnhaus of doctoring the stenographic notes Ohnhaus had taken during the "confession" in the marshal's office.

Chatterton obtained Ohnhaus's original stenographic notes and reviewed them with his secretary, who knew the form of shorthand Ohnhaus had used. Chatterton concluded that they corresponded with the testimony at the trial. More startling is his determination that the notes were complete. Chatterton felt that Horn's only defense was that the entire conversation with LeFors was a "josh." He agreed with the Supreme Court that it was the jury's prerogative to determine if Horn was sincere in his statements.

The defense countered with affidavits presented to the governor in Horn's behalf. Glendolene Kimmell presented a lengthy statement in an affidavit[3] made on October 13, 1903, before notary Laura M. Walker in Jackson County, Missouri, stating that Victor Miller was the killer and that both he and his father had admitted as much to her.

She also indicated that Jim Miller told her how Joe LeFors had approached him to join forces to finger Tom Horn:

> After James Miller and I had gotten back to the Miller Ranch from attendance at the frontier celebration in Cheyenne Miller privately told me that while he had been in Cheyenne, Joe LeFors had approached him with the proposition that if he (Miller) would make out an affidavit implicating Tom Horn as the murderer of Nickell..., if he (Miller) would take the stand against Tom Horn; that Joe LeFors would personally see to it

Fenimore Chatterton. (Wyoming Division of Cultural Resources)

that neither Miller nor any member of his family would be held responsible for the murder of Nickell, and that further, LeFors would give Miller five hundred dollars—one-half of the reward money. Miller further said to me that he had replied to LeFors that he wasn't making it his business to run down the murderer of William Nickell; that the voters and tax-payers elected and paid officers for that purpose.... Miller further said to me that he saw through LeFors's game; that LeFors didn't care anything for him; that if he did what LeFors wanted him to and Tom Horn was convicted, he would never get any of the money, and he might get hanged "alongside of Tom Horn."

Walter Stoll had Kimmell arrested and indicted for perjury, and she was placed under house arrest until after Horn's demise. Stoll, however, dropped the charges after the hanging when he "discovered that according to Wyoming law perjury could only be committed in court."[4]

Three affidavits damning other parties were filed as part of Horn's appeal concurrent with Kimmell's statement:[5]

Edward T. Clark [formerly part of Horn's defense team], being duly sworn deposes and says that on or about February 11, 1903, Joseph LeFors and he, the deponent, while in the smoking compartment of a train on the B. & N. railroad between Sheridan, Wyoming, and Alliance, Nebraska...LeFors said to this deponent that Stoll had advised the county commissioners not to pay the reward offered by the county for the arrest and conviction of Tom Horn to him (LeFors) until the appeal had been decided by the Supreme Court. That he (LeFors) had learned that Stoll had said that he wished to withhold the payment of the reward in order to keep him (LeFors) in line. LeFors then said that Stoll had better be careful how he treated him since he [Stoll] knew that LeFors had knowledge of evidence which would clear Tom Horn. He said that if he had been working on the other side of the case he would have cleared Tom Horn.

Albert W. Bristol, Jr., swore before notary Jennie M. Tupper a statement that:

> ...He is acquainted with the two Miller boys, Victor and Gus Miller, though he does not clearly distinguish one from the other; that some time about the time when Tom Horn was tried for killing Willie Nickell, that is to say, about the month of October, 1902, the said two Miller boys were at the ranch of Albert W. Bristol, the father of this affiant, for the purpose of getting some bulls that had been sold to the Millers by Albert W. Bristol. While there affiant asked one of the Miller boys... whether he thought Tom Horn was guilty of killing Willie Nickell, and the said Miller, whether Vic or Gus affiant cannot say, answered, "No, Tom Horn never killed the boy. I happen to know who killed him."

On November 3, Alfred Cook swore an affidavit in Albany County that John (Jack) Martin had made a statement incriminating the Millers:

> That about October 1901 and some months prior to the arrest of Tom Horn for the murder of Willie Nickell, Joe LeFors came to this affiant and inquired where he could find [Jack] Martin, and affiant told him. Thereupon the said LeFors hunted up Martin. The next night Martin repeated to this affiant what he said, the exact words of which affiant does not now remember, but such statement is in words as follows, that "Joe LeFors can come to Martin, stating to him that he (LeFors) had been investigating the killing of Willie Nickell and that his investigations came close to Jim Miller and his family, and that Jim Miller had paid him (LeFors) five hundred dollars to cease his investigations of Miller, and his family.

In addition, Martin at that time repeated a conversation with LeFors, something to the effect that (LeFors speaking), "It would be an elegant opportunity to cinch Tom Horn...."

Cook continued that he had known Martin for fifteen years and he believed that Martin would not make a false statement and that his reputation for truth and veracity was good when speaking in earnest, although he had the reputation of "engaging in contests in the way of imaginary stories in a jocular way."

Martin's statements seemed to twist around each other. While LeFors, of course, denied everything Martin had said about him, others said that he was in general an honest man and could be believed. One of Martin's statements, the one about having seen Horn in Laramie the day after the shooting, was to Horn's detriment.

Most of the major cattlemen who had previously employed Horn quietly distanced themselves. Ora Haley insulated himself further by signing an affidavit that bolstered Martin's statement about the day he had seen Horn. Haley said, "affiant has known the said John Martin for at least fifteen years...and he knows the reputation of the said John Martin in the community in which he resides,...for truth, veracity and integrity is good."[6]

Other prominent men of good standing similarly spoke highly of Martin. However, he had boasted that he was part of the Younger brothers gang of Missouri and had played a prominent role in the posse that pursued the Wilcox train robbers. Regardless of his truthfulness, as the appeal process moved swiftly ahead it became more apparent that the governor had made up his mind.

Glendolene Kimmell had four meetings with the governor in his office. He became convinced that she was simply attempting to gain a commutation of Horn's sentence to life imprisonment, intending to deny later that Victor had made the confession to her. Kimmell's words were by now worthless since they amounted to diametric opposition to her earlier testimony in the inquest which had helped exonerate the Millers. Chatterton wrote:

> If the Kimmell affidavit be true, a great deal of the other matter presented in support of the application [to commute Horn's sentence] is irrelevant and could only be construed as an endeavor to create a suspicion or feeling of uncertainty in my mind. Certainty is what I have been looking for. If the Kimmell affidavit is true, it is all that is required, and Tom Horn should be pardoned. [But,] if this affidavit is true,... should not the facts have been presented to the court rather than to me?[7]

The governor decided that if the assertions in Kimmell's statement were true, the defense should and would have known of them before the trial ended. (She commented after Horn's execution that she had made her findings available to Horn's lawyers, but they had told her she would not be needed. Realistically, they would have known that she was a legal hot potato since she had already cleared the Millers during the inquest.)

Further, Chatterton felt that many of her assertions were nothing more than theories, and even if they were statements of fact, they could have been presented to the Supreme Court before that body reached its decision. If public opinion could be judged by newspaper editorials both in Wyoming and other states, his decision was correct.

The papers in Cheyenne had been neutral during Horn's trial, doubtless wanting to support the winning side regardless of the verdict. After it was rendered, however, the *Leader* editorialized that it reflected a new step toward a more civilized society.

Following the announcement of Chatterton's conclusions, the *Cheyenne Tribune* stated:

> The masterly manner in which Governor Chatterton handled and eventually decided the application for a commutation of sentence for Tom Horn is highly commendable.... He gave ample evidence, not only of the fact that he is an able chief executive, but that he is also one of the ablest lawyers of the Far West.[8]

Despite this type of praise, the prophecy by the cattlemen's anonymous representative that Chatterton would be defeated in any further attempts at high office was correct. Although generally supported by the public and the press, he was defeated at the Republican State Convention by what he called the "Machine" (the Francis E. Warren political machine), and the nomination went to Bryant B. Brooks of Casper, a cattleman. Brooks went on to win the election in 1904.

Years after Chatterton's decision on Tom Horn's fate, family members spoke of an ominous sound the acting governor had heard while walking home from his office after a day's deliberations on the matter. It was snap of a rifle hammer from behind a tree.

Chapter Twenty-seven

ESCAPED!

TWO EVENTS, ONE perhaps more a fiction created by the local
newspaper and the other certainly fact, contributed to the failure
of the appeals initiated by Tom Horn's lawyers. Any effort by
Horn to escape, whether imagined or real, reminded citizens that he
was a dangerous man who should be dealt with once and for all. An
attempt to escape seemingly would acknowledge his guilt.

The first came in the form of a newspaper article reporting that a
plot to spring Horn from jail had been foiled by the authorities.

In November 1902 a young cowpoke named Hubert Herr was
jailed in Cheyenne for thirty days for stealing a saddle. The suspicion
was that Horn's employers, including John Coble, had arranged for
Herr to deliver plans to Horn for his escape.

The story the newspaper proffered went like this: as Horn exer-
cised on a catwalk in front of his cell on the upper tier of the jail, he
dropped wadded-up notes he had written on pieces of toilet paper to
young Herr. Herr, who was enjoying a degree of freedom in the jail
yard due to the mild nature of his offense, passed these notes to Tom's
conspirators. The notes detailed a plan to deposit five sticks of dynamite at the base of the masonry jail wall.

The night before the jail was to be blown, a snowball would be
placed on the windowsill of St. John's hall across Ferguson Avenue
(now Carey) from the jail to the east. Horn, visible in a window as he
took his evening exercise, would light a cigarette to confirm he had
seen the signal.

The next day an unbranded horse would be hitched at a specific
rack, with warm clothes, mittens, shoes, and a six shooter hidden in
an adjacent alley. That evening, when he lit his smoke, the dynamite
would be ignited.

But Hubert Herr lost his nerve. Fearful that Tom's friends would double-cross and kill him to prevent him from telling of his complicity in the plot, when he was released he went straight to the newspaper. The *Daily Leader* broke with the story the next morning. That was the end of the cabal's plans, if any really did exist, to spring Tom from jail by means of explosives.

The only evidence of a man named "Herr" in Cheyenne jail records is an entry that a "T.P. Herr" from Lincoln (probably Lincoln, Nebraska) was jailed with a sixty-day sentence for grand larceny on November 17, 1902, and discharged on January 21, 1903, after serving sixty-four days and paying $3.45 in court costs.[1] So, indeed, he was in the jail at the same time as Horn.

In later years, speculation was that the newspaper had made the whole thing up. Perhaps looking for a good story, the editor was said to have approached young Herr with an offer of cash plus a train ticket to San Francisco in exchange for use of his name and the story. The truth will never be known, but Hubert Herr disappeared, adding more to the legend of Tom Horn.

In the meantime, Attorney Lacey had achieved the delay of Tom Horn's execution date originally scheduled for January 9, while he prepared for the appeal.

An accomplished thief and safecracker by the name of "Driftwood" Jim McCloud was imprisoned in the cell adjacent to Horn's. McCloud, along with Tom O'Day and Earl Shobe, had collaborated in breaking into the post office in Buffalo early in 1903, where they blew the safe with black powder. O'Day previously had drifted in and out of Butch Cassidy's Hole-in-the-Wall Gang, while Shobe was a known horse thief and accomplished bronc rider in the rodeo circuit.[2]

Shobe and McCloud were also implicated in the murder of a prominent sheepman by the name of Minnick in the Big Horn Basin. Shobe, though wounded, escaped the posse, but McCloud was captured and jailed in Thermopolis. Tom O'Day intended to mount an effort to free him, but became less emboldened when he saw the size of the lawmen's contingent. McCloud was sent to Cheyenne, partly to prevent the jailbreak and partly to prevent a threatened lynching.

In Cheyenne, McCloud complained of stomach problems, and a medicine was prescribed for him to take with warm water. Twice a day, Deputy Sheriff Dick Proctor brought a cup of water to McCloud's cell.

The remote mechanism that opened McCloud's cell door also opened Tom Horn's at the same time. On Sunday, August 9, at eight that morning, the unarmed deputy opened the doors and ascended the steel steps to the upper level where the convicts' cells were located along the west wall. The jail yard was below to the east.

Proctor found his two charges sitting on a bench on the catwalk. He opened another door that provided access to the catwalk and reached in to hand the water to McCloud. At that, both prisoners sprang and pinned Proctor's arm between the door·and the jam.

The three struggled ferociously, with Proctor at one point lifting McCloud and nearly throwing him over the railing to the concrete floor on the lower level. Horn, however, had a stranglehold around Proctor's neck, and he was forced to relent.

Binding Proctor with window cord, Horn and McCloud led him down to the sheriff's office, where they made a desperate search for weapons. They either overlooked or could not unlock a cabinet next to the door, where five thirty-thirty Winchesters were stored. McCloud then found a rifle on top of the cabinet, but no ammunition.

At the time, Deputy Les Snow was sunning himself on the steps at the south entrance to the complex. Desperate to find ammunition and fearful Snow might appear, McCloud and Horn threatened to bash Proctor's skull in with the butt of the rifle unless he found weapons and ammunition. Proctor, playing a delaying game, told them ammunition was locked in the safe, where he knew a handgun was hidden. The two prisoners loosened the bonds on Proctor's hands, so that he could work the combination lock.

Proctor fumbled with the dial, hoping help would arrive. In the meantime, McCloud discovered that the Winchester he held was loaded, and seeing through Proctor's delaying tactics, said, "Open that door, you son of a bitch, or I'll blow your brains out." Proctor opened the safe, but asked McCloud to get the key to the inner door of the safe from a desk drawer. As McCloud turned toward the desk,

Deputy Sheriff Les Snow in Sheridan, Wyoming, some years after his retirement. (Wyoming Division of Cultural Resources)

Proctor grabbed the handgun hidden in the safe. Horn, however, had been eyeing the deputy and leaped before he could make use of the weapon. The three then struggled for ten minutes, according to the *Cheyenne Daily Leader*, until Les Snow sauntered into the building and down the hall.

McCloud heard Snow's footsteps, and with Proctor now subdued, waited inside the door with the rifle at the ready. Snow opened the door but immediately slammed it shut and ran out of the building, firing his rifle into the air to attract attention. McCloud then abandoned Horn and Proctor and ran out through a west door. He ran to a stable where a buckskin horse was in a stall, threw a bridle over the animal's head, and led it out.

Sheriff Ed Smalley, who lived in the sheriff's residence adjoining the jail to the north, heard the shot fired by Snow and stepped out his front door to Ferguson Street. He also heard a warning called by Ed Durbin. Colonel E. A. Slack, who lived nearby, shouted to Smalley that someone was leading a horse out of the stable. At that, Smalley fired a shot, which frightened the animal and caused it to rear back.

McCloud attempted to control the animal and keep it between him and Smalley, but the sheriff fired twice more. McCloud then dropped the rope, ran west through the alley and turned north on Eddy Avenue (now Pioneer). Smalley ran into his office to get a rifle.

A mail clerk, Pat Hennessey, heard the commotion and realized there was a jailbreak. He grabbed a double-barreled shotgun, ran into the street, and bumped into McCloud. But, not knowing who the escapee was, he hesitated. McCloud sensed Hennessey's confusion and said, "Tom Horn broke out of jail. Have you seen him running this way?"

Hennessey replied, "No. Which way did he go?"

McCloud did not bother to reply, but ran into an alley between Twentieth and Twenty-First Streets, jumped a fence, and ran into a barn behind a residence. A girl who was employed there saw him enter the barn and alerted a police officer, John Nolan, who had arrived with Oscar Lamm. Lamm was armed with a rifle, which he pointed at the barn while he yelled, "There he is! I can kill him now." Lamm could not see McCloud, but the bluff worked. McCloud stepped out with his hands up, leaving the rifle behind. Nolan and Lamm led him back to the jail.

Tom Horn, meanwhile, had continued to struggle with Dick Proctor for a few minutes more before Horn twisted the pistol out of Proctor's hand. Proctor had, however, already slipped the safety on the gun, an automatic, with which Horn was not familiar. The newspaper reported that Horn then attempted to shoot the deputy two or three times, but the gun did not fire.

Horn ran out the same door McCloud had exited, but hearing the commotion in the alley, ran to the south toward the front of the courthouse. A crowd of roughly fifty people had assembled after hearing church bells sound the alarm and saw him turn and run east toward Capitol Avenue.

Sheriff Ed Smalley. (Wyoming Division of Cultural Resources)

The operator of a merry-go-round that had been in town about a week, O. M. Aldrich, was in a tent across the street south of the courthouse. He grabbed a small caliber Iver Johnson revolver, walked across the street, and spotted Horn when he ran around the corner heading east. Aldrich snapped a shot at him. Horn turned and again tried to fire the automatic. When it did not fire, he ran east on Nineteenth Street before turning north at Capitol. He jumped the fence of a residence, ran north across the yard toward Twentieth and vaulted a fence.

Aldrich was right behind him and fired the small pistol again. The shot creased Horn's head, stunning him, and he fell face down. He struggled to his feet and again attempted to fire at Aldrich. At that point Robert LaFontaine, who lived nearby on Ferguson Street, arrived on the scene. He and Aldrich tackled Horn.

Tom Horn (center) being escorted back to jail down Ferguson (now Carey) after his failed escape. (Wyoming Division of Cultural Resources)

Aldrich struck Horn several times on the back of the head and neck with his small revolver, drawing blood, and giving rise later to reports that he had been shot. Police Officer Otto Ahrens reached the scene. Horn surrendered the pistol and said, "Well, Otto, I guess they have got me, all right."

A second officer, named Stone, approached, and he and Ahrens walked with Horn between them west on Twentieth and south on Ferguson. Les Snow, who had long harbored animosity toward Horn, approached on horseback and tried to hit Horn on the head with the butt of his rifle. Stone warded off the blow with his arm. Several citizens then disarmed Snow, creating "another ripple of excitement," the *Leader* reported the next morning.

After McCloud was brought back to the jail, a mob started to howl for a lynching. With the arrival of Horn back at the jail, the furor

grew. Kels Nickell, at the forefront of the trouble makers, "did everything in his power to excite the people up to the lynching point. He
loudly berated the officers for what he considered the lax discipline at
the jail and for permitting the men to escape. He talked wildly and
gesticulated frantically during his inflammatory utterances.... Nickell
was told to leave the area," the paper said.

That afternoon and evening there was more talk of lynching. Ed
Smalley, however, had quietly gathered a dozen men as deputies to
guard the jail during the night. In the end, cooler heads prevailed,
and no mob action ensued.

Later, speculation arose that the jailbreak was a setup engineered
by some of Tom's former employers to help establish Horn's guilt
even further. Alternately, others speculated that the cattlemen wanted
to get Horn killed before he implicated them or that they genuinely
were trying to spring him.

C. B. "Charley" Irwin, along with John Coble, were among the
few friends who stood by Tom Horn until the end. Charley's granddaughter, Betty Steele, stated[3] that a stool pigeon had been planted in
the Laramie County jail to advise the authorities about any impending break by Horn. "He never had a chance," she said. She was right.

Chapter Twenty-eight

HANGED BY THE NECK

O N NOVEMBER 14, 1903, six days before the hanging, the
Rawlins Republican reported that Bob Meldrum had written
to Horn:

Tom Boy Mine, Telluride, Colo.
Nov. 3, 1903

Tom Horn, Esq., Cheyenne Wyo.

Dear Tom: I see by the daily press that things are coming your
way at last, which pleases me very much. Lots of people here
want to see you clear and in fact are positive that you will. By
the way if the worst come to the worse YOU WILL NEVER
HANG, as I know of a way that will get you out of that, so
don't lose any sleep on that part of the programme....

Now, remember what I tell you. It will be all OK. I got it
STRAIGHT AND I MAY BE THERE TO SEE IT.[1]

The letter was not delivered to Horn, the *Republican* said.

Horn meanwhile wrote John Coble a letter with an air of finality
on November 17, 1903:

Dear Johnnie:

Proctor told me that it was all over with me except the
applause part of the game.

You know they can't hurt a Christian, and as I am prepared, it
is all right.

I thoroughly appreciate all you have done for me. No one
could have done more. Kindly accept my thanks, for if ever a
man had a true friend, you have proven yourself one to me.

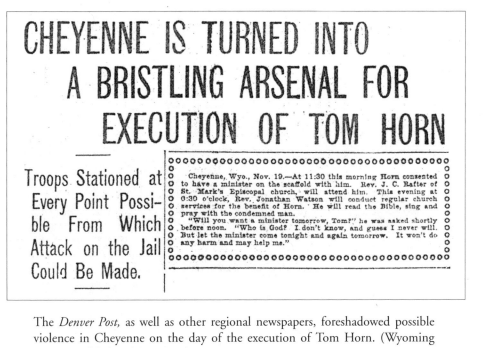

CHEYENNE IS TURNED INTO A BRISTLING ARSENAL FOR EXECUTION OF TOM HORN

Troops Stationed at Every Point Possible From Which Attack on the Jail Could Be Made.

Cheyenne, Wyo., Nov. 19.—At 11:30 this morning Horn consented to have a minister on the scaffold with him. Rev. J. C. Rafter of St. Mark's Episcopal church, will attend him. This evening at 6:30 o'clock, Rev. Jonathan Watson will conduct regular church services for the benefit of Horn. He will read the Bible, sing and pray with the condemned man.

"Will you want a minister tomorrow, Tom?" he was asked shortly before noon. "Who is God? I don't know, and guess I never will. But let the minister come tonight and again tomorrow. It won't do any harm and may help me."

The *Denver Post,* as well as other regional newspapers, foreshadowed possible violence in Cheyenne on the day of the execution of Tom Horn. (Wyoming Division of Cultural Resources)

Remember me kindly to all my friends, if I have any besides yourself. Burke and Lacey have not shown up.

I want you to always understand that the stenographic notes taken in the United States Marshal's office were all changed to suit the occasion. The notes read at the trial were not the original notes at all. Everything of an incriminating nature read in those notes was manufactured and put in. It won't do any good to kick at that now, so let 'er go.

If any one profits by my being hung, I would be sorry to see them disappointed.

It would, perhaps, be somewhat of a trying meeting for you to come to see me now. Do as you like. It might cause you a good deal of pain. I am just the same as ever, and will remain so.

The governor's decision was no surprise to me, for I was tried, convicted and hung before I left the ranch. My famous confession was also made days before I came to town.

The militia preventing curiosity seekers from approaching the courthouse. The building in the rear is the Masonic Temple, as seen from in front of the courthouse east along Nineteenth Street. (American Heritage Center, University of Wyoming and Wyoming Division of Cultural Resources)

I told Burke to give you some writing I did; be sure and get it. You will not need anything to remember me by, but you will have that anyway. Anything else I may have around the ranch is yours.

I won't need anything where I am going. I have an appointment with some Christian ladies tomorrow, and will write you of their visit tomorrow night.

I will drop you a line every day now, till the Reaper comes along. Kindest to all.

> Yours truly,
> Tom Horn[2]

Newspapers were full of rumored plots to set Horn free by illegal means. According to two sources, on November 18 Tom learned that an effort to spring him free would be made the next day. Butch Cassidy, it was said, would be the leader. While the rumor grew, and it is possible the two knew each other, they seem an unlikely alliance.

Nevertheless, the morning of the nineteenth a message appeared in the snow outside Horn's cell, "Keep Your Nerve."[3]

Sheriff Ed Smalley had no intent of allowing his most infamous prisoner to escape. With assistance from the governor, he arranged for armed troops to surround the block where the jail and courthouse were located. A Gatling gun from Fort D. A. Russell was mounted on the roof, with Sergeant Mahon, "an expert gunner of the Thirteenth Artillery" stationed in the jail every night.

Sheriffs from other communities were stationed in the complex, armed with shotguns and repeating rifles. Cheyenne's mood was apprehensive. Cattlemen gathered at the Cheyenne Club. Saloons boomed, with bets being placed on whether Tom Horn would hang or not. Small groups whispered their hopes, fears, and—for some—plans.

The Friday morning of November 20, 1903, dawned cold, gray, and windy for the last legal execution in Laramie County. The gallows had been erected within earshot of Horn's cell, but was obscured from his view by a canvas curtain. The sound of its construction was in itself a grim omen to the condemned man. The structure stood in the northeast corner of the jail, with a nine-by-eleven-foot area in front of it for witnesses. To reach it, Horn would have walk to the north and make two right-hand turns.

Cheyenne architect James P. Julian had designed the gallows in 1892. He developed the device, adapted from a design used in Colorado, so that it did not require an executioner to spring the trapdoors.

The Julian gallows operated when the weight of the condemned man depressed the two leaves of the trapdoors, the edges of which were held slightly above the level of the surrounding platform. The weight pulled a plug from a can full of water, which was at the opposite end of a board from a counterweight. As water drained from the can, its weight diminished. When the weight became less than that of the counterweight, the counterweight dropped.

Attached to the counterweight was a rope that ran through a pulley; the other end of the rope was attached to a vertical four-by-four inch post that supported the trapdoors. The four-by-four was hinged at two places; when the counterweight dropped the rope jerked the post at the hinges, springing the trapdoors.

The gallows, in the "before" and "after" positions. (Steve Brown, author's photos)

Father Kennedy from Saint Mary's Catholic Cathedral and Reverend Watson of Saint Mark's Episcopal Church, accompanied by three women, visited Horn the day before the hanging. The minister conducted a short service for condemned prisoners, and the three women sang a hymn.

Horn awoke early, ate a big breakfast brought to him by Dick Proctor, and spent the rest of the morning writing letters.

The upper platform of the gallows was at the same level as his cell on the second floor of the jail. Shortly before eleven, he walked from his cell, accompanied by Cahill, Smalley, and Proctor. Newspaper reporters were crowded into a small area at the end of the platform adjoining Horn's cell, while visiting sheriffs and other witnesses were below on the lower level of an open area.

Glancing at the sheriffs below, Horn said to Ed Smalley, "Ed, that's the sickest looking lot of damned sheriffs I ever seen."

Horn had requested that Charley and Frank Irwin, who were on the lower level, sing "Life's Railway to Heaven," a favorite hymn. Charley said, "Would you like us to sing, Tom?"

"Yes, I'd like that," Tom replied.

As Dick Proctor buckled the straps around Horn's arms and legs, the two brothers sang—loudly—some said extra loudly so that if Horn confessed or made any last-minute statement implicating his employers, he would not be heard. Horn remained silent to the last.

A clergyman read a prayer for the dying. Ed Smalley asked Tom, "Would you like to say anything?"

"No."

Charley Irwin asked, "Tom, did you confess to the preacher?"

"No."

Proctor placed and adjusted the noose around Horn's neck and drew a black hood over his head. Smalley and Cahill lifted the condemned man onto the trap.

Witnesses could hear the sound of water draining from the can. Ed Smalley buried his face in the crook of his arm which rested against the gallows, and he was trembling.

From beneath the hood came a calm voice, "What's the matter, getting nervous I might tip over?"

Horn said to Cahill, "Joe, they tell me you're married now. I hope you're doing well. Treat her right."

Thirty-one seconds after he was lifted onto the trap it sprang, and Tom Horn dropped four and a half feet, leaving his head and shoulders above the upper level of the gallows. His body made a one-half turn, so that it faced away from the spectators. Newspaperman John Charles Thompson's report stated that the heavy hangman's knot had knocked Horn unconscious as he fell. Although his neck was broken, he died of strangulation, the cause of death in most hanging executions. His heart continued to beat for sixteen minutes, at which point he was declared dead by two attending physicians. Horn's body was cut down after another four minutes.

Dick Proctor had calculated the length of the drop required carefully, fearing that with a man of Horn's weight a longer fall would tear his head off. Proctor may have been influenced by an earlier event in Newcastle, when a mob lynched Diamond L. "Slim" Clifton for the murder of a young couple, Louella and John Church. A plaque at the location of the lynching at the Belle Fourche River reads:

Tom Horn. This photo is believed to be the last taken of him. (Wyoming Division of Cultural Resources)

People throughout northeastern Wyoming, angered by the grisly deed, stormed the jail, took the prisoner from Sheriff Billy Miller at gunpoint, and dragged Slim to the bridge. Masked men slipped the noose around Slim's neck and dropped him from the bridge, neatly decapitating him. Such was frontier justice.[4]

Horn's body was taken to the Gleason Mortuary in Cheyenne. His brother, Charles, who lived in Boulder, Colorado, had the Boulder County sheriff transport the body on the Union Pacific via Denver to Boulder for the funeral there.

The sadness felt by Tom Horn's family during the entire episode is reflected in letters to him from his sisters. Nancy Adams wrote to him from Granger, Missouri, on November 28, 1902:[5]

My Darling Brother—

This is Thanksgiving. Do you ever remember that it was observed when we were children? I don't & we are not so very old either. Now-a-days it is very generally observed here. We have so much to be thankful from this year. Bountiful crops, good prices & good health. Welton is so much better this fall. He has worked considerable. I have gotten so fleshy and rheumatic I can't help out of doors much this fall; I hope you are well. My grandchildren all have the whooping cough. Does it seem odd to you that I have grandchildren? Last winter one of my daughters had the small pox, also her baby.

Do you hear from any of the family? I haven't for such a long time, except Charley [Charles Horn, Tom's older brother, who lived in Boulder, Colorado]. Lizzie [Charles's wife] wouldn't let him come to your trial. He drinks so hard & she was afraid he would get into trouble....

We were all so sure you would be acquitted, & the boys [family in Missouri] were all so busy over the election they could do nothing. But they will go to work in earnest now. I find we have none of our influence even though our father is gone. You must be worn out waiting for something to turn up. These trials are such tedious things and so uncertain....

Good bye for this time. You will hear from some of us soon.
"Be of good cheer."
With love,

Sister Nancy

A younger sister, Maude Simpson, wrote from Easton, Washington, on January 28, 1903: [6]

Nan wrote to me some time ago that you had been convicted, and I have tried a number of times since to write but I just couldn't do it. I have not seen any papers concerning your affairs. Matt has kept them all from me.

Why haven't you written to me or had your lawyer write?

I am expecting Mother in a few days. She does not know that you have been convicted and I don't want her to know. I can make her believe you are all right and I shall do so.

I can't write a cheerful letter, Tom, for I haven't had a cheerful thought since I heard of your conviction. Matt promised me I should come and see you. Do write me or have your lawyer write for I want to hear from you so bad....

P.S. Your little namesake, Tommie, is quite sick with the "grip."

Alice Horn Loney, his youngest sister, wrote from Elgin, British Columbia: [7]

Elgin, BC. November—[date illegible] 1903.

To my dear brother Tom: You may never see this letter as I am told your sentence is for the 20th. However, I am hoping that things are all for the best and that you may at the last moment be proved guiltless which I believe you are, or pardoned. However, if it is God's will that you should be martyred for another crime, we must learn to say, "Thy will be done." I have often thought I would write you, but I have forgotten when I wrote last and I don't know if I told you that Aus [Austin] was lost while out sealing last year. He left April, 1903, and went to the Bering Seas. They had a fine catch and it was fine weather so their schooner stayed longer than the rest and when the fine

Tom Horn's body was removed under a rubber sheet to the waiting horse-drawn hearse. His brother, Charles, had obtained the assistance of the Boulder County, Colorado, sheriff, at right, to escort the body to Boulder for burial. (Wyoming Division of Cultural Resources)

weather broke it broke with a terrible storm and he was lost. He and all aboard. No one lived to tell the fate of ship or crew. Poor boy, how I miss him. Maud [*sic*] hoots at the idea of my wearing mourning for him, but I feel as if I could never wear anything but black again. Maud is here with her two children. Two girls, one is my girl and one yours [refers to their given names]. One is Alice and one Thomasine. They are both nice children but Thomasine is a fine child. Perhaps a little willful, but very cute and can say anything. Well, Tom, I can't write tonight so good-bye. Good-bye it may be forever, but I am trying to be very hopeful. Both that God's blessing rests upon you now and always is the wish of your sister, Alice.

The funeral was held on Sunday, November 22. According to the *Boulder Daily Camera* issue of the next day, Reverend G. Lane conducted private services at the Buchheit Undertaking Rooms. The

Denver Post reported that the procession to Columbia Cemetery was one of the largest ever in Boulder, with 2,500 people in the assembly. Tom's mother, Mary, was seventy-two at the time. She lived in Boulder next door to one of the pallbearers, W. B. Inglefield, a bartender.[8]

John Coble paid for the coffin, gravestone, and all funeral expenses.

Tom Horn's grave is in the southwest quadrant of the Pioneer Cemetery at Ninth and Walnut, adjacent to that of his brother Charles Horn and Charles's wife, Elizabeth.

The Laramie County Commissioners arranged for a permanent historical exhibit to be placed at the approximate location where Tom Horn's execution took place. It can be visited on the second floor of the south wing of the present historic Laramie County Courthouse.

Chapter Twenty-nine

TERRIFYING, RUTHLESS, A FINE FELLOW

NO QUESTION, THERE was blood on the moon by the time Tom Horn arrived in Wyoming. He arrived ten years too late. The "times, they were a-changin'" and neither his employers nor he fully grasped how he became the focal point of the social and economic conflicts of the late nineteenth and early twentieth centuries. Glendolene Kimmell saw it clearly when she wrote in the epilogue of his 1904 autobiography: "Riding hard, drinking hard, fighting hard, so passed his years until he was crushed between the grindstones of two civilizations."

Yes, Tom Horn was an instrument of big business in its efforts to turn the clock back…guilty of other murders. …taking the law into his own hands…intimidating…terrifying…ruthless…hated…and very, very good at what he was hired for.

And who killed Willie Nickell? We will never know for sure; no eyewitnesses came forward. The only hard evidence is Glendolene Kimmell's affidavit, which is hardly hard at all because she changed her story from her earlier sworn testimony. Yet one name lingers and is the one that most often surfaces as the likely suspect: Victor Miller.

Another question has lingered. Here we had a man who earned an exemplary reputation for his work with the army in the Southwest—at least what we know of it. People who knew him well, really well, spoke highly of him: "a fine fellow"… "kind to children…."

Did something happen to him? Was there a shift, a degradation in character that Doc Shores observed? No conscience? Did something get into him? Did something go wrong?

Was it from the frustration of never having accumulated wealth? Was it an unconscious decision, fueled by resentment and alcohol, to use his abilities to earn big fees without regard to the means?

Thanks to Dr. Courtney Brown, a psychiatrist and an acquaintance of the author, it is clearer now that all these characteristics were already present, but had not always been observed. Horn's latent, abusive nastiness evidenced itself in childhood, transferred from his father. He administered it to the small ranchers he investigated and his victims.

                           ❦

The retrial of Tom Horn in the historic Laramie County Courthouse[1] occurred on September 16 and 17, 1993. Several years beforehand, Peter G. Chronis, a reporter for the *Denver Post,* had suggested the retrial. Unofficial retrials had been conducted for Henry Plummer, a Montana sheriff and outlaw, and for Dr. Henry Mudd, the army doctor who had set John Wilkes Booth's broken leg after Booth assassinated President Lincoln.

The presiding judge was retired Wyoming Supreme Court Justice C. Stuart Brown. Robert Skar, County Attorney for Wyoming's Hot Springs County, was prosecutor, and Joseph W. Moch, a trial lawyer from Grand Rapids, Michigan, represented Horn as counsel for the defense.

Despite a thorough and assertive effort by the prosecution, the jury found Tom Horn innocent. The principal thrust of the defense was an attack on the transcription of Horn's confession. When Charles Ohnhaus documented Horn's remarks, he did not try to write down every word; he recorded only the parts he felt were most important. Horn's attorney surmised that Wyoming people have a strong feeling for fairness, so he emphasized the incomplete nature of the transcript. He pointed out the jury had a right and a duty to know the full extent of Horn's conversation with LeFors, not just the parts Ohnhaus chose to write down. Jurors who spoke with the author after the retrial consistently confirmed that they found the incomplete transcript troubling.

Another component of the defense mentioned by some observers, more subtle but perhaps equally powerful, was Attorney Moch's inclination to stand next to the jury box with the jurors to his immediate right. His position placed him diagonally across from the witness stand. In effect, he was inviting the jurors to ally or unite with him. Subtle perhaps, but effective.

Tom Horn's name eclipses all others in Wyoming's history, and he remains one of the most enigmatic figures of the West. You might or might not want to call him a friend. You would not want to have him as an enemy.

HE KILLED PLENTY OF OTHER PEOPLE

FTER KELS NICKELL was shot, he sold out to Frank Shiek and
fled with his family to Cheyenne, where they lived in a house
on East Twenty-third Street. The house stood at the present
location of the parking garage for United Medical Center West. Frank
Shiek sold the original Nickell property to the Two Bar Ranch who
later sold it to Gus and Victor Miller.

While living in Cheyenne Nickell worked as a night watchman for
the Union Pacific. He remained in Cheyenne until after Horn's execution. Later, he moved to Encampment, Wyoming. He died in
Kentucky in 1929 while visiting relatives and is buried in Cheyenne's
Lakeview Cemetery adjacent to Willie's grave. Mary Nickell died in
1935 and is buried at the same location.

Fred Nickell, who found Willie's body, died in Rawlins, Wyoming,
on September 17, 1974.

Julia Nickell Cook Gjervick, who was with her family in the aftermath of Willie's death and who rode for help when their father was
shot and wounded, died on February 12, 1967, in Evanston,
Wyoming. She is buried northeast of Willie's grave in Cheyenne, next
to the body of her second husband, Erik Gjervick.

Jim and Dora Miller turned their ranch over to Gus and Victor.
They moved with their younger children to Noble, Oklahoma,
around 1905 after their home at Iron Mountain burned down from
an overheated stove. Jim Miller died in 1917 and is buried in Noble.
Dora later married M. W. Futrell. She died in 1929 from injuries suffered when she was hit by a car.[1] She is buried in an unmarked grave
in Noble next to that of her first husband.

Ruth B. Martin Miller was the last living member of the immediate families who were parties to the Nickell-Miller feud. She passed

away in 1994. In a daylong conversation with her on July 4, 1990 the author's first question was, "What do you think of the whole Tom Horn-Willie Nickell deal?"

She replied, "Well, Joe LeFors was the guiltiest one of the whole lot! Tom Horn never killed that kid. He was too smart, too good a shot, and he never would have made a mistake like that."

Ruth, who was born in Boston, married Gus Miller in 1920. Her father had worked for John Coble before they married. Gus died in 1965 and is buried in Wheatland.

Victor Miller married Eleanor Gobleman, a teacher, in 1913. At first they lived at the Miller ranch at Iron Mountain, and there again at times in later years. In 1914 they moved to Colorado, in 1922 to Casper, and to Denver in 1942. He died in 1964 and is believed to be buried in Denver.

Joe LeFors and his wife Bessie had five children, Reba B., Ruth J., Earl G. (to whom LeFors dedicated his autobiography), Clarice M., and Francis, a son who died at four months of age on August 7, 1905. Francis is buried in Cheyenne's Lakeview Cemetery about seventy-five feet northwest of the Nickell grave.

Bessie divorced Joe in 1912. Bessie and the other children eventually left Cheyenne.

LeFors later married Nettie Waegele and lived in Buffalo, Wyoming, until his death on October 1, 1940, at the age of seventy-five. He and Nettie are buried in the Waegele family plot in the Willow Grove Cemetery in Buffalo.

John Coble, who financed a major part of Tom Horn's defense, was for many years in partnership with Frank Bosler in the Iron Mountain Ranch affairs. They parted company, according to Frank Bosler, Junior, because Coble had diverted money Bosler sent him to buy steers to pay the initial retainer to Horn's lawyers.[2] After Coble and Bosler dissolved the partnership, Bosler sued Coble, but the latter prevailed in an appeal to the Wyoming Supreme Court.

Coble established a ranching business in the western region of Wyoming. The company suffered serious setbacks. Apparently desperate, he wrote Bosler several times asking for help and threatened suicide if Bosler would not give assistance.

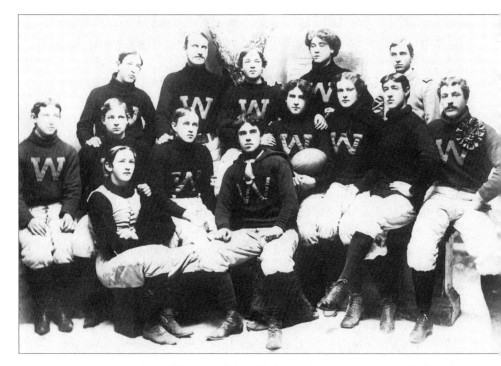

University of Wyoming "Never Defeated" football team. Louis Bath is at far right.
(American Heritage Center, University of Wyoming)

Overwhelmed by financial difficulties and suffering from health problems, John Coble took his own life in 1914 in Elko, Nevada. He is buried in Cheyenne northeast of the Nickell graves.

Hi Bernard, who had documented the Brown's Hole conspiracy engineered by Wiff Wilson, Charley Ayer, and Ora Haley, died in 1924 in Rock Springs, Wyoming, of the heart condition that had plagued him for several years. The obituary[3] in the local paper indicated he was between sixty-five and sixty-eight years old, and he had no immediate relatives. It stated he had come to Wyoming in 1879. At the time of his death he resided in Brown's Park and had had a partnership with Charles Sparks in a cattle operation.

Louis Bath who was jailed for rustling in the Langhoff incident, played football for the 1896 University of Wyoming on "The Never Defeated Team," and participated in Cheyenne Frontier Days rodeos. In 1924 he moved to Pasadena, California, where he worked in the movie industry for four years, appearing in "Ben Hur" and "The Sign of the Cross."

Otto Plaga, the young cowboy whose testimony might have provided an alibi for Tom Horn, had won the saddle bronc championship in 1901 in Cheyenne. After Horn's subsequent conviction and hanging, Plaga continued his involvement in rodeo, and rode Wyoming's infamous bucking horse "Steamboat." Steamboat was probably among the horses Horn escorted to Denver for the Festival of Mountain and Plain in late September that year. Years later when the horse contracted blood poisoning in 1914, coincidentally, Tom Horn's Winchester was used to end his misery.

Plaga later embarked on a career that was marked largely by professional law enforcement. At various times he was a secret service agent in Mexico, a special agent for railroads, a prohibition officer, and a local lawman in several towns in Wyoming. He also served as a justice of the peace.

Walter R. Stoll, Horn's prosecutor, was born in Deckertown, New Jersey. In the November election that followed Tom Horn's conviction in 1902 he was the sole Democrat to win in the face of a county-and-statewide Republican landslide. He died of myocarditis in Cheyenne in 1911 at age fifty-three. His remains were transported to Denver for cremation.

John W. Lacey, Horn's chief attorney, was born in Indiana in 1848. He came to Wyoming when he was appointed Wyoming's first territorial Supreme Court justice by President Chester Arthur in 1884, and became the general counsel of the Union Pacific for its Mountains and Plains Division in 1889. His wife was the sister of Willis Van DeVenter, at one time his partner who became a Justice of the United States Supreme Court. Lacey was the defense counsel for Harry Sinclair in the Teapot Dome case when the federal government canceled Sinclair's lease in the 1920s. He died in 1936 and is buried in Cheyenne.

T. Blake Kennedy was the youngest attorney on Horn's defense team. Kennedy was born in Michigan in 1874. He studied law at Syracuse University, where he became friendly with Roderick Matson and practiced there for two years. The two decided to pursue opportunities away from Syracuse and wrote to a number of cities to inquire what their prospects might be. The reply from Cheyenne was the most favorable. Kennedy was the first to move to Cheyenne in 1901 and urged Matson to join him there, where they became partners.

He was the first to see Tom Horn after his arrest, and apparently became better acquainted with the detective than did the rest of his lawyers. He commented in his memoirs[4] that Horn "was a very pleasant fellow." He became judge of the U.S. District Court and was the presiding judge in the Teapot Dome case, retiring in 1955. Kennedy died in Cheyenne in 1957 and is buried in Cheyenne. His obituary noted that he was an avid professional baseball fan and had attended twenty-six World Series.

When asked by his successor, Ewing Kerr, if he thought Tom Horn had killed Willie Nickell, Kennedy responded that he didn't know, "but he killed plenty of other people."[5] When he retired, Judge Kerr was cleaning out the office and came across a pair of shoes wrapped in a newspaper. Kennedy told him they had belonged to Tom Horn and were intended to be used as an exhibit in Horn's trial, but were never entered. These may have been shoes that would demonstrate that footprints at the Nickell murder site were smaller than could have been made by Horn's shoe. The shoes are in the Wyoming State Museum archives.

Richard H. Scott, the presiding judge in Horn's trial, was born in Minnesota in 1858 and was a graduate of Annapolis. Scott came to Wyoming in 1886 and established a law practice in Sundance. He was a member of the statehood constitutional convention in 1889 and was elected the first judicial district judge in 1890, a position he held until 1906 (he ran unopposed in the 1902 election after Horn's conviction), when he was appointed a Supreme Court justice after the death of Jesse Knight. He was elected and re-elected to the bench every four years, dying while a justice in 1917. Scott is buried in Cheyenne.

Charles J. Ohnhaus, the court stenographer who recorded Tom Horn's confession, was born in Cheyenne in 1878. Near the turn of the century he acted as the secretary to the Indian agent of five tribes in Muskogee, Oklahoma, before returning to Cheyenne. He became Clerk of the U.S. District Court in Cheyenne, and died suddenly in Judge Kennedy's chambers in 1952. Ohnhaus is buried in Cheyenne.

The home in Atascadero where Glendolene Kimmell and her mother lived. (Vicci Stone, author's collection)

After Tom Horn's execution Glendolene Kimmell eventually returned to Missouri. Her name appeared in the Hannibal, Missouri city directory in 1907, 1909, 1911 and 1912.

In 1913 her mother, Frances Pierce Kimmell, sold the family home and it was demolished. Mrs. Kimmell then lived with her sister, Aurelia, at 905 Paris Street in Hannibal for a short period of time. Mrs. Kimmell then bought property in Atascadero, California, a city that was founded as a real estate "colony" for investment purposes. She moved there and lived in a tent city while her home, which cost $1,390, was built.

The 1920 census reflects that a roomer, seventy-year-old Frank T. Wheeler, lived at the Kimmell Atascadero home as well. Originally from Indiana, he was a self-employed painter.

Glendolene remained in Hannibal until 1927 and then followed her mother to Atascadero and lived with her. Her mother died there on October 11, 1930. Glendolene accompanied her remains back to Hannibal.

Immediate family there was now less plentiful. Consequently, after her mother's funeral Glendolene returned to Atascadero. In 1946 she was declared incompetent, probably because of blindness since she had applied for state government blind aid. She was placed under guardianship, and her real and personal property in Atascadero was publicly sold for $2,300 to provide support on June 17, 1946.

The guardian, Constable Dale G. Poole, paid seventy-five dollars monthly from the estate to a caretaker who provided a home for her in San Pedro in Los Angeles County, near Long Beach. Poole requested his removal as her guardian early in 1948, possibly because the funds for her care were becoming depleted; only $152 remained in the estate and she was approaching the point where the state would support her. When the funds were exhausted she was placed under public guardianship and supported by public assistance.

She died in the Sun Flower Haven Rest Home in Long Beach on September 12, 1949, at age seventy, never having married. The cause of death was "generalized atheriosclerosis." She is buried in in an unmarked grave in Westminster Memorial Park in Long Beach.[6]

Glendolene Kimmell's Affidavit

*Glendolene Kimmell wrote a statement, several pages in length, which
appears as a supplementary chapter in the back of Tom Horn's autobiography,* Life of Tom Horn. *This, however, is a separate affidavit, which
has been published only in the author's book on Joe LeFors, which is out
of print.*

*Kimmell generated this affidavit[1] before notary Laura M. Walker in
Jackson County, Missouri, on October 13, 1903, five weeks before Tom
Horn was scheduled to hang. S. B. Willock and E. M. Willock attested to
the affidavit.*

I, Glendolene Myrtle Kimmell, being first duly sworn, upon my
oath, depose and say that:

1. Victor Miller, of Iron Mountain, Laramie County, Wyoming, killed William Nickell of said Iron Mountain. On three different occasions I have overheard Victor Miller and his father, James E.
Miller, talking about the killing of William Nickell—in each of these
three conversations, both James and Victor Miller making statements
that incriminated Victor Miller as the murderer of William Nickell.
Twice James confessed to me that Victor Miller had confessed to him
that he (Victor) had killed William Nickell. Once Victor himself confessed to me that he had killed William Nickell.

The first direct evidence I had that Victor had killed Nickell was
one evening in the first part of September, 1901. It was milking time.
Mrs. Miller and Gus Miller were at or about the corral; Eva and
Maud were at the milk-house; the younger Miller children were playing outdoors. I did not know where Victor was, but took for granted
that he was doing some chore outdoors. James and I had been sitting
in the parlor, but I got up to go to my room (adjacent to the parlor),

and James got up and went into the dining room (adjacent to the parlor). I stayed in my room just a minute or so, then returned to the parlor. As I was opposite the door between the parlor and the dining room, Victor entered the back door of the dining room (slamming it after him), glanced toward the eastern part of the dining room (which was out of my view), and then with considerable noise quickly walked in that direction. I took for granted that Victor saw James in that part of the dining room, or in James' bedroom (which adjoined the eastern side of the dining room). Victor did not see me, and with my customary quiet I walked across the parlor and stood in the front doorway. The front door of the parlor approximately faces the East, and is directly at the side of the one window of the dining room, which was then open. In an excited way, Victor asked James if anyone had been at the ranch that afternoon. James replied: "No," and then said: "Now, Victor, there ain't the least use in you keeping in sich a tarment. Nobody suspicions you no more. I tell you, everybody thinks Tom Horn done it, and it'll just blow over."

Victor answered: "But you know Tom Horn didn't do it; and if they ever have a trial, he can clear himself all right; then they'll jump on me. What I'm afraid of is that somebody might have been in the hills and seen me, when I shot Will—and maybe they're just laying low."

Then ensued a discussion between James and Victor regarding the exact spot Victor met Nickell, the exact spot at which Nickell had been killed, and the exact route Victor had taken when he left the scene of the crime and returned home.

Victor said he had not seen anyone but Nickell in all that time, and James said: "And no one saw you, I tell you, or we'd've heard from it long ago."

Just then Eva and Maud came in the rear door of the dining room and the conversation between Victor and James closed. Both men used modulated tones during the conversation just detailed; but it was perfectly quiet at the house, and I listened intently, so I missed not one word.

The second time I overheard a conversation between James and Victor incriminating Victor was one night during the latter part of September, 1901. Only the Miller family and I were at the ranch.

Mrs. Miller and the younger children had been in bed about two hours. The rest of us had been sitting around the dining room table reading some story papers that had been brought to the ranch that evening from the post office. Then Eva and Maud went to their bedroom, and I to mine. About half an hour later, Gus went out to the tent where he slept, leaving James and Victor alone. I did not light my lamp as the moon shone in my window, and in my night clothes was sitting there thinking. The rest of the Miller family sat around the dining room table reading and playing cards.

While they were reading and playing they got to talking about the change in the sheriffs of Laramie County. They discussed what effect it would have on the investigation of the murder of William Nickell. Both were much worried, and they fell to discussing just what evidence the officials had discovered against James and Victor. They went over the whole affair, from the time Nickell had been killed down to the present, and summed matters up, agreeing that suspicion pointed as strongly against Tom Horn as against themselves; that it was evident no one had seen Victor when he killed Nickell or when he was returning from the scene of the crime; that nobody but they (James and Victor) knew Victor had killed Nickell; and that Victor had his youth in his favor. Then each went to his bed.

During this entire conversation between Victor and James they modulated their tones; but as soon as the conversation began I got up and stood at my door-way (there being only a portiere between my room and the parlor), and I heard every word plainly.

The third time I overheard a conversation between James and Victor incriminating to Victor was the night immediately following the night on which I heard the second conversation just detailed. I spent the entire evening in my own room writing letters. The youngest four children were put to bed early. The rest of the Miller family sat around the dining room table reading and playing cards. While they were reading and playing they got to talking about the change in sheriffs of Laramie County and the coming fall election, and they talked very bitterly against all of the officers—particularly Walter Stoll. Then Gus went out to the tent where he slept; and in a few minutes Mrs. Miller, Eva and Maud went to the out house, staying about 15 minutes. As soon as James and Victor were left alone they talked over the same matter they had discussed in their conversation of the night before—dwelling particularly on the facts that no one had seen Victor in the vicinity of the crime the morning he had killed Nickell, and that there was nothing to implicate Victor except that he had had quarrels and fights with Nickell. Then Mrs. Miller, Eva and Maud came in, and Victor went out to the tent. During this entire conversation between Victor and James they talked loudly (just as they had been talking when the rest of the family were with them), evidently forgetting all about my proximity.

A few days after this third conversation, James made his first confession to me implicating Victor. It was Saturday afternoon, and all of the older members of the Miller family were working except James. I had nothing to do, so James and I took a walk. We went about 400 yards southeast of the house, keeping on Miller's deeded land. After a while we got to talking about the murder of Nickell. Then James made several remarks that plainly showed he was trying to throw suspicion onto Tom Horn. I replied: "Now, look here, Jim Miller, Tom Horn didn't kill that boy—and you know it; and I'm not going to stand for your side-tracking the crime onto him. Victor killed Nickell."

Then I told James how three different times I had heard him and Victor discussing the murder of Nickell, in all of which conversations they had made statements that incriminated Victor as the murderer. James was taken completely by surprise. He stammered out a denial at first; but when he saw this would not "go" with me, he said he and Victor had just been joshing. I told him there was no use in his trying to make me believe that, for he and Victor had been very serious when they held these three conversations; that I had no desire and no intention of making any of the Miller family any trouble as long as they kept quiet; but if they attempted to side-track the crime onto Tom Horn, or any innocent person, I should certainly tell all that I knew about the Millers' criminality. Then James broke down, and assured me that the Millers were going to keep quiet and not attempt to incriminate any innocent person.

A few nights after this, when we were breaking up to go to bed, I distinctly heard a policeman's whistle at the side of the house, and a second later, an answer from the rocks back of the house. I told the Millers, but they had not heard it (having been moving around and talking). We put the lights out, and watched and listened for a long time; but discovered nothing. Then all went to bed except James and me. After a while we got to talking in whispers. James brought up the subject of the murder of Nickell, and repeated all he had said to me in his first confession. In addition, he told me that Victor and Nickell had met accidentally, and had resumed their old quarrel; that they quickly came to blows, and that Victor, having his gun with him, shot and killed Nickell. Miller and I sat up until about 12:00 o'clock that night.

On October 10th, 1901, I left the Miller Ranch and went to Cheyenne. Victor drove me down to John L. Jordan's where I took the train. On the way between Miller's and Jordan's, Victor told me his father had told him that I had overheard three conversations between his father and him, in which both of them had made statements that incriminated him as the murderer of Nickell; that his father had further said that I had said I would cause the Millers no trouble as long as they attempted to incriminate no innocent person.

I replied that I had said all this; and then Victor wanted to know if I intended to stick to this intention. I assured him I did, and then he confessed to me the same facts James had told me regarding the murder of William Nickell—how Victor and William had accidentally met, resumed their old quarrel, come to blows, and Victor had killed William.

2. Before I had any of the direct evidence above detailed regarding the murder of William Nickell, I strongly suspicioned Victor to be the murderer, my suspicions being based on the following facts.

Victor was late at breakfast on Thursday morning, July 18th, 1901, the morning Nickell was killed. During the several months I lived at the Miller Ranch it was an unusual thing for anyone to be late at breakfast, so I noticed his tardiness that morning. I have long been cognizant of a serious misapprehension regarding my testimony about breakfast at the Miller Ranch on July 18th, 1901, as given at the first session of the coroner's jury. A careful perusal of this testimony will show that I did not establish a "complete alibi" for the Millers, or any certain member of the Miller family. Breakfast at Millers was never at a stated time, but varied all the way from seven to nine. Not having any reason for noticing the time of breakfast of July 18th, 1901, I did not do so. However, I distinctly remember that Victor Miller, and he alone, was late.

On July 19th, 1901, a few minutes after Kels Nickell and Joe Reid had left the schoolhouse, Victor came there and wanted to know what Nickell and Reid had wanted. Victor's actions and manners on this occasion impressed me at the time as being "knowing;" and that was the main reason I was so careful to question him, and to tell him nothing until I had him, and Gus, and Mrs. Miller together.

When I did get Mrs. Miller, Gus and Victor together and told them of the murder, Mrs. Miller began to talk about the trouble between the Millers and the Nickells. Then Victor told her to keep quiet as I would go to court and bring up everything they said against them [the Nickells].

This coming from an unsophisticated country boy like Victor Miller strongly increased my suspicions. At the first session of the coroner's jury, I testified that so far as my knowledge extended the Millers had always spoken tolerantly of the Nickells. At that time this was the absolute truth. At the second session of the coroner's jury, I made it plain that James Miller and Kels Nickell were both bad men, but I testified that I had never heard the Millers make any threats against the Nickells. During the interval between the two sessions, I learned through my own experience that Nickell and Miller were both bad men; but the Millers were very guarded in their statements before me, so at that time this testimony was the absolute truth. Had there been a third session of the coroner's jury at any time after the middle of September, 1901, I could have testified that I had heard all the older members of the Miller family make strong threats against the Nickells, and speak in the most malignant way possible concerning the Nickells. Either the Millers wanted to make a good impression on me and so were very careful in what they said before me until they thought I was their friend; or else they ceased to guard their tongues after the second session because they thought the affair had blown over. Several times that I know of the Millers tried to work off schemes tending to exonerate themselves and incriminate Tom Horn regarding the murder of William Nickell. These schemes I will detail in full upon the desire of the proper authorities. Several times, Victor, Gus and James E. Miller, individually and collectively, have said to me, "It's all right to let suspicion fall on Tom Horn. He don't care, and it might help us."

3. The moment I had read over the testimony of LeFors, Snow and Ohnhaus, as given at the preliminary trial of Tom Horn, I knew (without being in possession of any of the facts surrounding that conversation) that Tom Horn's talk to Joe LeFors was nothing but a huge "josh," my reasons being based on the following facts:

According to Ohnhaus' stenographic report, Tom Horn said, "She (referring to me) wrote me a letter as long as the Governor's message, telling me in detail everything asked her by Stoll, the prosecuting attorney. I got this letter from the girl the same day I got my summons to appear before the Coroner's Inquest."

I deny this statement of Tom Horn's absolutely and unqualifiedly. The first session of the coroner's jury was open to the public; and I had the sense to know that if Tom Horn wanted to know about the proceedings of this session he could have found out much more quickly and explicitly than by a letter from me. At the second session, Tom Horn and I were both in Cheyenne.

According to Ohnhaus' stenographic report: "LeFors said, 'Did the schoolmarm tell everything she knew?' Tom Horn said, 'Yes, she did. I wouldn't tell an individual like her anything—not me.'"

I deny that the last sentence of this statement of Tom Horn's has any foundation in the truth. Tom Horn told me the whole history of his life, informing me of many things known only to his intimate friends, and I can prove this statement of mine. According to Ohnhaus's stenographic report: "Tom Horn said, 'She told me to look out for you' (referring to LeFors). She said, 'Look out for Joe LeFors. He is not all right.' She said, 'Look out for him. He is trying to find out something.'"

I deny absolutely and unqualifiedly that I made this statement, or any similar to it, to Tom Horn. I had talked with Joe LeFors very little before I discovered he was trying to work up a case against Tom Horn. I told Tom Horn several things Joe LeFors had asked about him and several things LeFors had remarked about him, all of which questions and remarks plainly showed he was trying to incriminate Tom Horn; but I never gave Tom Horn any specific warning in regard to LeFors. Tom Horn understood LeFors' attitude toward him long before I knew LeFors, and the understanding that existed between Tom Horn and me in regard to Joe LeFors was simply a matter of intuitional perception.

According to Ohnhaus's stenographic report: "I (Tom Horn) said 'What is there to this LeFors matter? She said Miller didn't like him, and Miller said he would kill the son of a bitch if God would spare him long enough.'"

I deny absolutely and unqualifiedly that I made this statement to Tom Horn. I did not know until after Tom Horn's trial that there had been any trouble between LeFors and James E. Miller. Up to the time I left Wyoming, on October 10th, 1901, there had not been a particle of trouble between Miller and LeFors; and it stands to reason that after I left Wyoming I could not have told Tom Horn of trouble that occurred between Miller and LeFors after I had left Wyoming.

There is no connection whatever between my alleged warning of Tom Horn against LeFors, and Miller's dislike of LeFors and threats against him. According to Ohnhaus's stenographic report: "She (referring to me) was there at this time, and of course we soon paired ourselves off." Now, I do not know what Tom Horn calls "soon;" but we certainly did not "pair off" at Miller's and after he left Miller's, we did not meet until the second session of the coroner's jury. According to Ohnhaus' stenographic report: "Tom Horn said, 'She (referring to me) was one quarter Jap, one half Corean [*sic*], and the other German. She talks almost every language on earth.'"

I deny absolutely and unqualifiedly that this statement of Tom Horn's has any foundation in the truth. I can produce many prominent people (who have known my people for years and who have known me at the various stages of my life) who can and will testify that I have not a drop of Japanese or Corean blood in my veins; and that I speak only one language (English), and have a theoretical knowledge of but two others (Latin and German). It stands to reason that if I could "talk almost every language on earth," I would never have made my living by teaching at the Miller-Nickell school.

Knowing as I do that practically everything Tom Horn said about me is false, I firmly believe the whole alleged confession to be simply a huge "josh;" for it stands to reason that no one has the right to put his finger on one part of the alleged confession and say it is strictly, literally true, and to put his finger on another part and say it is a "josh." Being unable to accept the whole alleged confession, every word of it, word for word, literally and strictly, I reject the entire alleged confession as a coarse "job."

4. I know Tom Horn very well, and understand his nature perfectly. I have seen him in all stages of intoxication, and know just how liquor affects him. He is highly imaginative, and even a little liquor acts as a strong stimulus to his imagination.

When sober, he is quiet and not noticeably talkative; when he is drunk, he is very talkative, and often has a deliberateness of manner not natural to him—commonly called "drunken gravity." Liquor has practically no apparent effect upon him physically. He never staggers, never trembles, never hesitates for a word; when he has reached his highest degree of intoxication, he goes to sleep—on his feet if he has no place to sit down.

Many times that I have been with Tom Horn when he was drunk, he has told me long tales (going into minute details) which I knew from surrounding circumstances were simply products of his imagination. I will relate some of these tales at the desire of the proper authorities.

As for the tale Tom Horn told LeFors about the murder of William Nickell, and also about the murders of Lewis and Powell, I myself heard the same tales long before Tom Horn's alleged confession. When Tom Horn was at the Miller Ranch, I heard James Miller tell Tom Horn the identical tale about the murders of Lewis and Powell that Tom Horn repeated to LeFors.

From the first conversation I had with James E. Miller after the murder of William Nickell down to the time I left Wyoming, Miller always advanced the same explanation in regard to the murder of Nickell that Tom Horn advanced to LeFors. Indeed, everyone (excepting officers) who called at the Miller Ranch from the time Nickell was found dead up to the time I left Wyoming put forward the same theory in regard to the murder of Nickell that Tom Horn gave LeFors. These tales, or theories, were the common property of all the ranch people of Iron Mountain and neighboring districts. Tom Horn had heard them repeatedly.

Tom Horn, being under the influence of liquor at the time he made his alleged confession to LeFors, his imagination quickly yielded to LeFors' adroit questioning, and he gave out as his own the tales that were the common property of all the ranch people in or near the Iron Mountain country.

5. After James Miller and I had gotten back to the Miller Ranch from attendance at Cheyenne Frontier Days, Miller privately told me that while he had been in Cheyenne during Cheyenne Frontier Days, Joe LeFors had approached him with the proposition that if he (Miller) would make out an affidavit implicating Tom Horn as the murderer of Nickell; when Tom Horn was brought to trial, if he (Miller) would take the stand against Tom Horn; that Joe LeFors would personally see to it that neither Miller nor any member of his family would be held responsible for the murder of Nickell, and that further, LeFors would give Miller five hundred dollars—one-half of the reward money. Miller further said to me that he had replied to LeFors that he wasn't making it his business to run down the murderer of William Nickell; that the voters and tax-payers elected and paid officers for that purpose; and that then he had walked off from LeFors. Miller further said to me that he saw through LeFors' game; that LeFors didn't care anything for him; that if he did what LeFors wanted him to and Tom Horn was convicted, he would never get any of the money, and he might get hanged "alongside of Tom Horn."

Prosecuting Attorney Walter Stoll of Cheyenne sent attorney William B. Ross of Cheyenne to Kansas City for the purpose of inducing me to attend Tom Horn's trial as a witness for the prosecution. From the start I told Ross that I knew absolutely nothing incriminating Tom Horn, and in truth knew many things in his favor, and that consequently I would not attend Tom Horn's trial as a witness for the prosecution. Ross wanted me to go anyway, and argued, bribed, begged and threatened. He repeatedly said to me, "Why, you'll make money by going. Stoll told me to tell you that besides the customary mileage to and from Cheyenne, besides the customary witness fee of two dollars per day, you will have your expenses paid at the Inter Ocean Hotel (or wherever you care to stop). As long as you are held as a witness, you will have bought for you anything you need, *and besides this you will get other money* [emphasis Kimmell's] if you will go out there and take the stand against Tom Horn."

He told me that Stoll had said to him that unless I took the stand against Tom Horn they wouldn't have testimony strong enough to convict Tom Horn. Ross further said that Stoll would be terribly angry if I didn't take the stand against Tom Horn, and would probably cause me a great deal of trouble.

6. It was on the night of October 10th, 1901, I arrived in Cheyenne from the Iron Mountain country; having resigned my teaching assignment at the Nickell-Miller school. I was staying at the Inter Ocean Hotel on the corner of 16th Street and Capitol Avenue. I remained in it until morning.

The next morning I had some shopping to do, so that my time was fully occupied until about 11:00 a.m. Then I went over to the office of Prosecuting Attorney Stoll with the intention of telling him all that had come to my knowledge regarding the murder of Nickell since the second session of the Coroner's Jury. I had decided that after all the best thing for me to do would be to lay all the facts before Stoll; and then it would not be likely that any innocent person would be convicted.

Stoll's clerk, a young lady, said Stoll was at court. She wanted me to leave my name, but I said I would probably return that afternoon.

Then I went on up to Mrs. Elizabeth S. Hawes' [the county superintendent of schools], and stayed with her until the middle of the afternoon. Mrs. Hawes returned downtown with me, and went with me on several little trips about the hotel and the shops that I had to take.

I said to her, "There is just one more thing I have to attend to before we go to the depot. I want to see Walter Stoll, and tell him of some things that have taken place since the second session of the coroner's jury." So Mrs. Hawes and I went to the building [presently the Atlas Theater on 16th Street] in which Stoll's office was located. She waited on the pavement at the foot of the steps while I went up to his rooms. The same clerk that I had seen that morning told me Stoll was again at court. Thus I was prevented from laying my knowledge before the prosecuting attorney. It was then about a half hour of train time, or I would have had ample time.

After I got to Kansas City I never wrote to Stoll about the matter, because I went back to my original decision to keep quiet as long as no innocent person was put to trial. I looked at it this way: Kels Nickell and James Miller are both undoubtedly very bad men. These two men, together, were the original cause of the feud between the Miller and the Nickell families; and in my opinion, the real culprits are Kels Nickell and James E. Miller. Hanging Victor would not bring William Nickell to life; and I felt sorry for Victor because he had been reared in the midst of quarreling and strife, and he was young.

These ideas, coupled with the fact that Tom Horn's attorneys were confident of acquitting him at the trial, constitute the reason I did not attend Tom Horn's trial and testify concerning all the above facts detailed in this affidavit.

The statement that Tom Horn's attorneys did not want me to attend his trial for fear I would prove an alibi for Victor I denounce as an unqualified and malicious lie gotten up by Tom Horn's enemies. After Tom Horn had been convicted in the District Court, I made out an affidavit for presentation to the District Court; but owing to my ignorance of the law—solely owing to this—I made out the affidavit in a form too general to be of any use to Tom Horn's attorneys. Before I had time to make out a new affidavit, the time which the law allows for the filing of an affidavit (disclosing new testimony) in the District or the Supreme Court had elapsed.

This affidavit I am making out at my own suggestion, and with my own free will. I am actuated solely by the desire of saving the life and the liberty of an innocent man—Tom Horn.

7. If a new trial is granted in this case of the State of Wyoming versus Tom Horn, I will attend such trial and testify with facts as above stated.

JUDGES T. BLAKE KENNEDY
AND EWING KERR

T. Blake Kennedy came to Cheyenne in 1901 after completing law school at Syracuse University.

Judge Kerr spoke of Kennedy's recollections of Tom Horn, "He said he was a very pleasant fellow to deal with."

Judge Kennedy's memoirs[1] not previously published for the public, provide further insight into events that surrounded Tom Horn's trial:

He [Tom Horn] was tall, a trifle round-shouldered and had a black, beady eye which was intensely piercing. He had a marked degree of humor for one so concerned in the more dramatic affairs of life. His capacity for becoming familiar with the great open spaces of the West and Southwest, for withstanding hardships upon the open range and mastering to the highest degree the weapons of defense of the pioneer's life, his fearlessness as to both man and beast and his acquiring knowledge of the many hazards which confronted the pioneer of the great western plains all gave him the background for a colorful and useful life.

It had become a sort of custom for the owners of the great herds of cattle, in the attempt to protect themselves against cattle rustlers who were very prevalent, to employ a detective for the protection of their interests. It is undoubtedly true that Horn was so employed. He operated in various places in Colorado and Wyoming, and sometimes before the Horn case came up two men in Routt County, Colorado, were killed, Dart and Rash, and one by the name of Powell in Wyoming. Efforts were made to apprehend the murderer, but without the definite ascertainment of facts upon which to base a charge, were unsuccessful, although suspicion was directed strongly toward Horn as the killer. It had been reported that at a coroner's inquest the small son of the murdered man [Powell], who was perhaps five years old, made the remark in identifying Horn, "That's the man that killed Daddy." No prosecution, however, took place.

"On July 18, 1901, Willie Nickell, 14 years of age, and son of Kels P. Nickell, who had run a band of sheep into the cattle country, was killed adjacent to his father's ranch in Laramie County. The community was very much aroused and again suspicion was directed toward Tom Horn. Nothing definite came out of this investigation until sometime in January of 1902 when Horn was arrested by the then Sheriff, Edwin J. Smalley, while sitting in the lobby of the Inter Ocean Hotel. It was something of a surprise to most people that Horn could be arrested without a shooting affray as he usually went heavily armed.

It was even more surprising that I should become associated as counsel in his defense. One night I was called over the phone by Harry Hynds, who asked me to come down to his place of business, which I did. There I was introduced to John C. Coble, who was the manager for a company in which he [Hynds] was himself heavily interested [financially], owning several ranches in Albany and Laramie Counties. He had told Harry Hynds that he was interested in securing an appropriate defense for Tom Horn and asked for advice in the matter of securing counsel. He recommended me to Coble as a young man who would give him good service and that he should at least have me on the staff of attorneys in defense of Horn. I sometimes think that Harry either liked me very much personally or that he might have thought Horn was guilty and would not have much of a defense. However the retainer was a high spot in my young life as a lawyer.

I was the first attorney employed for Horn and the first to interview him after his arrest.

Later John W. Lacey and Timothy P. Burke were retained, which also brought into the picture Ed Clark, Burke's partner, and Roderick Matson, my partner, all of whom took an active part in the defense of Horn. Other attorneys performed special services including M. A. Kline and Clyde M. Watts, although I do not remember upon which side they were engaged. [Kline and Watts were part of the prosecution.]

At a subsequent meeting of counsel some days later the fee which was to be paid by Coble was disbursed among counsel, and I received as my share as a retainer fee One Thousand Dollars. This was the first real money in a substantial amount that I had had in my practice up to that time. I certainly felt proud of my achievement in being able to connect with—in those days—so handsome a fee. Matson and I still had the tail-end of our college debts hanging over us and we immediately proceeded to 'clean house' by paying off all our creditors, my expenses being somewhat in excess of One Hundred Dollars and his probably less than Three Hundred. At least we felt a relief because we were then even with the world.

[Judge Kerr indicated in a conversation with the author, "I knew Mrs. Coble. She showed me a cancelled check for ten thousand dollars.... It was made out to John W. Lacey, as his first payment. That was a lot of money back in those days."]

Next followed, in due course, the preliminary hearing at which the evidence of the prosecution was revealed, proof of Horn being in the vicinity where the murder occurred, and principally an alleged confession made by Horn to one Joe LeFors, a Deputy Marshal connected with the United States Court. LeFors, when Horn was drinking heavily, induced him to go with him to the Marshal's office one night and they exchanged stories of their prowess in the handling of guns. Quite cleverly LeFors led up to the Nickell killing and remarked to Horn that he was very clever in being able to cover up his tracks in that matter in which it was stated that Horn had said in the conversation that it was the best shot he ever made but the dirtiest trick he ever did. To make the confession more binding, a stenographer [Charlie Ohnhaus] was posted at the door into an adjoining room and took down in shorthand the remarks of Horn made in the conversation which was likewise produced at the hearing.

One of the most amusing incidents in this alleged confession was in connection with a little school teacher who was teaching school at Iron Mountain by the name of Kimmell, whom Horn had met at some dance, and who became greatly interested in Tom's behalf and so remained during the entire subsequent proceeding. The statement made by Horn to LeFors was in substance: "The little school teacher tells me, 'Look out for Joe LeFors, he's not alright.'" As it turned out the schoolteacher was smarter than Tom because if Horn had obeyed her injunction he might never have been connected with the murder sufficiently to have secured a confession or conviction.

The result of the preliminary examination was that Horn was bound over for trial. Then followed the preparation of the defense. Being the youngest of counsel it became my duty to perform the greater portion of messenger service, interviewing Horn at the jail, looking up evidence and the like.

When the panel of jurors was selected for the trial, after securing a list of the names from the Clerk, I found that it contained quite a number of ranchmen in the County whom Horn might possibly know. I went over the list very carefully with him and he took a pencil and marked on a slip of paper those on the panel whom he would be willing to have act as jurors and, strange as it may seem, six of those on the original panel were selected as trial jurors in whom he expressed himself as having confidence.

I made a special trip to the Iron Mountain country to interview a number of people who were supposed to know something of Horn and his habits in the community. I went by train to Bosler and stayed overnight at the Coble ranch house. It was in January and the weather was very cold. The next morning we prepared to set out on horseback across the mountain range through the Sybille country to interview witnesses. Coble, I remember, brought in a pair of chaps for me to put on. I was not familiar with cowboy regalia and started to put them on with the "open space" in front, at which Coble summoned the cowboys while I was in the act and said, "Look at the tenderfoot."

I made the trip with Duncan Clark who was then foreman for the Iron Mountain Ranch Company. On the trip we stopped at several ranches and at one point I ran into a cowboy by the name of Otto Plaga, whose parents lived in the mountain country, and whom Horn had mentioned as being a possible witness, having seen him at about the time the killing occurred. Plaga gave me an affidavit to the effect that he had seen Horn on horseback at a point where it was practically impossible for him to be, had he been at the spot where the killing

Joe LeFors late in life. (American Heritage Center, University of Wyoming)

took place, which I thought was very valuable evidence; and it would have been except that Horn, when testifying himself upon the trial, not willing to subdue his passion for "braggadocio" responded to a question that he supposed it would not be impossible for a man who was a good rider and knew the country to cover the ground between where the killing took place and where Plaga had testified he saw him.

In company with Judge Lacey and Mr. Burke I visited the place where the killing occurred and the entire surrounding country, and came to the conclusion that the boy was killed by a shot from a clump of rocks which was perhaps 30 yards from the gate which the boy was attempting to open at the time he was killed. Horn in his alleged confession to LeFors, in bragging about the shot, said that he had killed the boy from the head of a draw 300 yards away. As a matter of fact there was no head of a draw 300 yards away from which the gate could be observed.

A proceeding was instituted to attack the manner in which jurors were selected which was before the Supreme Court, and Horn's counsel were permitted to intervene as *amicus curiae*.[2] This effort, however, was unsuccessful. The trial took place on October 10, 1902, and was concluded on the 24th, resulting in his conviction of first-degree murder. So in the end six of the men whom Horn had vouched as satisfactory to him voted to hang him.

Then came the motions for a new trial, which being overruled an appeal was made to the Supreme Court, likewise being unsuccessful, and subsequently an appeal for executive clemency to the then acting Governor Fenimore Chatterton but who refused to intervene. Horn in the meantime was confined in the Laramie County jail in the old courthouse which stood upon the site of the present courthouse.

An effort was made for a jail delivery in which another prisoner, McCloud, and Horn hit the jailer over the head and grabbed his keys, making their escape into the open. The escape was particularly sensational and played up in the papers, inasmuch as it was alleged [the previous winter] that Horn had assistance from the outside, and that a snowball had been placed on the window across the street which was observable from Horn's cell in the jail as a signal, and that Horn's fully saddled and bridled horse was standing hitched in the alley for several days across the street behind old St. John's Hall. Horn came into possession of Proctor's gun, but it was equipped with a safety latch which he did not understand, and he was therefore prevented from using it. When the hue and cry was given that Horn had escaped he had gone across the street, but being unable to protect himself without firearms, the proprietor of a circus who was conducting a small show on an adjacent lot apprehended him without a fight, and he was led back to jail.

In an attempt to save his life I made several trips to interview the jurors who had served on the case. Among these was one Homer Payne who worked for the Two Bar outfit in and around Chugwater. I went to Chug and without revealing my mission, proceeded to interview Payne at the ranch seven miles above. Al Bowie, then manager of the Swan Land and Cattle Company holdings, to my surprise offered to drive me up. In a short time we were on the way with snappy bays hooked up to a good working buckboard.

Digressing for a moment, it was on this trip that I got my first and most lasting impressions concerning the immensity of the great cattle ranges. Rather innocently I asked Mr. Bowie, "How many cattle do you have?" To this he replied, "Well, you know we never know just how many cattle we do have, but to give you something of an idea, we have branded considerably over 10,000 calves this year." This was indeed revealing for I reflected that for every calf a "mama," with a generous distribution of "papas," then the yearlings, two year olds, three year olds and four year olds, many of the latter being held for marketing at that time.

I found Payne and got a rather comforting affidavit as to the things seen and heard by him while on the jury as to the seeming demands upon them by an enraged public to do their duty, but it was all lost motion so far as accomplishing results were concerned.

The hanging was set for November 20, 1903, at the County Jail at 19th and Carey. I was the only one of Tom's rather numerous counsel whom he personally invited to the hanging, which invitation however I did not accept. One of the most dramatic things perhaps at the "hanging party" as told to me by persons present, was the song sung by Charlie and Frankie Irwin just before the principal event took place: "Keep Your Hand Upon the Throttle and Your Eye Upon the Rail." Incidentally, as many here may know, the Irwin boys had good voices. Charlie was a true friend and helper to Tom Horn to the bitter end. [Judge Kerr, in our conversation, remarked that Judge Kennedy told him, "The Irwin brothers sang. They sang so loud—they were afraid he'd make a confession involving other people right at the last—so they wouldn't hear him."]

It was likewise related that Tom was the coolest of those present when preparations were being made for his demise. It was reported that he inquired of Joe Cahill who was assisting the Sheriff in the preparations: "How are your wife and children?" and also: "Joe, you seem to be shaking a little."

Tom was about 45 years old at the time he ignominiously passed out of this world, and many people have expressed doubts as to his being hung. Actually there can be no doubt about it.

In the conversation with LeFors it was recorded that Tom said, "Killing men is my specialty. I look upon it as a business proposition, and I think I have a corner on this market." As practitioners it was not a pleasant experience to lose the case, especially if one's client is to be hung, but out of the gray shadows arising from the memories of over 40 years, one is prone to adopt a philosophy that, technicalities aside, the world is better off without a man who could be the father of the thought last above quoted.

2. Troublesome

1. Some documents show the name spelled "Hardman," but he always spelled in with a "t." His descendants spelled it with a "d."
2. Scotland County, MO, Circuit Court Recorder case #2061.
3. *Chancery:* A court of public record or equity.
4. The reason for Harris Thompson being named as a co-defendant is not clear, but John's lawyers may have suggested including him if only because he was part of the foursome in which John lost out.
5. Knox County, MO, record of proceedings in the Court of Common Pleas, entered as part of case 2061.
6. Quotations from Knox and Scotland County court records.
7. Case 2061 affidavits.
8. Conversations with researchers Sandra Remley, Barbara Howard, and LeAnn Russell, Memphis.

3. Bound to See Trouble

1. Tom Horn, *Life of Tom Horn*, first printing, 17. Note references herein correspond to the original version.
2. Nye was the founder and publisher of the Laramie newspaper, the *Daily Boomerang.*
3. Sandy Remley, from public records.
4. Horn family member and genealogist John Weihing.
5. Probate records, Scotland County Courthouse. The list of assets in the probate record includes a note due from Thomas Horn, which had been scratched out, apparently to delete that asset. Thomas was the administrator of his father's estate.
6. Courtesy Cathy Hernandez, Horn researcher, who obtained information in Ohio source materials.

7. Census Records, family chronicles, State Historical Society of Missouri and research by Remley, Howard, Russell and Hernandez.

8. Charles, who moved to Boulder, Colorado, was closest geographically to Tom during the period 1890–1903. He had married Elizabeth Blattner in 1887 and moved to Boulder around 1890.

9. Etna Cemetery records, Scotland County Circuit Court Recorder files.

10. Records conflict on the names.

11. He is referred to as "Ben" Markley in Horn's autobiography. Tom wrote about Ben scornfully. Horn, 6-7.

12. Horn, 17-18.

13. Horn, 18.

14. Horn, 20.

15. Horn, 23.

16. Information provided by Professor Larry D. Ball, Arkansas State University, from his continuing research into Horn's early life for a forthcoming book.

17. Horn, 26.

18. Colorado census, courtesy Larry D. Ball.

19. Larry D. Ball.

20. Census document, June 14, 1880.

21. Letter dated June 5, 1924, to Mrs. John C. Coble in Cheyenne from Daly in Washington, D.C. John Coble became Horn's close friend and his last employer before Horn's involvement in the Willie Nickell killing.

22. National Archives, courtesy Larry D. Ball.

23. An interesting connection between Emmet Crawford and Cheyenne appeared in the Cheyenne *Daily Leader* on July 23, 1880. Under the headline "Base Ball":

"A game of baseball was played on the grounds at Fort Russell yesterday which resulted in a victory for the Cheyenne Club, four innings only being played. Some excellent playing was done by Capt. [Emmet] Crawford making three home runs and knocking the ball into the guard house on two occasions."

24. The letter has not previously been published other than in the Memphis *Reveille* on March 4, 1886. Located in the Scotland County Memorial Library.

25. *Tom Horn, Chief of Scouts,* by Horace E. Dunlap, one who knew him, *Arizona Historical Review,* April 1929, 73-85.

26. Larry D. Ball.

27. British Columbia census document, courtesy Claudia Cole.

28. Loney provided the "Maricha" maiden name, doubtless a mistake.

4. Black, Shifty Eyes

1. C. W. Shores, *Memoirs of a Lawman,* 261.

2. Ibid., 261.

3. Ibid., 265.

4. Horn, 259-260.

5. Horn, 260-261.

6. Horn, 261-262.

7. *Reno Evening Gazette,* April 10, 1891, p. 3. On file at the Nevada State Archives and Library.

8. *Daily Nevada State Journal,* July 15, 1891, p. 3. On file at the Nevada State Archives and Library.

9. *Reno Evening Gazette,* July 17, 1891, p. 3.

10. Ibid.

11. *Daily Nevada State Journal,* September 30, 1891, p. 3.

12. Ibid., October 2, 1891, p. 3.

13. Ibid.

14. Arizona Historical Society

15. Horn, 262.

16. Horn, 287.

17. The injunctions were to prevent a cattle roundup that was not authorized by the Wyoming Stock Growers Association.

18. Crossthwaite Commission Report located at the Wyoming Division of Cultural Resources.

19. Microfilm H191 at the Wyoming Division of Cultural Resources, Correspondence from the U.S. National Archives.

20. Ibid.

21. Vertical file H71-111 at the Wyoming Division of Cultural Resources.

22. Written perspective provided to the author by Don Patterson.

5. Considerable Cattle Stealing

1. The name was alternatively spelled "Langholf" and "Langhoff" in early family records.

2. Murray L. Carroll, "Tom Horn and the Langhoff Gang," *Annals of Wyoming*, Spring 1992.

3. 1880 Census on file at the Wyoming Division of Cultural Resources.

4. Records of the Laramie County District Court located at the Wyoming Division of Cultural Resources.

5. Leslie Sommer, *History of the Sybille Country*, on file at the Wyoming Division of Cultural Resources.

6. Ibid.

7. Ibid.

8. Carroll, "Tom Horn and the Langhoff Gang."

9. Sommer, *History of the Sybille Country*.

10. Records of the Laramie County District Court.

11. Gus Rosentreter, *Memoirs*. filed at the Wyoming Division of Cultural Resources.

12. Letter to the author, December 1989.

13. Harley Axford figured in a minor role in the Willie Nickell incident.

6. No Better Man

1. Tregoning had been convicted of killing George Henderson on John Clay's 71 Quarter Circle Ranch on the Sweetwater River in a dispute over wages on October 7, 1890, and sentenced to life at hard labor. See Elnora Frye's *Atlas of Wyoming Outlaws at the Territorial Penitentiary*, 121.

   Henderson, a former Pinkerton operative, was the stock detective who was indirectly involved in the lynching of "Cattle Kate" Ellen Watson and Jim Averill in 1889. William Jackson, a witness in Tregoning's trial, stated that a juror, William Frederick, said that Henderson's murder was a direct result of Watson's and Averill's deaths. See George Hufsmith's *Wyoming Lynching of Cattle Kate 1889*, 179, 209, 212, 274-275, 277.

2. Copies of letters furnished by Dan Thrapp in the author's possession.

7. A System That Never Fails

1. John Rolfe Burroughs, *Guardian of the Grasslands: The First Hundred Years of the Wyoming Stock Growers Association*, 154.

2. Ibid., 155.

3. Charles B. Penrose, *The Rustler Business*, 55-56.

4. Dean Krakel, *The Saga of Tom Horn*, 5.

5. Mark Dugan, *Tales Never Told Around the Campfire*, 203.

6. Issue housed at the Wyoming Division of Cultural Resources.

7. *Laramie Daily Boomerang*, October 3, 1895. The *Boomerang* itself covered Clay's arrival and Horn's telegram from Glenrock, indicating he would arrive in Cheyenne. He was in town the evening of October 2.

8. The Desired Effect

1. "Family Traditions" by Mark Dugan, *Annals of Wyoming*, Volume 64, Number 2, Spring 1992, 45.

2. Mark Dugan, *The Making of Legends: More True Stories of Frontier America*, 255-256.

3. Dugan, "Family Traditions, 47.

4. Virginia Cole Trenholm, *Footprints on the Frontier: Saga of the Laramie Region*, 185.

5. Issue housed at the Wyoming Division of Cultural Resources

9. No Cure, No Pay

1. National Archives: Adjutant General's Office, document files #29451, courtesy Britt W. Wilson.

2. Ibid.

3. Courtesy Britt Wilson.

4. Issue on file at the Arizona State Historical Society.

5. Phillip G. Nickell, "Tom Horn in Arizona, or Who Killed Old Man Blevins?" *Quarterly of the National Association and Center for Outlaw and Lawman History*, Volume XIV, Numbers 3 and 4, 1990, 21.

6. Horn, 245.

7. Larry D. Ball, in his chapter in the book *With Badges & Bullets*, 71-86, based on research in the National Archives. The book is edited by Richard Etulain and Glenda W. Riley.

8. Ibid.

9. Ibid.

10. National Archives.

10. Kill Him and Be Done with Him

1. Statement by Nelson Wren at Wilcox June 2, 1999.

2. Accounts vary on the amount stolen, but most now point to $50,000..

3. Joe LeFors, operating as a Pinkerton agent, was assigned the cipher (code name) of "Pulet." Other prominent figures in turn-of-the-century annals who were Pinkerton operatives were assigned various ciphers. A few were Frank A. Hadsell, U.S. Marshal, who was assigned "Log;" Peter Swanson, Rock Springs sheriff, was "Stone;" Creede McDaniels, sheriff in Rawlins, was "Hamper;" Thomas Horton, also a sheriff in Rawlins, was "Muff;" R.D. Meldrum, deputy sheriff in Dixon, was "Cigar;" and Charles Ayer, stock association inspector, Dixon, was "Stamp." There is no record of Horn's cipher.

4. Edmund C. Harris was himself Canadian-born. U.S. Census of 1900, Laramie County, Vol. 3, Sheet B, E.D. 36, Line 88, located at the Wyoming Division of Cultural Resources.

5. Ghent was a well-known figure who was allied with the lawless element in Johnson County.

6. Hadsell file on microfiche, Wyoming Division of Cultural Resources.

7. Hadsell vertical file, Wyoming Division of Cultural Resources.

8. Cited in Robert K. DeArment's *Alias Frank Canton*, 353.

9. Cheyenne *Daily Leader*, November 20, 1903.

10. See Margaret Brock Hanson, Powder River Country: The Papers of J. Elmer Brock, 454.

11. Don't Say Anything

1. Donna B. Ernst and Dan Davidson, Museum of Northwest Colorado.

2. Rawlins *Republican*, November 17, 1900. Courtesy Dan Davidson and Bill Mackin.

3. Horn's comment about the "visionary show" apparently refers to a visit to a nest of soiled doves.

4. John Rolfe Burroughs, *Guardian of the Grasslands*, 196.

5. Jay Monaghan, *Last of the Bad Men: The Legend of Tom Horn*, 157-159.

12. The General Welfare

1. Dart spelled his name "Isam" when signing documents according to Dick and Daun deJournette in *100 years of Brown's Park and Diamond Mountain*, 373.

2. Brown's Hole is more commonly known as Brown's Park. Tom Horn used the former term, which will be used throughout.

3. Contemporary newspapers pointed to Haley's prominence and wealth. In 1879 the *Laramie Weekly Sentinel* reported that Haley was a member of the Territorial Legislature in 1871 and Postmaster in Laramie in 1875. It added that "Messrs. Sudduth and Montgomery purchased Ora Haley's entire herd of 1700 cattle." In 1905, according to the May 17, 1905, Laramie *Daily Boomerang*, Haley and his brother, Frank, of Rifle, Colorado, bought thirty-five thousand head of cattle from a cattle speculator at the Dupree ranch near Van Horn, Texas. The purchase amounted to $420,000. The *Boomerang* commented that it would take almost one hundred trains to transport them from Texas, figured at eighteen head of cattle per car and twenty cars per train. Materials based in the Ora Haley file, American Heritage Center, University of Wyoming.

4. Quotations are excerpted from "Confidentially Told," typescript written by Frank Willis from his recollections of living with Hi Bernard in 1919, filed in the Colorado Historical Society collection. Bernard made it a condition that his comments not be released until after his death. He died in Rock Springs, Wyoming in 1924, leaving no descendants or relatives.

5. Ibid.

6. Ibid.

7. Ayer has at times been spelled "Ayres" by parties not familiar with the correct spelling.

8. The Iron Mountain Ranch Company's headquarters had moved from Iron Mountain, east of the Laramie Range, by 1900.

9. "Confidentially Told."

10. Ibid.

11. John Rolfe Burroughs, *Where the Old West Stayed Young*, 203.

12. Carey wrote of the episode to John Rolfe Burroughs, as cited in *Where the Old West Stayed Young, 203.*

13. Letter from Burman to his son, Bobby, December 20, 1944, located in the Burman Collection, American Heritage Center, University of Wyoming.

14. Courtesy Museum of Northwest Colorado.

15. deJournette, 373.

16. Transcript of an oral history by Chuck Stoddard, late 1950s, housed at the Museum of Northwest.

17. Ibid.

18. "Confidentially Told."

19. Ann Bassett Willis, "Queen Ann of Brown's Park", *The Colorado Magazine*, Volume XXIX July 1952, Number 3, State Historical Society of Colorado.

20. "Tales of the Old West Retold" by C. A. Stoddard, as told by Carl Davidson. No date shown. Courtesy of Dan Davidson, Museum of Northwest Colorado, Craig.

21. Records in the file of *State of Wyoming, Plaintiff, vs. Tom Horn, Defendant,* Laramie County District Court, Gerrie E. Bishop, clerk.

22. Stoddard manuscript.

23. Ibid.

24. According to Dan Davidson, at the Museum of Northwest Colorado, considerable question exists as to whether Wallihan's story about seeing Horn from his wildlife photography blind is true. However, this account has been published many times. Wallihan's roadhouse was at Juniper Springs, near Lay, fifteen miles east of Craig. If Horn did in fact stop at the roadhouse, it could have been to try to heal his wounds in the springs, after his initial recuperation from the fight.

13. More Trouble Ahead

1. 1900 Census. Dart may not have known the exact year he was born.

2. Burroughs, *Where the Old West Stayed Young*, 24-30.

3. Letter from Sweetwater County Museum to *The Denver Post*, April 1, 1970, citing *The Wyoming Historical Blue Book* by Marie H. Erwin.

4. Court records on file at Wyoming Division of Cultural Resources.

5. deJournette, from the probate file of Isam Dart.

6. Frank Hadsell named White River Charley in a diary entry as one of the killers of Sheriff Joe Hazen in his pursuit of the Wilcox robbers. Information in the Hadsell vertical file, Wyoming Division of Cultural Resources.

7. Materials courtesy of the Museum of Northwest Colorado.

8. Museum of Northwest Colorado.

9. Letter courtesy the American Heritage Center, University of Wyoming.

14. Killed to Get Them Off the Range

1. Transcribed oral history courtesy Dan Davidson, Museum of Northwest Colorado, and Bill Mackin Colorado historian.

2. Housed at the Museum of Northwest Colorado.

15. The Intention Was to Get Me

1. "Winnemucca Revisited," by Mike Bell, *The Journal of the Western Outlaw-Lawman History Association,* Vol. IX No. 1, Spring 2000.

2. *In Wyoming,* Vol. 4, No. X, October/November, 1977. On file at the Wyoming Division of Cultural Resources; also found on the Internet at www.nickell.tierranet.com.)

3. Julia Nickell Cook Gjervick died on February 12, 1967 in Evanston, Wyoming..

4. Fred Nickell died in Rawlins, Wyoming on September 17, 1974.

5. Census records at the Wyoming Division of Cultural Resources.

6. Two of Kels's granddaughters provided the description to the author.

7. Ibid.

8. Oral history recording of Howard E. "Mick" Miller, September 28, 1979, in which he said the family moved to the Iron Mountain country in 1884, on file at the Wyoming Division of Cultural Resources.

   Ruth Miller, Mick's mother, said the family moved to Wyoming from Greeley in 1883. Ruth, the daughter of George S. Martin, was born in Boston and moved with her parents to Wyoming. Her father and brother-in-law, Victor, worked for Coble for several years.

9. 1900 Census at the Wyoming Division of Cultural Resources.

10. Additional information provided in this passage courtesy of Ruth Miller Ayers. There is a pillar indicating the year of Frank's death in the Miller private cemetery at Iron Mountain.

11. *Wheatland World*, August 24, 1900.

12. Nettie Jordan, typewritten notes from her black notebook. Courtesy Teresa Jordan.

13. Smalley was not actually the sheriff at the time but he may have been part of the investigating party.

14. Conversation with the author, 1994.

15. Accounts offered in Willie Nickell's inquest differ as to the timing.

16. Information provided verbally to the author by Nickell family members.

17. Letter from Henry Daly to Mrs. John C. Coble located at the National Archives, courtesy Larry D. Ball. Daly had been transferred to Camp Carlin (Fort D. A. Russell) near Cheyenne after the Arizona campaigns.

18. Horn's testimony in the inquest that followed Willie's murder.

19. The story of Horn always marking the spot where he killed a man was used in newspaper accounts coinciding with his trial. Over the years the "flat rock legend" has persisted despite little basis in fact.

20. Transcription from the inquest.

16. Nobody's Family is Safe

1. Cheyenne jail records at the Wyoming Division of Cultural Resources.

2. In LeFors's testimony in Horn's trial.

3. Tom Horn later said to LeFors in the "confession" on January 12, 1902, that she had written to him, "Watch out for Joe LeFors. He is not all right."

4. Conversation with the author, July 4, 1990.

5. Scroder's testimony in the inquest.

6. Biango's inquest testimony.

7. In conversation with the author, Julia's daughter, Virginia Cook James, described her as "outspoken, very outspoken," and a niece, Viola Nickell Bixler, indicates she was "feisty." Mrs. James also indicated in a conversation and correspondence that Julia desperately wanted people to like her, probably because Kels was so disliked.

8. The prosecution convincingly used Martin's testimony on the July 19 sighting date during Horn's trial.

9. In August 1992 a group of volunteers conducted an archaeological survey at the site of the Nickell homestead, under the direction of Mark Miller, Wyoming State Archaeologist. Using metal-detecting equipment, a number of artifacts were uncovered under approximately four inches of soil. They included two stove fronts, a blacksmith's tongs, a watch face, part of a lantern, an ax head, and copper sheathing from the roof. The conclusion reached was that the family would not have left articles of intrinsic, utilitarian value unless under great pressure to leave the country quickly.

17. He Was Going to Kill Me on Sight

1. The association was the Sybille Canyon Protective Association. See records at the Wyoming Division of Cultural Resources.

18. Of Course, They Had Trouble

1. The sources for the Pierce and Kimmell family information are Roberta Hagood, Hannibal researcher and authority, who obtained the information from local government, church and cemetery records; and Vicci Stone, Atascadero researcher; and the California Department of Vital Statistics.

2. Cheyenne *Daily Leader*, November 1, 1903.

3. Horn, 287.

4. Horn, 287.

5. Inquest, 80-98, 355-376.

6. Horn, 309. Written by Kimmell in Denver, April 12, 1904.

7. Nettie Jordan notes in her black notebook. Courtesy Teresa Jordan.

19. Pretty Pronounced Thieves

1. Inquest, 283-301.

2. Durbin was a major figure in the cattle business in the Sweetwater country to the west. He had earned the enmity of the homesteaders through his complicity in the lynching of "Cattle Kate" Ellen Watson and Jim Averill in 1889.

20. A Confession?

1. Tom Horn's movements are derived from his testimony in the inquest and that of others.

2. In the trial.

3. Carpenter was the brother-in-law of Duncan Clark, foreman of Coble's ranch.

4. The brand, which at the time was owned by Tom Coble, John's brother, passed to Carpenter and finally to the Harding-Kirkbride outfit, which still uses it on cattle in the Chugwater area.

5. Frank Stone described Horn's attire in the trial.

6. While in jail for the Nickell murder.

7. 1900 Census filed at the Wyoming Division of Cultural Resources.

8. The marriage ended in divorce in 1912. LeFors later married a widow, Nettie Waegele. He died in 1940 in Buffalo, Wyoming, and is buried in the Willow Grove Cemetery south of town.

9. From the unpublished manuscript by George and Peggy Stumpf, "United States Marshals, Deputy United States Marshals of the Territory and State of Wyoming," Cheyenne.

10. It was, coincidentally, at this fair that year that Wyoming's most famous bucking bronc, Steamboat, made his rodeo debut. It is probable that Steamboat was part of the herd.

11. Ironically, Corbett's last professional fight took place about ten years later in Cheyenne.

12. Montana authority Hank Mathiason.

13. W. G. Preuitt was a prominent Montana cattleman and an official of the Montana cattlemen's association.

14. LeFors contended that he met Horn at the Union Pacific depot Sunday morning, and inferred that was when Horn arrived in Cheyenne. In Horn's trial, however, numerous witnesses said they had seen him at different locales Saturday night and early Sunday.

15. Joe LeFors, *Wyoming Peace Officer.*

16. Chip Carlson, *Joe LeFors: "I Slickered Tom Horn,"* 223-224, from LeFors's *Wyoming Peace Officer.*

17. Frank Bosler and Coble were partners in the Iron Mountain Ranch operation, which was also known as the Bosler Cattle Company. Bosler was also from Carlisle, Pennsylvania.

18. Carlson, 227.

19. *Annals of Wyoming*, Volume 13, No. 1, 72.

20. LeFors vertical file, American Heritage Center, University of Wyoming.

21. *True West*, date illegible. Tom Horn file, Wyoming Division of Cultural Resources.

22. *Joe LeFors: "I Slickered Tom Horn,"* 231, from LeFors's *Wyoming Peace Officer.*

21. Hung Before I Left the Ranch

1. This letter is located in the Horn vertical file at the Wyoming Division of Cultural Resources.

2. 1900 Albany County Census.

3. 1900 Laramie County Census. The census record indicates that the children are "grand nieces," but the data was given by Davidson's uncle, for whom the children would have been great-nieces.

4. John D. Clark, *John W. Lacey: A Memorial.* Courtesy Bill Babbitt.

5. On file at the Wyoming Division of Cultural Resources.

6. Payne arrived in Wyoming in 1895. He was Platte County Sheriff 1920–1922 and died in Jackson, Wyoming, on May 8, 1944. He is buried in Pinedale. Material on file at the Wyoming Division of Cultural Resources.

7. Hiram W. Yoder was born in Elkhart, Indiana in 1863. His family moved to Creston, Iowa, where he graduated from college. He arrived in Wyoming in 1887 and worked for the Swan Land and Cattle Company and the Bear Creek Land and Cattle Company. He became a prominent businessman and community leader in Torrington. A three-term mayor, he died on July 13, 1925. From documents at the Wyoming Division of Cultural Resources.

8. Kennedy's memoirs, made available to the author by Judge Ewing Kerr in 1990.

9. Irwin had tangled with Horn over suspicious cowhides.

22. I Knew Perfectly Well What I Was Saying

1. Kennedy, *Memoirs.*

2. W. C. Carpenter was married to Duncan Clark's sister, whose family ranched on Horse Creek northwest of Cheyenne. Information received by the author from the Clark family.

3. The horse's name was Pacer, and he was branded Lazy TY.

4. Microfilm files at the Wyoming Division of Cultural Resources.

23. Guilty!

1. One theory now gaining credence is that one or more of the Millers had sneaked over to Nickell's home the night before the murder.

While discovering that there were three adult men there, the Millers learned that Willie would go to the gate the next morning.

2. The *Denver Post*.

3. Laramie County District Court records.

24. He Talked Too Much

1. Tom Horn vertical file, Wyoming Division of Cultural Resources.

2. Ibid.

3. Ibid.

4. Records at Wyoming Division of Cultural Resources.

5. Ibid.

6. Ibid.

7. Conversations with Bill Babbitt, a friend, in the early 1990s.

8. J. Anthony Lucas, *Big Trouble: A Murder in a Small Western Town Sets Off a Struggle for the Soul of America*

9. Ibid, 727

10. Charles A. Siringo, *Riata and Spurs*, 269-270.

11. Joseph W Moch and Lori A. Kreuter, *Against the Wind: Our Client Tom Horn*, 66.

12. Horn, 263.

13. Horn, 315.

14. Horn, 317.

15. Microfilm of the *Denver Post*, Denver Public Library.

16. *Phrenology:* the study of the conformation of the skull as indicative of mental faculties and traits of character," a hypothesis propounded by F. J. Gall, 1758–1828 (Webster's third new international dictionary, 1976, G. & C. Merriam Company).

17. Larry Jordan is the grandson of John L. Jordan, a prominent Iron Mountain rancher and one of Tom Horn's occasional employers.

18. Denver Public Library microfilm.

19. Files at the Wyoming Division of Cultural Resources.

20. Ibid.

21. D. H. Grover, *Debaters and Dynamiters*, 262, citing B. A. Botkin, *A Treasury of Western Folklore*, 336-338, "The Hanging of Tom Horn." Quoted from Westerners Denver Posse *1945 Brand Book*.

25. How is the Horn Case?

1. Horn vertical file, Wyoming Division of Cultural Resources.
2. *Cases decided in the Supreme Court of the Wyoming from August 3, 1903 to April 25, 1904*, 80-166. Information at the Wyoming State Law Library, courtesy Kathy Carlson.
3. Horn, 232.
4. Files at the Wyoming Division of Cultural Resources.
5. Ibid.
6. Ibid.

26. Law and Justice?

1. George Hufsmith, *The Wyoming Lynching of Cattle Kate 1889*, 267, 271.
2. Fenimore Chatterton, *Yesterday's Wyoming: The Intimate Memoirs of Fenimore Chatterton, Territorial Citizen, Governor and Statesman..*
3. Information from public records provided by Alice Cornelius.
4. Horn vertical file at the Wyoming Division of Cultural Resources.
5. Tom Horn vertical file and the T. Blake Kennedy vertical file at the Wyoming Division of Cultural Resources.
6. Horn vertical file at the Wyoming Division of Cultural Resources.
7. Chatterton, 83.
8. Ibid., 71.

27. Escaped!

1. Cheyenne jail records at the Wyoming Division of Cultural Resources.
2. In 1908, Shobe, under the alias of Dick Stanley, suddenly appeared at Cheyenne Frontier Days with a girl on each arm. He rode Wyoming's infamous outlaw horse Steamboat to a standstill and was the only rider ever to stay on the horse while spurring it. To appear in public then was an act that reflected incredible nerve, an excess of alcohol, or poor judgment, because there was a five-thousand-dollar reward on his head. Known as the "man of mystery," he was challenged to a rematch the following year, but never appeared. He died in a rodeo accident in California in 1910, with federal warrants

still out for his arrest for the post office job. From records of the U.S. District Court, Cheyenne.

3. Conversation with the author, April 22, 1990.

28. Hanged by the Neck

1. Museum of Northwest Colorado.

2. Horn, 281-282.

3. Dee Brown, *American West*, 344-45; Richard Patterson, *Butch Cassidy: A Biography*, 200.

4. Files at the Wyoming Division of Cultural Resources, and Susan C. Carlson, *Wyoming Historical Markers at 55 MPH*.

5. Horn vertical file at the Wyoming Division of Cultural Resources.

6. Ibid.

7. *Denver Post*, November 20, 1903.

8. Boulder City Directory, 1903; *Denver Post*, November 21, 1903.

30. Terrifying, Ruthless, a Fine Fellow

1. The 1902 trial occurred in the original courthouse, which was razed in 1916 and replaced with the City-County Building, where the retrial occurred. The latter structure was refurbished and is now known as the Historic City-County Building.

Afterword: He Killed Plenty of Other People

1. Report written by Ruth Martin Miller, Gus Miller's widow. Courtesy Ruth Miller Ayers.

2. Conversations between Frank Bosler and the author. The fact has been cited elsewhere.

3. *Rock Springs Rocket*, February 1, 1924.

4. *Memoirs*, courtesy of Judge Ewing Kerr, U.S. District Court.

5. Conversation with the author.

6. Information provided by Vicci Stone, Atascadero researcher, from cemetery records.

Appendix A: Glendolene Kimmell's Affidavit

1. Affidavit provided by Alice Cornelius, researcher.

Appendix B: Judges T. Blake Kennedy and Ewing Kerr

1. Provided by Judge Kerr, in his library in the U.S. District Court, Cheyenne.

2. *Amicus curiae:* a bystander who suggests or states some matter of law for the assistance of a court; specifically: a lawyer that files a printed brief or makes an oral argument before an appellate court on behalf of a person affected by or interested in a pending case but not actually a party to it.

Bibliography

Books

Bakker, Johan P. *Tracking Tom Horn*. Union Lake, MI: Talking Boy Press, 1994.

Bromberg, Walter MD. *The Mold of Murder: A Psychiatric Study of Homicide*. New York: Grune & Stratton, 1961.

Brown, Dee. *The American West*. New York: Charles Scribner's Sons, 1994.

Burns, Robert Homer; Gillespie, Andrew Springs; and Richardson, Willing Gay. *Wyoming's Pioneer Ranches*. Laramie, Wyoming: Top-Of-The-World Press, 1955.

Burroughs, John Rolfe. *Guardian of the Grasslands: The First Hundred Years of the Wyoming Stock Growers Association*. Cheyenne: Wyoming Stock Growers Association, 1971.

Burroughs, John Rolfe. *Where the Old West Stayed Young*. New York: William Morrow and Company, 1962.

Canton, Frank M. *Frontier Trails: The Autobiography of Frank M. Canton*. Boston and New York: Houghton Mifflin Company, 1930.

Carlson, Chip. *Joe LeFors: I slickered Tom Horn: The History of the Texas Cowboy Turned Montana-Wyoming Lawman—A Sequel*. Cheyenne: Beartooth Corral, 1995.

Carlson, Chip. *Tom Horn: "Killing men is my specialty...": The Definitive History of the Notorious Wyoming Stock Detective*. Cheyenne: Beartooth Corral, 1991.

Carlson, Susan. *Wyoming Historical Markers at 55 MPH: A Guide to Historical Markers and Monuments on Wyoming Highways.* Cheyenne: Beartooth Corral, 1994.

Chatterton, Fenimore. *Yesterday's Wyoming: The Intimate Memoirs of Fenimore Chatterton, Territorial Citizen, Governor and Statesman. An Autobiography.* Powder River Publishers & Booksellers, 1957.

Clay, John. *My Life on the Range.* New York: Antiquarian Press, Ltd., 1961.

Clay, John. *The Tragedy of Squaw Mountain.* John Clay, privately published, 1921.

Clark, John D. *John W. Lacey: A Memorial.* Privately published, 1937. Courtesy of Bill Babbitt.

Cowan, Bud. *Range Rider.* Garden City: The Sun Dial Press, Inc., 1930.

Davis, John W. *A Vast Amount of Trouble: A History of the Spring Creek Raid.* Niwot: University Press of Colorado, 1993.

DeArment, Robert K. *Alias Frank Canton.* Norman: University of Oklahoma Press, 1996.

Dugan, Mark. *Tales Never Heard Round the Campfire: True Stories of Frontier America.* Athens, OH: Swallow Press/Ohio University Press, 1992.

DeJournette, Dick and Daun. *One Hundred Years of Brown's Park and Diamond Mountain.* Vernal: DeJournette Enterprises, 1996.

Dugan, Mark. *The Making of Legends: More True Stories of Frontier America.* Athens, OH: Swallow Press/Ohio University Press, 1997.

Engebretson, Doug. *Empty Saddles, Forgotten Names: Outlaws of the Black Hills and Wyoming.* Aberdeen: North Plains Press, 1982.

Ernst, Donna B. *Sundance, My Uncle.* College Station, TX: The Early West/Creative Publishing Company, 1993.

(Edited by) Etulain, Richard W. & Riley, Glenda. *With Badges and Bullets: Lawmen and Outlaws in the Old West.* Golden, Colorado: Fulcrum Publishing, 1999.

Frye, Elnora L. *Atlas of Wyoming Outlaws at the Territorial Penitentiary.* Laramie: Jelm Mountain Publications, 1990.

Grover, D. H. *Debaters and Dynamiters: The Story of the Haywood Trial.* Corvallis: Oregon State University Press, 1964.

Hanson, Margaret Brock. *Powder River Country: The Papers of J. Elmer Brock.* Kaycee, Wyoming: Margaret Brock Hanson, 1981.

Henry, Will. *I, Tom Horn.* Philadelphia: J. B. Lippincott Company, 1975. New York: Bantam Book reprint, 1992.

Horn, Tom. *Life Of Tom Horn: Government Scout & Interpreter, Written by Himself.* Denver: The Louthan Book Company 1904. Norman: University of Oklahoma Press, 1964.

Hufsmith, George W. *The Wyoming Lynching of Cattle Kate 1889.* Glendo, WY: High Plains Press, 1993.

Kelly, Charles. *The Outlaw Trail: A History of Butch Cassidy and His Wild Bunch.* New York: The Devin-Adair Company, 1959.

Krakel, Dean F. *The Saga of Tom Horn: The Story of a Cattlemen's War.* Laramie: Powder River Publishers, 1954.

Kouris, Diana Allen. *The Romantic and Notorious History of Brown's Park.* Basin, WY: Wolverine Gallery, 1988.

Lamb, Bruce F. *Kid Curry: The Life and Times of Harvey Logan and the Wild Bunch.* Boulder: Johnson Books, 1991.

LeFors, Joe. *Wyoming Peace Officer: An Autobiography.* Laramie, Wyoming: (Printed by) Laramie Printing Company, 1953.

LeFors, Rufus. *"Facts As I Remember Them": The Autobiography of Rufe LeFors.* Edited by John Allen Peterson. Austin: University of Texas Press, 1966.

Lukas, J. Anthony. *Big Trouble: A Murder in a Small Western Town Sets Off a Struggle for the Soul of America.* New York: Simon & Schuster, 1997.

McClure, Grace. *The Bassett Women.* Athens: Swallow Press/Ohio University Press, 1985.

McPhee, John. *Rising From The Plains*. New York: Farrar Straus Giroux, 1986.

Meadows, Anne. *Digging Up Butch and Sundance*. New York: St. Martin's Press, 1994.

Moch, Joseph W. and Kreuter, Lori A. *Against the Wind: Our Client, Tom Horn*. Grand Rapids, Michigan: Privately published, 1999.

Monaghan, Jay. *The Legend of Tom Horn: Last of the Bad Men*. Indianapolis: Bobbs Merrill Company, 1946.

Morn, Frank. *"The Eye That Never Sleeps": A History of the Pinkerton National Detective Agency*. Bloomington: Indiana University Press, 1982.

Moulton, Candy Vyvey and Moulton, Flossie. *Steamboat—Legendary Bucking Horse: His Life & Times and The Cowboys Who Tried to Tame Him*. Glendo, WY: High Plains Press, 1992.

Nunis, Doyce B. Jr. *The Life of Tom Horn Revisited*. Los Angeles: The Los Angeles Corral of the Westerners, 1992.

O'Neal, Bill. *Cattlemen Vs. Sheepherders: Five Decades of Violence in the West*. Austin, TX: Eakin Press, 1989.

Paine, Lauren. *Tom Horn: Man of the West*. Barre, Massachusetts: Barr Publishing Co., 1965.

Patterson, Richard. *Butch Cassidy: A Biography*. Lincoln: University of Nebraska Press, 1998.

Patterson, Richard. *The Train Robbery Era*. Boulder, Colorado: Pruett Publishing Company, 1991.

Penrose, Charles B. *The Rustling Business*. Douglas, Wyoming: (Printed by) The Douglas Budget, 1982.

Pointer, Larry. *In Search of Butch Cassidy*. Norman: University of Oklahoma Press, 1977.

Progressive Men of Wyoming (a compilation). Chicago: A. W. Brown & Co., 1903.

Rollins, George Watson. *The Struggle of the Cattleman, Sheepman and Settler for Control of Lands In Wyoming, 1867-1910.* New York: Arno Press, 1979.

Shores, Cyrus W. "Doc" (Edited by Wilson Rockwell). *Memoirs of a Lawman.* Denver: Sage Books, 1962.

Siringo, Charles. *A Cowboy Detective.* Lincoln: University of Nebraska Press (Bison Book), 1988.

Smith, Helena Huntington. *The War on Powder River: The History of an Insurrection.* Lincoln: University of Nebraska Press (Bison Book), 1966.

Trenholm, Virginia Cole. *Footprints in the Frontier: Saga of the La Ramie Region.* Douglas, Wyoming: (Printed by) Douglas Enterprise Company, 1946.

Webb, Walter Prescott, editor. *The Handbook of Texas.* Austin: The Texas State Historical Association, 1952.

Weston County, Wyoming. Dallas: Weston County Heritage Group, 1988.

Periodicals

Burroughs, John Rolfe. "Bob Meldrum, Killer for Hire." *Empire Magazine*, The Denver Post, September 23, 1962: 10-13.

Cahill, T. Joe (as told to Dean Krakel). "I Hanged My Friend, Tom Horn." *Empire Magazine*, The Denver Post. Page numbers and date not legible, 1960. (Wyoming Division of Cultural Resources).

Carroll, Murray L. "Tom Horn and the Langhoff Gang." *Annals of Wyoming*, Volume 4, Number 2, Spring, 1992.

"Cheyenne City Guide, 1902." (Wyoming Division of Cultural Resources).

Chisum, Emmet D. "The Wilcox Train Robbery—Newspapers and Instant Mythmaking." *Annals of Wyoming*, 55, (Spring 1983).

Dunlap, Horace E. "Tom Horn, Chief of Scouts." *Arizona Historical Review*, April 1929, 73-85.

Jessen, Kenneth. "Tom Horn—He Was A Pinkerton Agent." *The Journal of the Western Outlaw-Lawman History Association* (WOLA), III, (Winter 1993).

Kindred, Wayne. "Harvey Logan's Secret Letters." *True West*, (October 1994).

Lamb, John A. "Harvey Logan's Lost Journal." *True West*, (October 1994).

MacAllister, John. "Tom Horn: Interesting Episodes In the Life of Notorious Early-Day Badman." Boulder: Daily Camera *Focus*, September 14, 1969: 7-12.

Nickell, Dennie Trimble. "Who Were Tom Horn's Victims? The Story of the Nickell Family." *It Happened In Wyoming*. Month not legible, 1977: 23-38. (Wyoming Division of Cultural Resources.)

Nickell, Phillip G. "Tom Horn in Arizona Or—Who Killed Old Man Blevins?" *Quarterly of the National Association and Center for Outlaw and Lawman History*. Volume XIV, Numbers 3 & 4 (1990): 15-22.

Smith, Helena Huntington. "The Truth About The Hole-in-the-Wall Fight." *Montana—The Magazine of Western History*, (April 1961).

Contemporary newspapers of the era, 1895-1903: Cheyenne *Daily Leader*, *Wyoming State Tribune*, Laramie *Daily Boomerang*, Laramie *Republican*, Cheyenne *Daily Sun*, *Denver Post*.

Unpublished Manuscripts

Bailey, Rebecca Williamson Carter. "Wyoming Stock Inspectors and Detectives, 1873-1890" (thesis). Coe Library, University of Wyoming.

Carlson, Chip. "Recollections of Judge Kerr, November 8, 1989" (recorded conversation), November 8, 1989.

Jordan, Laura Jeannette (Nettie) Liggett. Typewritten talk in Nettie's black notebook and handwritten notecards. Courtesy Teresa Jordan.

Kennedy, T. Blake. "Memoirs," Chapter VI; pp. 201-211. Courtesy the Honorable Ewing T. Kerr, Cheyenne.

Rosentreter, Gus. "Memoirs." Courtesy Laurence Rosentreter.

Shores, Cyrus W. Papers. Denver Public Library.

Sommer, Leslie. "The History of the Sybille Country." Unpublished manuscript dated June 22, 1941. (Wyoming Division of Cultural Resources).

Stumpf, George and Peggy. "United States Marshals, Deputy United States Marshals of the Territory and State of Wyoming." Cheyenne.

Thompson, John Charles. "The Hanging of Tom Horn: Frontier Justice." Presentation given at a meeting of the Westerners in Denver, no month indicated, 1945. The writing from which he read was the only one ever used as he preferred to speak extemporaneously. (Wyoming Division of Cultural Resources)

⊷⊷⊷⊷Public Documents⊷⊷⊷⊷

Department of Commerce, National Oceanic and Atmospheric Administration, National Weather Service. "Original Monthly Record of Observations at Cheyenne, Wyo.," for the months of July 1901 and November 1903.

Department of the Interior, U.S. Geological Survey. 7.5 and 15 minute topographical maps, 7.5 minute diazo photos.

Laramie County Records Center Department, Cheyenne. Resolution of the Board of County Commissioners" (for the $500 reward for the arrest and conviction of the killer of Willie Nickell). July 23, 1901.

"Coroner's Inquest In the Matter of the Killing of William Nickell." (Incorporated into "State of Wyoming vs. Tom Horn"). Laramie County District Court, Gerrie E. Bishop, Clerk.

"State of Wyoming, Plaintiff, Vs Tom Horn, Defendant." Complete transcript of testimony, with accompanying affidavits, motions, notations of exhibits, May 21, 1901–October 27, 1902.

"Tom Horn, Plaintiff in Error, Vs State of Wyoming, Defendant in Error." Various Briefs, 1903.

"Wyoming Reports: Cases Decided in the Supreme Court of Wyoming from August 3, 1903, to April 25, 1904." Reported by Charles N. Potter (Justice). Vol. 12, pp. 80-167.

Wyoming State Livestock Board. Brand Records.

Letter from Tracey Stoll to Solar Productions, Inc. (associated with the Steve McQueen movie, "Tom Horn"), December 14, 1978. (Wyoming Division of Cultural Resources).

Personal Correspondence

Ayres, Ruth Miller. Miscellaneous correspondence, 1999.

Bindschadler, Helga H. Letter to the author, April 13, 1990.

Buffalo Bill Historical Center (Christina Stopka, Librarian/Archivist). Letter to the author, November 13, 1989.

Burlington Northern Railroad (W. N. Joplin, Director Public Affairs). Letter to the author, January 3, 1990.

Carroll, Murray L. Letter to the author, November 17, 1989.

Cox, Gary L. Letter to the author, October 10, 1989.

Department of the Army, U.S Army Military History Institute, Carlisle Barracks, PA (John J. Slonaker, Chief, Historical Reference Branch). Letter to the author, December 18, 1989.

Gressley, Dr. Gene M., American Heritage Center, University of Wyoming. Letter to the author, November 28, 1989.

Hagood, Roberta. Miscellaneous correspondence, 1998 and 1999.

Hirsig, Glenna, letter to the author, December 1, 1990.

Johnson County Library, Buffalo, Wyoming (Patty Myers, History Librarian). Letter to the author, January 17, 1990.

Laramie County Records Center Department, (Dan Siglin, CRM). Letter to the author, November 13, 1989.

Meschter, Dan. Letter to the author, December 9, 1989.

Rosentreter, Laurence. Letter to the author, December 12, 1989.

Union Pacific Railroad Company (George R. Cockle, Research Assistant). Letter to the author, January 25, 1990.

✦✦✦✦✦Miscellaneous✦✦✦✦✦

Bosler Collection, American Heritage Center, University of Wyoming.

Diagrams and maps from the personal files of T. Blake Kennedy, showing the site where Willie Nickell was killed. (Wyoming Division of Cultural Resources).

Conversations with L. W. Jordan (grandson of J. L. Jordan mentioned in the transcripts), 1990.

Conversation with Betty Steele (granddaughter of Charles B. Irwin), April 22, 1990.

Conversations with Bill Babbitt, 1990.

✦✦✦✦✦Collections✦✦✦✦✦

Wyoming Division of Cultural Resources, Cheyenne: Tom Horn, T. Blake Kennedy, Frank Hadsell.

American Heritage Center, University of Wyoming, Laramie: Archives on Joe LeFors, T. Blake Kennedy, Wyoming Stock Growers Association, Wilcox train robbery, Ora Haley, Walter Stoll.

★━━━━━Acknowledgments━━━━━★

I am truly indebted to and grateful for their assistance to a lot of people. There are really two who first come to mind, and I must give them credit first.

First I want to thank Dr. Larry D. Ball at Arkansas State University and Nancy N. Curtis at High Plains Press. To Larry, many thanks for your assistance and generosity with research materials. Anything Larry writes about Tom Horn is "must reading."

And to Nancy, I can say that working with you has truly made me realize what a difference an outstanding editor/publisher makes. You have earned all the compliments I have heard from your authors.

And once again thanks to Larry and Jan Edgar, whose Western art and friendship have made living in Wyoming just that much better.

Others I wish to acknowledge and thank are, in alphabetical order, Ruth Miller Ayers, Miller family historian; Johan Bakker, Michigan historian and author; Larry K. Brown, Wyoming author and friend; Gerry Bishop, Clerk of the Laramie County District Court; Viola N. Bixler, Nickell descendant and family historian; Carol Bowers of the American Heritage Center; Carolyn Bowler; Jean Brainerd, LaVaughn Bresnahan, and Cindy Brown of the Archives Section, Wyoming Division of Cultural Resources; Dr. Courtney Brown, psychotherapist; Sharon Brown of the Scotland County Circuit Court; Claudia Cole, researcher in British Columbia; Jeanette Corbin-Guzman, Nickell family genealogist; Kathy Carlson of the Wyoming Law Library; historian Murray L. Carroll; Yvonne Chalifour of the Archives Section; Pete Chronis, Denver historian; Alice Cornelius; Jim Darden; Dan Davidson at the Museum of Northwest Colorado; Dan Davis, John and Betty Dilts; Dean P. Edmundson for his advice on copyright matters and the friendship, Tracy Eller at High Plains Press; Donna B. Ernst; Rick Ewig at the American Heritage Center; Ron Franscell at the Denver Post, Elnora Frye; Clay Gibbons; Gene Gressley; Curtis Gruebel; Roberta Hagood; Carl Hallberg; Cathy Hernandez, Horn family researcher; Kathy Hodges; Alvin and Barbara Howard in Memphis; Larry Jordan; Teresa Jordan; Sandy Landers; Bill Mackin; Hank Mathiason; Lee and Judy Miller; Brenda Meyer; Joe Moch; Patty Myers; Patsy and Don Parkin; Don Patterson; Sandy Remley in Memphis; LeAnn Russell in Memphis; Celia Schadel; Melissa Schuster; Steve and Laura Smith; Vicci Stone, researcher in San Luis Obispo County; George and Peggy Stumpf; Dave Taylor and the Wyoming State Historical Society; Anita Watkins; John and Shirley Weihing, Horn family genealogists; Judy West; and Britt Wilson.

Many, many individuals have assisted with my research over the years, and I offer an apology if I have inadvertently missed anyone's name here.

Chip Carlson.
(photo by Graig Marrs)

AUTHOR CHIP CARLSON was born in Pennsylvania near Carlisle, coincidentally where many of the early powers in the Wyoming cattle business originated. He is a graduate of Colgate University with a BA in philosophy. Before moving to Wyoming in 1977 he lived in Latin America, Canada and the Midwest while working in marketing capacities.

He has invested over twelve years into researching the history of the Tom Horn episode in Wyoming, as well as other aspects of the early ranching business. A frequent contributor to national and regional publications, his two previous books are *Tom Horn: "Killing men is my specialty..."* and *Joe LeFors: "I slickered Tom Horn..." – A Sequel.*

Carlson and his wife, Susan, live north of Cheyenne and can be reached at beartoothc@worldnet.att.net.

This book was simultaneously released in three editions.

A *collectors' edition* of only 50 copies was Smyth sewn and bound in Mocha Grand Levant, embossed with copper foil, and wrapped with a four-color dustjacket. The endleaves are a special marbled stock exclusive to this edition.

The *collectors' edition* contains a High Plains Press limited edition bookplate, designed and hand-printed from a woodcut on Mohawk Superfine archival paper by Richard Wagener. Each bookplate is signed by the author and hand-numbered.

A certificate, signed by the author at the gate at Iron Mountain on July 18, 2001, one hundred years after the murder of Willie Nickell, authenticates each book of the *collectors' edition.*

A *limited edition* of only 500 copies was Smyth sewn, bound in cinnabar Arrestox B cloth, embossed with copper foil, and wrapped with a four-color dustjacket. Each is signed by the author and hand-numbered.

A *softcover trade edition* was issued simultaneously with the two special editions. It is covered with a twelve-point stock, printed in four colors, and coated with a special matte finish.

The text of all editions is Garamond by Adobe. Display type is Post Mediaeval by Adobe and Way Out West by P22.

The book is printed on sixty-pound Joy White, an acid-free paper by Thomson-Shore.